FV

306.89 C371f
CAUHAPE
FRESH STARTS : MEN AND WOMEN
AFTER DIVORCE
                              16.50

St. Louis Community College

Library

**5801 Wilson Avenue
St. Louis, Missouri 63110**

Fresh Starts

FRESH STARTS

Men and Women After Divorce

ELIZABETH CAUHAPÉ

Basic Books, Inc., Publishers

NEW YORK

Library of Congress Cataloging in Publication Data

Cauhapé, Elizabeth.
  Fresh starts : men and women after divorce.

  Bibliography: p. 315
  Includes index.
  1. Divorced people—United States. I. Title.
HQ834.C37 1983   306.8'9   82-70845
ISBN 0-465-02553-6

I dedicate this book and I blow a kiss to

Nina and Sara

and

Duncan and Tom

Contents

Preface

THIS RESEARCH and my hopes to do a book have involved the support of many people. When I was a student, Leonard Schatzman, Virginia Olesen, and Jackie Wiseman taught me important lessons about doing social research. Carroll Estes was one of my role models, and she, Leonard Schatzman, and John McNamara gave me the teaching assistantships and research consultancies that both enhanced and helped to fund my training. I am also grateful to Marjorie Fiske who directed UCSF's Adult Development Program in Psychiatry, and Dave Chiriboga, with whom I began my study of divorce aftermaths. As a pre-doctoral research training fellow, grants from the National Institutes of Aging and Child Health and Human Development advanced and supported my work.

My indebtedness to Anselm Strauss is a special one. He always encouraged my developing line of analysis and his intellectual perspective frames and informs mine.

Leonard and Sylvia Schatzman's friendship sustained me. I would be very pleased if the intellectual mentorship and human qualities of these foregoing people were to sometimes shine through in my life.

Preface

Other valued associations have also influenced my decision to undertake this book. At the New School, where I began my doctoral studies, I benefited from the friendship and theories of Stanford Lyman and Arthur Vidich. At San Jose State University, (where I earned my Master's degree), my friends Jacqueline Fullerton, Henry Pitchford, and Bob McNair taught me humanistic sociology and were colleagues when I began to teach. More recently, it has been my luck to know Lillian Rubin. Her book on working class marriage, *Worlds of Pain*, is a classic in the field. It was she who sent me to Basic Books' copublisher and executive vice-president, Jane Isay, who became my editor and brought my book to life. She saw at once what I was attempting to do and showed me what was yet undone. Her energy sparked mine. My task was much assisted by the copy editing of Barbara MacAdam and Ann Cambra's courtesy and competence when typing the manuscript.

I have always been fortunate in having the company of good friends to cheer me on. I admire the generosity of Bill and Carol Churchill, William Bennett, Jr., Shirley (Shoshana) Zimmerman, Thom Sturm, and Laura Stenson Brown. I am also indebted to Stephen Diamond, Anna Barnes, Arlene Daniels, Karl and Helen Felperin and Eva Laskin, Greg McGinnis, and Lorrie Berg. And I thank Bruce and Louise Smith-Donals, Beth Huttman, Mae Ann Waller, Christopher and Barbara Hendrickson, Pete Wilson, and Maris Dravnieks.

Long ago, I was aided by having my family's blessings. My parents, James William and Esther Broadhurst (Morehouse), believed in university training for women, and my mother always supported all of my professional goals. After my father's early death, I often thought about his parents' decision to come to American from England's Midlands and that decision's influence on my life. Another source of courage was my sons'

Preface

early acceptance of my educational plans; my return to school became parameters for their lives, too. Thus, I thank Duncan (and JoAnn) Waldrop for forbearance in having a preoccupied graduate student mother, and my son, Tom Waldrop, for his intellectual companionship, concern, and my first insights into the "New Age." I also owe a large debt to the children of my "intentional family," Nicholas and Sara Baz, who opened their hearts and homes to me many times.

Lastly, I must acknowledge the wit, warmth, and advice of Marian Kazman Richards and William Reid Smith. These comrades have stood by me through a very long struggle. Simply put, the commitment each of them made to my welfare and to this book has made all the difference.

In closing, I want to salute the study's subjects who shared so much with me and taught me about passage, and the memory of Arthur Burton, Jungian extraordinaire, who first accompanied me on the journey that led into the work.

Claremont Canyon
Berkeley
February 8, 1983

Fresh Starts

1

Introduction

A DIVORCE can be a powerful crisis in middle age; but, while we know a great deal about the disruption of losing stable moorings at this stage of life, we know very little about the fresh starts people make. This book grew out of my research to see if people "recover" after divorce and if so, how? I wanted to discover the means by which men and women rebuild their social worlds at mid-life after undergoing a divorce.

This is not an account of the lives of exceptional Americans, but rather a book about upwardly mobile professional men and women with origins in the middle, lower-middle, and working classes. When I studied them throughout the 1970s and early 1980s, they were casting about for and locating avenues by which to adapt to their divorces. In varying degrees they had been persistent strivers who believed in the American dream of "success." Their several married decades devoted to hard work and achievement gave them new levels of affluence. The "good life," however, brought them problems as well as pleasures. In addition, although many of these people left marriage voluntarily, all of them had to start over again to create new social identities and satisfying new existences.

The picture that follows reports my study's central finding: divorced men and women can master their circumstances and take power over their lives. This book describes the range of options my research subjects considered and the paths they finally chose. Some, for instance, set out to find another partner; but others, for reasons I will discuss, preferred to remain single. Either way, some form of response to the issue of partnering again is one of the earliest decisions people make.

But before people make any choices concerning their futures, they first make assessments about what kinds of possibilities seem to be available to them and how desirable these appear to be. These appraisals are based on their perceptions of their life chances (or the odds for success), especially in terms of the social resources they already command or think they can assemble. One important social resource is the occupational role, for instance. Because expectations tend to determine outcomes, accurate judgments are crucial. In addition, people must select strategies or means which will be appropriate for achieving the ends they desire. The tactics they use to pursue goals may be rational and appealingly "safe"; or the strategies may be risk-laden gambles, such as subordinating all other interests to a partner search, even though this might jeopardize an occupational career that provides one with both economic and emotional security. Some of my research subjects made evaluations cautiously, but others acted quickly and confidently. People take stock of the "cards" they hold, as if life were a poker game; and one of the strongest cards I found anyone has to play is a personal history of adapting well to change.

Chapter 2 describes the research subjects and examines the significance of their mobility patterns. Many were children of immigrant families, carrying on hopes for new lives in the New World. A typical life pattern had been growing up in a small town (or, much less often, an ethnic neighborhood), working one's way through college, marrying someone who also aspired to "making it" in the city, and accomplishing this aim. These men and women learned early that deferring gratifications was a route to assuring a more abundant future; for instance, many women went to work or got more training in the midst of child rearing. As couples, these people were used to planning ahead, advancing gradually but steadily, and being ready to marshal all their resources when "a good opportunity" came along. Both upward (social) mobility and horizontal (geographic) mobility were elements in their histories directly linked to their financial successes. This kind of a history was, by the 1950s, becoming very common in American middle-class life.

By the 1950s, many couples were prosperous and, as heads of suburban families, situated in the kinds of lives they had earlier envisioned and sought for themselves and for their children. Few of them stopped to note that they had established families and assumed positions in the business world and the professions during a period of unprecedented national prosperity; their timing was lucky, like "catching the wind" when setting forth to sail. But for many of them, the next decade found the winds shifting. The 1960s were a time of disjuncture, because some of the social changes that emerged were as threatening as they were unexpected. Nevertheless, by the 1970s, many subjects had either incorporated new ideas into their lives or managed to withstand their impact. At best, however, there were unforeseen consequences of this period that complicated launching children or put family stability to the test and also brought to many forms of social relations a confusing fluidity, not the least of which was alterations in sex roles. Some of my subjects were puzzled or dismayed by what became a cultural transformation in the minds of many, but others applauded and hastened to utilize it for their own purposes. At any rate, either way, as these subjects divorced and had to find new social identities, the "times" helped some of them and hindered others. For each divorcing individual, life involves a matrix or a combination of one's personal history, stage of life, and a particular point in social history. All of my subjects had to deal with the implications of this fact in approaching the issue of the future. How a person responds to the convergence of these three factors (and what other influences he or she sees as important to consider) determines his or her course of action.

My research uncovered eight different and specific divorce aftermaths that characterize the most common range of choices among men and women like my subjects. I call the transitional paths that led to each outcome "passages" and describe them in chapters 3 through 7. In these chapters, I discuss, based on profiles of some of my subjects, which kinds of people are likely to be attracted to what sorts of aftermaths. Indirectly, these descriptions of a particular kind of person being interested in a specific life goal cast some light on the question of personality types. I make no pretext of giving a comprehensive picture, however. Extrapolating to personality types can only provide one with inferences. Nevertheless, I show in concrete terms the options most often selected by the subjects in my sample and the ways they overcame the circumstances they saw as obstacles.

To my surprise, I found the eight types of passage cluster into three main categories that are immediately related to a postdivorce transition's length. Two factors determine the amount of time an individual will devote to the transition: how long the person is willing and able to remain in a transitional state, and how long a passage is required for attaining a certain goal (aftermath). While some subjects could not tolerate the irresolution of an incompleted passage and said things like, "I can't *stand* being alone"; others seemed to enjoy irresolution and talked about "wanting to keep [their] options open." The fact that different sorts of passages take differing lengths of time was repeatedly confirmed. Clearly, some goals can be accomplished faster than others, even if two people in the same kind of passage move ahead at slightly different rates.

I found that passage termination appears to occur by choice. That is, termination is controlled by a person's decision that a goal is reached, and hence, no more time in passage is necessary. I regarded each passage as a means to a particular goal, because people used the transition in this way. My subjects chose an end goal at the beginning of the transitional period and then tailored their passages to accomplish the desired aftermath. In other words, the passage cannot be separated from the aftermath. At first, I did not consider such a possibility; but my subjects saw the logic of it and set out to build pathways that would be consistent with their choices.

All my subjects agreed that a passage is concluded when two desired conditions exist: first, the person has established a viable and comfortable social identity of the type sought from the beginning of passage, and second, the person has woven a satisfactory web of new social relationships that accord with his or her hopes for the future. Of course the second necessary condition relates to an individual's having already chosen the goal of an enjoyable singlehood or a pleasant partnership. Possession of a new social identity sufficiently solid to bring one either kind of desirable future (paired or not), indicates to each person that "life is good now" and the transition, over. Thus, even men and women in contrasting types of passages agreed on what constitutes the grounds for closure.

Everyone wants to undergo transition in the company of

others interested in the same type of passage and outcome, but people have a hard time sorting each other out and giving out cues about their own intentions that will not be ambiguous. This task is urgent for anyone seeking a new partner. Therefore, the problem of deciphering (en route to an outcome) what kind of passage an individual is in the process of undertaking can be critical to others and always was to my research.

While the length (duration) of different passages gave me my first clues about types, endpoints (aftermaths) also soon became useful. The points at which a desired end is attained can be fairly visible (marriages, for example, are public information), and people tend to talk about whether or not they have achieved their goals. I had only to ask my subjects if they considered themselves to be in transition, and if not, why? Were they satisfied with the outcome? If they were, I asked how they had successfully concluded the transition. Endpoints enabled me to get a "handle" on the problem initially, helping me to locate and eventually understand passage types. I found that after identifying endpoints and repeatedly working back from them over many cases, I could then investigate the passages people construct as bridges into their futures from either end of a transition. Sometimes, I was able to determine the type of passage in the middle of a transition because each kind displays its own characteristic patterns. Relying on a passage's conclusion in order to recognize or confirm its type wastes a lot of time, but as a researcher, this was a necessary first step. One of my motives for writing a book was to offer readers a general road map.

Chapters 3 and 4 examine brief passages, those taking from several days to around two years. The reason they are this brief is that the basic aim of the men and women who choose them is simply to get out of transition. They are selected by people who may or may not want another partner but who share a common aim: to "normalize" their lives. To these men and women, passage is merely the means to an end; it is never seen as a valuable experience in itself. I found three subgroups of people involved in brief passages, all characterized by a desire to leave passage as quickly as possible, given their goals. This they did with dispatch.

Chapter 3 describes two of these subgroups: the Immediate (Planned) Remarriers and the Graduates. The Immediate (Planned) Remarriers have already found a new potential mate before choosing to divorce. In most cases, it was the new relationship that precipitated the decision to act on what had been until then only a vague, long-held wish to divorce. The new lovers, in their concern that the spouse to be divorced will discover and be able to block the divorce plan and thus prevent a remarriage carefully begin executing a covert plan. This type of passage can be packed with action and drama. For instance, among my subjects, the suspicious husband of one woman, unwilling to relinquish control upon learning of her intentions, immediately left town with another woman, leaving many clues as to their destination but no forwarding address, possibly hoping to be begged to reconcile on his return. By so doing, he left the subject unable to serve him promptly with divorce papers. This is a dramatic example of some of the common problems encountered in divorce litigation that are also considered in this chapter.

The Graduates comprise a less colorful but equally determined subgroup. They hold very negative views of their prior marriage and of the process required to find or hold a second mate. They regard themselves as *lucky to be single again*, establishing themselves as singles immediately, emphatically, and permanently. After the final decree, they devote their resources to those roles they do regard as valuable.

Chapter 4 examines the last brief-passage subgroup, the men

and women I call Comfortable Courters. To Courters, the Noah's ark patterns of suburban life are "normal" and desirable, and they remarry fairly rapidly by locating several potential mates and courting and claiming one of them. Courters think that predictable, married futures are fundamental to one's well-being. To this end, they enlist the aid of sympathetic relatives, friends, or associates and usually end up marrying someone whom they did not know at all or knew only slightly at the time divorce papers were filed. In addition, this chapter emphasizes the characteristics shared by all men and women who select brief passages and also notes the distinctions among the three subgroups. Chapters 3 and 4 discuss the problems that are common to all brief passages, and how they are usually handled.

Chapter 5 describes the mid-length passages which range from about two to four years and usually involve children. These passages often reflect people's concern for their children. Sometimes, the children's existence is the motive for choosing such a passage in the first place; while other times, the children's needs become a motive for choosing this kind of passage after someone has been in transition for awhile. The basic aim of these men and women is to "stabilize" life. There are many reasons why these transitions take more time than the brief passages. For example, people who want to find a new spouse through a very cautious process, or men and women with very disrupted transitions, tend to choose mid-length passages.

There are two subgroups among the men and women who undertake mid-length passages: the Steadies and the Enforced Remarriers. The primary purpose of Steadies is the creation of a stepfamily. They proceed very carefully, testing out a particular, tentative partnership to measure its promise as a permanent, marital alliance. These men and women look around seriously for a dependable future spouse. Structuring a reconstituted family unit requires the patience to integrate a prospective mate gradually into the family and the neighborhood. Steadies and their prospects are home- and family-centered. Their courtships involve rounds of picking up children at the movies, having summertime barbecues, and "slowly sliding," as one put it, into remarriage.

Enforced Remarriers are those men and women for whom unforeseen problems continually arise. They leave passage somewhat reluctantly, but they do so because they feel they presently lack the skills and other necessary resources required to continue on their own, an appraisal which, generally, seemed to me to be accurate. Chapter 5 examines some of the problems that can destroy a person's hopes to remain in passage or to keep on functioning without a marital partner's aid. Abandoning a difficult romance in favor of a reliable admirer pushing for marriage, or abandoning a passage that is turning sour for one reason or another (for example, money difficulties), are ways by which such men and women can "cut their losses." While Enforced Remarriers, unlike most other people, do reset their goals in the course of a passage, it is the particular marriage partner, not the fact of remarriage, that is a disappointment for them. Enforced Remarriers tend to bargain for the second best kind of partner and are, at least temporarily, quite relieved to be removed from the stormy struggles of passage. Thus, mid-length passages tend to culminate in the fruition or (less often) the downward revision of hopes, but in either case, people recognize that they have options. Chapter 5 also notes some similarities among the men and women who choose either brief or mid-length passages, including their tendency to rely quite heavily on traditional social values, their deep concern about aging, and their lack of interest in social trends.

Chapters 6 and 7 examine long passages. These are generally

chosen by men and women who are self-consciously "modern" and who reinterpret middle age as a time of "opportunity and expansion," because for them, this is the case. The people drawn to these passages look back on the first marriage mainly as a duty-bound experience of trying to honor important (family) commitments. As one said, "Sometimes people make a lot of erroneous assumptions. For instance, if a man knows he pleases me, he is then apt to suspect I will try to maneuver him into marriage. But in my case, I associate marriage with obligations and self-sacrifice, not with happiness."

To these men and women, being in mid-life and in transition are both interesting experiences, because, for what seems to them virtually the first time in their lives, they turn their full attention to their own social and psychological needs. Among my subjects, the "pacesetters" comprising this subgroup were sharply divided over the repartnering issue, but they nevertheless resembled one another strongly on the basis of the personal attributes by which they managed passages and maximized their goals with considerable skill. These characteristics included: optimism, resilience, social ease, and self-possession (as personality traits); familiarity with innumerable, highly diverse social settings (as concomitants of cosmopolitan backgrounds); and a tendency to be independent thinkers who brought quite original perspectives to bear on the transitional process of self-definition (as part of a habitual posture toward change).

Long-passage men and women were the study's "social gymnasts." They felt that many social conventions straitjacketed people because they were stultifying, constricting, and inauthentic social forms which serve the major social institutions (as in the case of traditional sex role expectations)—but prevent healthy human growth. There are three subgroups in the long-passage category: Hunters-and-Sorters, Runners in Place, and Passionate Searchers. All of these people enjoy the latitude for personal and social exploration allowed them by this type of transition. In a general sense, they are not particularly concerned about the way other people regard mid-life singles; rather, these accomplished professionals are used to being well-received. They find their passages more challenging and pleasurable than stressful, and approach them with eagerness.

Chapter 6 describes Hunters-and-Sorters, those who devote a considerable amount of time and energy to a partner hunt that they almost amble through, without much sense of urgency. They tend to pair off tentatively, and then, pair again with somebody else. They hunt and sort their ways through a series of partnerships for two main reasons: they want to make a "really good choice," (and therefore, do not necessarily consider a brand new pairing as very likely to be permanent) and they place a high value on trying out a variety of partnering possibilities available to them. They tend to contract these (sometimes monogamous) alliances by living together rather informally. Hunters-and-Sorters, then, are often coupled.

The Runners in Place were the most glamorous and unfettered of my research subjects. Runners tend to take their relatively luxurious existences for granted. Their comparatively high incomes finance a considerable amount of leisure time; worldwide travel; a staff of helpers; and conveniently run daily existences, exemplified by habitual eating out. They enjoy active sports such as tennis, all kinds of social and cultural events, and being "on the go." Runners were the most socially active of the study's subjects. Although they are not interested in being partnered, their frequent out-of-town "dating time" revolves around such recreation as sailing, skiing, and tropical sunning in the winter. They are fascinated by physical fitness and interested in nutrition and/or holistic health care. Runners tend to live alone.

Long-passage subjects tended to "experimentalize" and "privatize" life during and after passage. One consequence was that they were slowly nudged toward further experiences of singlehood and innovative life-styles. Chapters 6 and 7 consider some of the difficulties that characterize these long passages and explain how they may be ameliorated. The subforms are compared and I make observations about the subjects' attitudes toward former partners, the ideology of singlehood, and the place given to sexuality, in each subgroup.

Chapter 7 reports my findings on the third subgroup in the long-passage category, the Passionate Searchers, those whose transitions focus on a theme of openness to change and personal transformation. They often are not only dedicated to incorporating into their lives many new social and cultural attitudes, but some of them are also engaged in contributing to these new developments in many of their ramifications. Their ideal is to emerge from transition in an intense pair bond with a partner whom they see as perfect for them. Searchers will undertake several trial unions to achieve this, usually ending up in a legal form of what is apt to be termed a New Age marriage, based on some version of egalitarian principles, such as sharing expenses and retaining separate property. Their pairings are marked by emotional closeness, sensuality, and a resolve to "work things through." In the process of searching, some men and many women revise their criteria for mate selection, often picking a person whom an old friend might consider to be a somewhat surprising choice. These people go to great lengths to separate intimate from professional life. They also find their pairings extraordinarily gratifying.

Chapter 8 summarizes the eight adaptive patterns of response to divorce at mid-life, showing how the ingenious handling of some of the properties of passage discussed in this chapter allows people to enjoy the diversity of aftermaths that match their disparate visions of personal destiny. I examine the implications for middle age as a stage of life, particularly as these are suggested by my analysis of data on long passages, and discuss several ways in which the tasks of mid-life have recently shifted. In the study, people's resourcefulness at overcoming the realities they defined as obstacles continually emerged, and none were more creative than the subjects in long passages. Their perspectives provide answers to middle-aged men and women who are divorced or contemplating such a break; they also offer interesting options for anyone presently dealing with the mid-life stage or anticipating it. I show how the vagaries of income or gender, the complications of what used to be "unusual timing" in being divorced at mid-life, or the influences of the mid-life stage itself are now being reinterpreted from the standpoint of their advantages.

I review some of the forms of problem-solving and some of the grounds for redefinition used in long passages, explaining why these efforts to prevail over more complicated and/or unfinished maturation tasks often succeed. Lastly, I argue that these developments are part of a major shift in cultural values in this country and may be regarded as encouraging indications of our capacity to honor and fulfill infinitely complex psychic needs during the entire course of adult life.

Stage of life—the fact that efforts to begin again must be undertaken in people's forties or fifties—is an implacable factor in the transitions studied. People must confront the fact of being in mid-life in order to master any form of passage and decide what this means to them. A person's judgments grow out of a set of attitudes to love, marriage, divorce, and singlehood. In addition, responses to the issues of sexuality, aging, emotional security, and the years yet to come, must be thought through and perhaps, reformulated from the perspective of middle age. Whether or not a person recognizes the fact, one's value system is the foundation for arriving at such judgments.

In addition to age, one's financial resources are conditions fundamental to making decisions during passage. I was surprised to find that age was the most difficult factor for men, and money, rather than age, for women. Other important problems are also linked to gender. For example, the experience of passage is qualitatively different for men and women in a general sense. At the study's onset, I considered concentrating my research on showing how gender often leads to a subjectively different experience. However, both my subjects and I were struck by the camaraderie of people in passage. In the main, everyone treated the transition as one more illustration of the human struggle for dignity and happiness. The kindness of other men and women, strangers to each other but all trying to manage their passages well, is quite remarkable if a person is at all receptive. Therefore, I chose to portray the whole experience, giving all possible information on the facts I uncovered about how problems were met.

In a general sense, I found that people elect a course in terms of their most treasured values, which requires them to face some difficulties directly but lets them ignore others at whatever costs they choose. In other words, there always are costs and tradeoffs, for men and women alike. Locating the tradeoffs that exist at mid-life as possibilities is an important component of transition management.

As a situational variable, the stage-of-life issue is at least implicit in the postdivorce decision-making process. For instance, the women in my study had worried about the prospect of aging so frequently and so early in life, that they simply tired of the topic and seemed relieved to say so. It appeared to be, at mid-life, an issue they had finally laid to rest. The men, however, appeared to have been "brought up short" at mid-life, as if bumping into something in the dark. They were not very comfortable with the topic of aging and tended to "clam up" and divert any discussion of it. However, there are other factors accounting for the variation in people's reactions to aging. Essentially, perceptions about the *social meanings* attached to age and to time are highly personal appraisals at the heart of making a choice.

Reorganizing life after mid-life divorce may demand intense effort and much trial and error. The core problem is to create or reintegrate one's social network (dyadic or otherwise); but no one has a map by means of which to get from the divorce to a desired outcome. People have to restructure their lives by themselves, and this may demand continual improvisation. Transition management is a dynamic process, especially in long passages. People have many roles, or "career lines," to enact— for example, occupational, familial, or sexual—and orchestrating them into a coherent, emergent identity is a complicated matter. For example, one takes to the office a "self" different from that one displays to a lover. After divorce, people must therefore be attentive to a *configuration of roles*, [1] trying to combine them into a whole with reasonable effectiveness. Over time, this constellation may change if one role becomes difficult to control or if a person decides to shift the emphasis among his or her roles.

The death of a marriage can provide a considerable jolt to both marriage partners, and the onset of passage often tends to reflect their loss of bearings, at least briefly. At this point, the problem of role alterations must be addressed at once. Usually, women have custody of children and may feel overwhelmed as single parents, speaking of everything being "too much" for them, but men more often speak in terms of (role) emptiness. The temporary sense of isolation that may follow a man like a hound, all day long, may not plague a harried, spouseless single mother until dinnertime, when no one comes home from work with her or to her. The following excerpt from a male subject in his forties sums up the feeling of being "dispensable" that some men feel initially,

> For a man, divorce can be sort of an inverse suicide. Instead of one's being dead—almost everyone *else* is. The divorced male is almost a ghost. He ceases to exist as far as most of his former world is concerned. You lose the primary Other, and the kids, and the house, the furniture, the friends, the life-rounds, and the total life pattern. You don't begin the day in the same way or in the same place. It's as if you are the only survivor!

This heartwrung description of one subject's feelings just after receiving the final decree leads us to the central question, "How do people cope?" If you begin passage as if you are in a race, running for your life, as this man felt, what sustains you? The answer in his case proved to lie in what he had to start off with. To put it another way, this subject was a man with a past, a history, and a set of values. As a soldier, logger, scholar, he had encountered change before; he survived it. Since he made those comments, he has been moving toward a goal that may yield a life unlike any he has known. He has already found, and convinced, his next wife. Goal attainment doesn't just happen to someone; he or she must instead remake a life. The aim of this book is to show how this can be done.

My investigation is based on six years of research during which I devoted thousands of hours to participant observation, talking to many people in my "natural role" as a separated and later divorced researcher, and hundreds of hours to intensive, open-ended interviews. These were collected in a long series for each of the thirty-four cases followed in depth over this six-year period. For ethical reasons, I always identified myself as a researcher to anyone with whom I talked.

Introduction

Obtaining subjects was not difficult. I found that people enjoyed having the opportunity to tell their stories and comment on their postdivorce situations to an interested listener. Some subjects were referred by their friends, while others I met at the activities of numerous singles events I attended continually. No one ever declined to be interviewed, and only one person among hundreds said, "Don't ever quote me."

To assure confidentiality, I used no research assistants, transcribed interview tapes myself, and filed case records under pseudonyms chosen by the subjects. I explained to all prospective subjects that I was originally interested in studying this particular form of transition because of its presumed relationship to mental health. Although I expected to encounter many cases of illness and breakdown, sleep disturbance was the only clear symptom of stress that consistentently appeared and was reported in response to my questions on health and job histories. Only one person was so disabled during transition as to need a period of psychiatric hospitalization. This subject recovered and became a staff member at a mental hospital, which was congruent with his professional training. Subjects were pleased to be treated as "normals" who might contribute to a better understanding of the mid-life postdivorce transition.

Of the many factors that helped put my research subjects at ease, foremost was the fact that I was in transition myself. Originally, I greatly underestimated how much the fact of my being in passage myself would legitimize the study to my research subjects. Because of the paucity of good books from research on the postdivorce period and the frequent assumptions in them that all formerly marrieds are "misfits" who could not cope with marriage and will continue to "fail," subjects tended not to trust the judgments of people who do not have a firsthand experience of divorce. One result of this is their interest in books on the postdivorce situation by its veterans, even when they are not trained observers.[2] To so decide to write a book simply out of one's life experience is, however, an excellent example of the way people innovate with respect to their social roles after divorce, itself a major theme of much of this book.

Furthermore, as a clinician, my practice as a marriage and family counselor has been and is devoted to assisting men and women in a variety of life transitions. Lastly, my affiliation with a well-known medical center and my work there in medical sociology and adult development also reassured subjects.

When my findings were tentatively reached, I convened a panel of representative subjects who analyzed and commented on the study's conclusions. Checking out my ideas by submitting them to the research subjects for comment was a technique I began using early in the study. As hypotheses emerged for testing or modification, I discussed them with many of my long-term subjects (those whom I followed in repeated interviews) as well as with new subjects whom I had not followed in this depth. I circulated the final drafts of this manuscript among some of my subjects. In all cases, my taxonomy of passage types was confirmed by the fact that my subjects knew of no middle-aged, divorced professional man or woman who did not fit into one of the identified categories.

Through the commonality of certain transition experiences —such as struggling to "read clues" from new friends, or attempting a new step only to encounter one's lack of skill at judging possibilities—my subjects and I felt we were on a shared journey. We spoke continually, not of the "right way" to conduct a passage, but of what we each saw as the "right way for *me*." The research subjects' perceptions of transition formed the basis for my representation of this postdivorce experience.

Divorce at mid-life both allows and forces improvisation, but

Introduction

many people hold changes to a minimum. Whatever their approach, however, most people are "winners" because they do achieve the futures they work to attain. These findings contradict popular images about the trauma or costs of divorce, especially in middle age. Success during the transition depends on people's capacities to turn problems into opportunities for enabling new self-definitions, and most people are equipped to do so.

Before you meet the men and women who opened their lives to me, I would like to state my position. To me, their stories do not reveal *levels* of coping, with some choices "better" than others; rather, I perceive them as demonstrating how people triumph over disappointment by making decisions on their own terms and on their own behalf. Men and women in the mid-life postdivorce transition *can* "turn things around." They do. And, the stories that follow are also love stories, of failed, faltering, or now flourishing relationships. Except in one case where I was otherwise instructed, all identities are concealed and all identifying details disguised, but these love stories are true.

2

The Subjects' Histories:

Time and Mobility

The Subjects' Social Characteristics

The research subjects not only often talked in terms of "our generation"; but also most were born into Depression-gripped families in the 1920s or 1930s. As college students, they were often the first family member to take a degree. They married very early, while still in or just out of school. These men and women accomplished much of their child rearing and the stabilizing of their families and careers during the relatively long period of postwar prosperity. When they divorced in the 1960s or early 1970s, their children were teen-agers or university students, still dependent upon them in important ways. To my subjects, the bomb at Hiroshima was the benchmark that the Kennedy assassination became for their children. They thought of themselves as a postwar or postbomb generation.

Since subjects married at different ages, remained married for differing amounts of time, and joined the study at various points, their progress through life and in the study also varied. Nevertheless, for a number of reasons, they had an "our crowd" feeling, a sense of being part of a collectivity. First, they all felt they had lived through quite unusual times accompanied by extraordinary changes in the world of ideas. Second, they also thought they had done "quite well" with much of it. This sense of mastery, deserved or not, which they brought to transition, was a personal attribute some of them would have to fight to keep.

A number of these people were horrified by the fact that they had suddenly become both middle aged and single, and they fled this reality by seeking refuge in a quick remarriage. Others looked around a bit and decided this might finally be an opportunity to do more of what they had always wanted to do—*all by themselves!* One spoke of it as "not always going ahead in the name of the company or as a member of a family, but *in my own right!*" Another declared, "I want to explore the boundaries of social experience, whatever that means." The refusal, on the one hand, to remain single, and the eagerness, on the other, to explore life as a single person, organized passage and provided an underlying motive power.

Receptivity to new ideas (or the lack of it) had a lot to do with whether or not people took a new direction after divorce. People responded differently to the changes that had been transforming American society. Some made decisions in opposition to the "new culture," because they found it alien; while others, fascinated by it, made choices from it. Too often people regard the cultural transformation as something that began and ended in the 1960s, but its influence on transition and on the origins of societal developments still resonating among us has enormous impact. Before noting the relevance to my subjects' histories of these broad cultural shifts, it is necessary to provide some additional background into their histories.

FRESH STARTS

The Experience of Mobility

A major theme in most subjects' histories was their recollections of money problems during childhood. Although the experiences of the few who came from homes where their grandparents had once been wealthy but lost much of their money may have differed from those of people who never had money, all the childhood stories focused on their parents going through "hard times." All subjects referred in some way to experiences of anxiety over money (status hunger) from early days. Nevertheless, their own experiences were of constantly enlarging opportunities. Most men had been officers in the military (women, their wives); at the least people went to college, especially men, who went on the GI Bill; and many secured a graduate or professional education. Initially, most went to second-rate schools, but many took advanced degrees at first-rank universities. A few had first attended preparatory schools.

The linchpin in the lives of these people was their decision not to return to small-town life after college: college was not to be an end but rather a means. College training was the mechanism that fed many couples into occupations that channeled them into upper-middle-class life, in a way few had foreseen. Many quickly attained solid, corporate posts. Others rapidly rose through law practices or the architectural firms they established, for example. It was "life's escalator, going up!"

Another fateful development that began with the college experience was geographic mobility: corporate life meant routinely accepting transfers. Couples moved through a succession of major cities, repeatedly setting up new homes. First, there were the housing developments; one subject started out in Levittown, for example. Then there were the "better suburbs" where houses varied architecturally and lawns were larger. Sometimes there was the architect-designed "house in the country." "But," as one subject said, "it was one of the few things that came off in the way I'd hoped."

Although their moves were not as far ranging as those in corporate life, self-employed couples also moved every few years, generally however into more expensive houses on the same city's outskirts. These couples described their moves in terms of a "better neighborhood for the children."[1] The shifts in residence were class linked, designed to assure their children the company of the "right children" and the "best experiences"; in short, to plant them firmly in the soil of upper-middle-class life, as a subculture. The "better neighborhoods" also very overtly reflected their financial success.

These couples were *proud* of having prospered. Some achieved more than others, but the point is, almost everyone in the study had "done well" as couples. They thought sometimes about how much better their children's childhoods were compared to the limitations of their own. Some couples argued about whether or not the kids "ought to have to work for it, just as we did." The more indulgent parent usually won, in practice, but these debates were common features of their social life as couples. The few subjects from homes where "old money" ran out, prided themselves on being able to "take a new tack" and sail on. When they were telling me their stories, almost all accounts began with a reference to college. In this book I began my discussion of their histories by noting the significance of the early fears of or fact of economic worries, but the subjects' inevitable reference was to college, where they thought it all started. In their minds, life had confirmed the dictum that the American dream begins with college.

All over the country, the suburbs were growing as a new social phenomenon, and people like my subjects moved into them in the manner of a new wave of migrants pursuing a gold rush—they were new social types. Later, this experience of moving became a favorite topic among them. A common question when people got together eventually became, "Do you have any place in the country that you now think of as *home?*" When someone would ask, "Where did you *grow up?*", some people would start to grin. One said, "All over the country." Many had a war story or two about moving; as they got older, these became reminiscences of a favorite town at a favorite time.

One woman apologized to her children for all the moving they had done and was surprised that their appraisals of the experience were unexpectedly positive:

> If we hadn't gone to the Middle West, we wouldn't have learned to ice skate; and if we hadn't moved to Southern California, we wouldn't have gotten to surf; and moving to the South was another good trip; so there's nothing we'd want to have left out.

She added that she had herself enjoyed each section of the country in turn, but that the experience had left her

> eternally vigilant—you know . . . feeling kind of *vulnerable.* So many things we had to face were unexpected, every time, every move. I had to grow up on each move. Sometimes I did, sometimes I didn't get far enough with that. It made us have to try to grow, but it made everything a little harder. It seems to have made me restless, or there was a rhythm I took on unconsciously. Seven years is about my limit now, before I start to look around and lay some plans. One result of the moving was my total drive to get my *own* house. I'd fight anybody for it—and I have.

The Subjects' Histories: Time and Mobility

After divorce, this mobility supplied the subjects with many conversational gambits through which they sized one another up as formerly marrieds. Thus the question "Where are (were) you from?" replaced the age-old query "Who are your folks?" Though they didn't discuss it as such, these moves not only reflected upward mobility, but also resulted from the nation's shift from a rural to an urban character. These people had left "down home" ways and became, in effect, transients.

This mobility did not prevent people from sustaining old ties through traveling on business and vacations (often combined). Old friends also came to visit them on both Coasts and in the large Midwestern city from which most subjects were recruited. They developed fairly wide acquaintance networks and a considerable familiarity with much of the country.

For many, these moves were enlightening and provided opportunities for a sense of camaraderie that would otherwise have been unavailable to them. One subject recalled,

> Denver was our longest stay. We formed a mission church there with three other couples. It got to be a great big family right down to kids, and we were all surrogate parents.

Another remembered,

> I had an Iowa farming community neighbor always baking bread and sewing. It made me feel unskilled and clumsy. But then we had a fire and her child almost died being born, and we became sisters from that time on. Much later her Charlie went into the New York office. I only saw her one more time. I'd gotten so down to earth and she was so citified and stylish; we laughed about all the changes.

Later on, when entertaining courting possibilities as individuals who had divorced along this road, mobility experiences gave everyone a place to start from. New partners might spend days discussing a city they'd both lived in as a factor they held in common from which to attempt a joint history. But sometimes their recollections of a region were vastly different, each having lived in a different part of an area and at different times. As one described it,

> All of that lovely, lolling-around summer, we talked about Chicago. But he talked about his classes and playing baseball and screwing the dean's daughter and beating out his friend—and I was talking about a house, and three kids, and a depression, out in Lake Forest.

An additional component of moving was its contribution to people's sensitivity to nuances of dress and speech. Many became skilled at "impression management," especially the "fast track" people. Manners, attire, and bearing had symbolic value and were important to couples who believed they had to "fit in." As "company people" they paid attention to their self-presentation. They trained themselves to "put a good face" on things and tried to cultivate in themselves the habit of adapting, right down to using local expressions or accepting local customs. Men and women who had been "good little boys and girls" and surely, good students, continued to study, emphasizing external factors in an effort to please or "to win." Carefully packaging oneself was just a sensible thing to do, in their judgment. Subjects later associated their financial success with what they called their "flexibility." One subject remembered a pact she had with her husband, when the children were young:

> If he gave me fifteen minutes notice before he brought home a client or a boss, I could pick up the front of the house, put out the makings of a drink, call the kids in from play and wash them, and change my clothes. Then Bill would walk in with the other

man and zap—the great all-American family, "interrupted" when cozily together at home.

Entertainment of business associates took many forms. In addition to the people who would fly in for a day of business, some might be entertained by a weekend of sporting events. Others would be brought in from the airport, served drinks at home, and be taken out for dinner prior to attending conferences the following day. When asked to describe these rounds of obligatory entertaining of what were mostly customers, one woman responded, "lonely." She thought a while, and then went on,

> One elaborate dinner in one overdone place after another. I'd ask the man if he had any snapshots from home; they always did. They'd get them out and light up—at least for the moment. I'd say something inane like, "Now that *is* a boy!" and pass them to Bill. And then they'd resume their business, and I'd excuse myself —"powder room"—and go to a pay phone and call all over the country, everyone I knew well who was in, and we'd kid and we'd laugh: "You can't imagine how *exciting* it is back here," I'd say, and we'd start laughing again. Having someone to call killed the time while they talked. One winter it must have kept me sane. Bill worked so hard, but he loved it. Going back from leaving the man at the motel the company used, we were always too tired to talk, and what did we have to say? At least our kids were with us, and not just in snapshots.

For these couples, married life was a continual repetition of settling into another neighborhood, another city, or new levels of responsibility and therefore, authority. Establishing themselves repeatedly and well, required being able to understand situations quickly. And playing politics well allowed one to *control* the next move. The possibility of moving to another city or another company was always a consideration, since "staying too long" could turn into "having to stay" which might come to mean the end of the upward mobility ride.

An apparent exception to this mobility pattern lay in subjects who "stayed put" after college as the children of locally important families. Nevertheless, these couples were *socially* mobile, because they made new occupational choices. They became the engineer sons or the professionally trained "late blooming" daughters of locally prominent merchants, settling into the "best part of town" in towns overtaken by fast-growing metropolitan centers.

All of the men and women viewed themselves as adventurers, compared to still-in-the-old-rut friends from childhood, who stayed behind to take over the family store. However, during periods when their careers or marriages may have been faltering or when they could afford to stop moving for a while, they would enjoy visits from those childhood friends and the chance to show them hospitality as well as their achievements. In the main, they tended to associate with other mobile people whom they met in their travels and with whom they had more in common (though this group was less likely to be impressed by the house, the pool, or the cars). But, as their marriages became increasingly unstable, all these associations tended to diminish. As one subject described this situation: "There were ten couples of us in all who started that company. Four of five years later, two of us were still married couples." An important function a few of these friends served was to be valued confidants during the divorce transition. Old friends gave them someone who was an intimate "back then." They delighted in having access to someone who "knew me before," and in this, these "good soldiers" were like military couples.

Most of my subjects wore their histories of moving as badges of honor. The fact of change was such a constant in their lives that it came to provide the foundation for many group myths;

changing was central as a life history theme, and their experience of social and geographic mobility was both concrete and symbolic. One woman discussed the significance of something so simple as a woman offering her hand to someone, because by this illustration, she had seen the importance of her being aware of regional customs, and her example showed how she had tried to recognize and meet other people's expectations as she moved around the country:

> In the East, you shake hands like a man if you're a woman; in the South, you loan a man your hand to hover over; but in the West, if you offer a man your hand, he sort of looks around, as if looking for your horse.

The final destination for large numbers of these men and women was the Sunbelt, particularly California. Some people who had been long-term mobiles did not want to undergo any more changes. But other people were ready and waiting for another good wind, as if they were hang glider converts. At any rate, all of my subjects got another chance at change, regardless of whether or not more change was welcome—the sixties were coming, like the Redcoats.

Alterations in Expectations: The Question of Recognition

Mobility was not the only factor to affect their marriages and influence their future postdivorce decisions. There was also a discrepancy between the traditional images of the family these people took into a first marriage and the *facts of family life*, as the subjects came to know it. The husband's job led them into rounds of job connected sociability. There were company cars, tax write offs, flight itineraries, company lodges in the North-woods, expense accounts, business-seminar vacations, and country clubs, or there were faculty clubs, conferences abroad, and admiring students. They had aspired to, and joined, an unfamiliar world. In this seductive, newly won experience of affluence, status considerations were prominent and gave rise to a common "language" nearly everyone could "read." As corporations, university faculties, and professions expanded, job advancement occurred more rapidly and with greater certainty.

On the other hand, in their parental roles, tangible positive recognition of their performance was often more elusive. One woman commented,

> I dropped a lot of my friends when our kids got close to college. Half of them had sons who went to Harvard or who then took graduate training on full scholarships, or daughters who married them—I didn't have much to report at the time.

The children of these subjects, instead of inheriting the hard-times legacy of their parents, had acquired a taste for good living. In the absence of family-owned firms or other substantial forms of property, "the good life" was about all most parents had to pass on. And, because they took their own accomplishments so seriously (not connecting them with the general effects of the country's increasing urbanization), they thought of themselves as "different" and special. Therefore, the upward-mobility drive was a gift people often attempted to impose on their children.

In many of my subjects' histories, along with the stories about "getting by in the Depression," there were memories of the ideas their parents impressed upon them about self-control and hard work. One man reported that his modest provider of a father was one of the few men in his hometown who was never without work. Another subject said she was surprised when her mother told her of a year during the Depression when her uncle and aunt had to live with their family. The subjects' own parents never forgot all the lean years, and these lingered on like echoes in the hopes and ambitions instilled in subjects by their parents. However, soon the "hard times" stories gave way before the standards of material comfort subjects came to possess, and their parents, to admire. The *meaning* of this was that something very good had happened, largely, people thought, by their own efforts. In other words, it seemed to them these rewards had been *earned;* therefore, they felt *entitled* to them.

From this emerged one example of what came to be called "the philosophy of entitlement." By the 1970s, there were many others. Throughout the sixties, newly permissive attitudes began to permeate many regions and many groups, especially on the East and West coasts. The media saw the "new culture" as amusing, while manufacturers perceived it as profitable.

Women returned to college, went out to work, or started to run for public office. A wealthy male subject complained, "At houseparties, all the women go to their rooms after dinner, to *study.*" The divorce rate rose. Traditional sex roles and many other bases of behavioral expectations began to shift. Rumor had it that many older formerly marrieds were, en masse, enjoying casual sexual encounters.

By the 1970s, long hair no longer signified ideological commitment, but perhaps the means to afford a hair stylist. "Hip!" became the justification for decreased effort. The image of the millionaire rock star or drug dealer, whose access to luxury appeared not to rest in deferred gratification, infuriated some hard working parents.

FRESH STARTS

Among other developments, in the early 1970s political activism turned to the civil rights of homosexuals. In some suburbs, people whispered that *"women* were leaving home for other women." One subject commented that lesbianism was a partial solution to the sex ratio disadvantage for women seeking partners, referred to by another subject as the "sex ration." The Gay movement emerged during the latter part of my fieldwork, and at the very least, its vitality meant that subjects knew quite well how much the social rules were changing.

Looking back on the 1960s, subjects commonly recalled the impossibility of explaining their parents and their children to each other. They regarded this function as an obligation which they often failed to fulfill. One stably married onlooker called his age group, the "first generation in history to be kicked by both their parents and their children," by which he meant, rejected.

Originally, as parents, my subjects probably intended to teach their children the values of the work ethic that had fueled them. However, many failed, in part because they took them for granted, and, in part, because circumstances had changed. By and large, the upshot was that they supplied their children instead with many things they had themselves gone without as children. Doing so was part of being successful. Some parents were still defensive or wistful about not having had the opportunity to learn to dance, sail, ride, or play tennis and saw to it their children had these opportunities. One subject said, "We defined these activities as part of a happy childhood as well as the normal way to acquire socially useful skills."

Many youths caught the emphasis on privilege, without understanding how to acquire the discipline necessary to secure these creature comforts by their own efforts. Others saw that plans had been made for them, largely without their being consulted. Lastly, as they got older, many children were baffled by their parents. They did not understand them, in many cases because they grew up after most of the parental triumphs were obtained. They had been too young to "really know" their parents on the "road up."

This is an old dilemma, but certain particulars of the parents' histories aggravated matters. Among them was the parents' preference for focusing on the expanded present rather than on their more modest beginnings. One subject remembered,

> We never said much about the early hardships as it was almost part of our code to make it all "look good," even with our kids. When they were little, there was almost no couple life. "Being on the road" meant calling to cancel most of the invitations we got, and when we planned a party, half the time Hank got called out on the road again. Finally, we used to go ahead anyway and wait for the last pair to leave, with all the cordiality still intact and all the laughing when they left. Everybody enjoyed Hank! When they'd pulled off in their cars, he just got in his, and maybe drove five hundred miles and went to work on his arrival. I cleaned up all the traces of the merriment, alone.

Another described the early struggle:

> We were awfully poor for a long time. I turned Frank's collars and learned to iron his shirts well. We tried to look like people who sent the laundry out, but we couldn't, for years.

Still another said,

> Part of our timetable was that we were looking ahead to putting a lot of this behind us, before time for the kids to go to school. Instead of saving money for that, we put our time and energies into it [getting the promotions].

According to their plans, couples wanted and expected to be rolling along on the momentum by the time the children started college. Part of the proof that they had made good choices would be their children going further and faster—more easily than they had. To this end, my subjects' firmly held but tacit expectations placed many of their older children in a double bind; the children were expected at the very least to "succeed" in their turn, but many of them had little idea of how to do it. The parents had the answer and stated it clearly: "college!" Enormous pressure was put on many children to get into a "good college," and much intergenerational conflict ensued. Some children met both parental timetables and hopes; a larger number refused, failed, or delayed doing so.

Among the other troubles was the fact that parents had produced so many offspring in so short a time that the "baby boom" resulted in a young mob competing for a limited array of services, such as college classes, and a smaller supply of social rewards, among them, good jobs.[2] This was not to claim that all children met with obstacles, balked, or were embarrassed by parents but, rather, to note an important fact. Child-launching time brought many parents to a halt. The escalator stalled. For many of my subjects, parenthood, family life, and middle age began to look alarmingly problematic.

What took place next was as unintended as it was unforeseen. Some parents joined hands with their children in the antiwar movement, but others virtually lost them, at least temporarily, to the youth movement. It was a volatile collective forum for students who romanticized, not the parental climb and the family history, but lower-class life. They adopted drug use, minority speech patterns, and working-class clothes and manners. They took up life in urban slums, particularly around their universities. At the same time, minority youths began the long march in the reverse direction: into college ranks and into the middle class.

In order to flout convention and authority, and "turn everything around," subjects' children began turning definitions on their heads. To be a "freak" was desirable, and it was "groovy" to gain an altered state of consciousness through hallucinogens, not a dangerous use of precious time. Parents heard permanence in relationships termed "neurotic dependence," rather than the capacity to honor commitments. Some almost grown children talked incessantly about "doing your own thing," clearly meaning *theirs,* and turned away from parents much as subjects had turned their backs on small-town life.

In the subsequent uproar, such topics as racism, pacifism, feminism, sexism, and violent political activism competed with the parents' plans as well as with middle-class notions about values, such as the proper definition of respectability and predictability. In recounting this period (when it had been an influence on their lives), some subjects mentioned in passing being affronted by the music, or the nudity, or frank sexuality of this period. Some were wounded by their children's apparent dismissal of family or national values, especially the fathers of conscientious objector sons. But many more subjects, particularly ones in long passages, talked about their families being united (intact, or not) by issues such as opposition to events at People's Park or Kent State or the wars in Vietnam and Cambodia.

Nevertheless, a potentially divisive factor lay in the contrast between what went on in their children's lives and in their own, at the time. Many subjects reported at least briefly some uneasiness about their children's existences or mounting distress at aspects of their lives in this era. Some subjects had adopted their children's music, pot-smoking habits, and attire, like blue jeans. But even many of these "hip" companions spoke of years of trying to understand and be supportive of rather distant children who went on to abandon them anyway, ultimately, often for new forms of quasi-families some of which made little sense to parents. These included Zen communities, the Moonies, fundamentalist religious sects, urban drug-oriented groups, and rural communes. After much of this experimentation partially severed many family ties, some adult children then set out on a trek into the Establishment without reconciling with parents.

Many of these departures were abrupt; some looked likely to be final. These withdrawals were frequently followed by the distress if not condemnation of grandparents, troubled by suggestions that they ought not to hold parents responsible for all of this. This state of affairs cut seriously into parental confidence, because it tore apart their assumptions about life and their places in it. Without the trust and appreciation of (or even contact with) blood relatives, subjects felt cut off and many of them regretted not being able to function as generational bridges to a now dispersed but once much closer family. One subject reported her daughter's response to a timidly tendered parental invitation: "Well, it's OK that you asked—but I don't think I'd want to come. I doubt that I'd be *comfortable.*"

These denials of custom did not end in a breakdown in American families across the board nor in a social revolution; but they did lead to a substantial erosion in traditional culture. It is usually discussed in terms of its effect on young adults, but it also had a major impact on parental lives, in many cases. It changed some subjects profoundly because it marked the overturning of many of their expectations for themselves, as well as the start of their search for substitute bases of life satisfaction and meaning. The resultant societal adjustments are still underway.

The Subjects' Histories: Time and Mobility

I have left for later mention the significance to many subjects of the social movements of the 1960s. Suffice to say here that these changes had been matters of great moment to some parents. Some had changed their careers or significantly changed the direction of their lives at this time. In addition, some men and women in my study had contributed to the creation of the "new culture" as wholeheartedly as had their children. One said, "That month, my daughter marched with Cesar Chavez and I was with the Kennedys in California." Some of my subjects had fostered many emerging ideals, such as self-determination for minorities and women. Many women had begun occupational careers of their own, for instance, before children were in high school and redoubled these career efforts in the sixties. And in addition to participating in the antiwar movement, many parents also shared their children's absorption in their music and general political stance.

If parents had learned *anything* from their experience of mobility, it was that social identities are continually being made and remade. The sixties had been another example of the truth of that fact, as well as another instance of change brought about in some of them by what they met in the wider world. Adulthood requires learning to negotiate one's way through the demands of meeting or evading a stream of expectations; but my research subjects also knew that, while a "real world" exists to be dealt with, many opportunities can be created within its parameters. Some subjects decided that they needed to remember that fact once again. Many long-passage subjects had been through psychotherapy and analysis, particularly in the Jungian, humanistic, or existential modes. They were interested in ideas about "self-actualization," and what eventually came to be regarded as the evolution of consciousness.

While some of my subjects looked back on the 1960s with regret, discomfort, or nostalgia over the loss of tradition, others rejoiced in what they saw more as the *loss of constraints* rather than the loss of supports. These latter people set out to enjoy and learn from the "new culture" and to use it as a vehicle for enhancing their lives to the degree that it offered them new goals and new perspectives. This contrast in response is extremely important for grasping the diversity in postdivorce choices, because, in large measure, as a factor in choice, it is a key determinant. Thus, to my subjects, finding themselves middle-aged and divorced in an era rife with cultural contradictions was either *extremely bad luck* or *great good fortune*, depending on how each individual saw matters.

The Social Meanings of Time, the Corporation, and the Future

During this tumultuous period, the meanings people had attached to time and work were also being attacked. The picture is more complete if some of these are now sketched. For one thing, while some research subjects had been self-employed, the corporate world was "home" to most, at least for a time. At any rate, the life-styles and assumptions in both sectors had been much the same. First, faith in upward mobility had originally helped these men and women accomplish their early achievements. Second, in turn, these early successes appeared to reinforce their beliefs in upward mobility as a valuable life motive. However, suddenly they found themselves in a position where they had to contend with critical commentaries on their lives that seemed to be coming from all sides and which seriously called into question the worth of achievement. For instance, some college-aged children pitilessly attacked their managerial fathers as mere corporate lackeys and their mothers as powerless victims of the continual moving that repeatedly uprooted families. Thus, what had for so long seemed a great boon now appeared possibly to be a liability. This took place just at the time when all of the struggle (presumably the down payment for the purchase of a good middle age) was supposed to end. If one's financial success seemed to have been won at the cost of losing one's children, or at the price of an unstable or arid marriage, the charges that parents had not chosen wisely were difficult to counter. Many subjects reported beginning to feel "lost" at some point, with nothing dependable to count on. Some couples insulated themselves from such anxieties, but other couples felt cheated after years of striving. The problem of having to face a relative vacuum in their roles was, for some, compounded by a sense of having followed a life map that was beginning to look ominously out of date.

In time, these worries were intensified by the newly disreputable image of business, government service, and the professions. Eventually even careerism itself, as a concept and a way of life, was devalued, hardly a minor setback for many of the subjects who had pursued the notion of Success the most avidly. Hence, at mid-life, some individuals discovered that they were not going to enjoy claiming the prizes for which they had thought they had laid the groundwork most carefully. This situation went well past the issue of familial values. If they could relinquish aspirations for the children, and indeed, manage to stop worrying about the children entirely, other important questions lingered. *"What,"* some subjects wondered, *"would be left* as possibilities to realize *for themselves?"* This could be a critical question, especially in view of the temporal dimensions of their lives. To some people, middle age was starting to look quite bleak, unlike the prime time they had expected. These men and women faced what was essentially a social/psychological problem of identity, and it had been building up for a long time.

At the problem's core were disturbing questions about meaning, for instance, about how one ought to judge the relationship between identity and Time. In some parent-youth contacts which had, up until then, frequently been harmonious or even enacted with mutual enthusiasm, the sense of mutuality ebbed away or the consensus collapsed. For example, the hip emphasis on "Do it!" and "Now!" was forcibly expressed by some college-aged children who failed to appear at home at the appointed time or in the agreed-upon week—or, at all. Furthermore, not only students but others proclaimed that drug use led to a "higher consciousness" manifested in altered experiences of Time and Self. (Parents who had themselves used hallucinogens tended to agree, if privately.) Worst of all, more and more young people, particularly the dropouts among them, took an increasingly casual approach to the temporal concept paramount to upper-middle-class life: the future. Youth claimed it was not necessary for everybody to prepare for one; rather one might better "stay in the moment." Many subjects knew they were regarded by their children not as "successful," but as people who had merely been "doing time" in occupational settings. Becoming increasingly concerned about their own futures, some parents began to suspect one of the resources they had misunderstood and misused was *Time*.

Research subjects who had been involved in managerial life during first marriages sometimes later recognized that they had felt stifled by the artifice of ostensibly social functions that were actually designed to facilitate the transaction of business. They were familiar with a ruthless level of competition for advancement, since this type of competition was a standard feature of business and professional life to which they'd long been accustomed. One woman spoke bitterly of this push to "get ahead," making an intentional joke by adding *"any-body's,"* to suggest a competitor's head on a platter. This is her retrospective summary:

> Looking back on it I understand it better. But I think we both were completely over our heads much of the time. We were great company performers, but it was the business of private life we couldn't get down to, or on with. There wasn't any *place* for it, or any *time* for it. I had a D and C finally. The doctor said, "You're trying to be a good sport about all the moving, but your insides are talking about how it is for you." I was astounded, and also a bit frightened, that he could meet me once, and tell all that. It meant I wasn't a good wife. On the next move, I got down to 85 pounds, and I was afraid to meet the neighbors. So I thought, "I'm supposed to *die* for Boeing?" And I left.

The instrumental character of much of this obligatory social life robbed it of any personal meaning; it became a matter of acting by "rote" when the husband and wife team was estranged or affluence no longer had much power to satisfy them in itself. This is what another woman subject said:

> Some of the women just gloried in big houses and all the hub-bub. I think I sort of sickened on all the competition and scramble for money after awhile. Nothing seemed to matter but the next contract.

Some of the people my subjects met on this road were very well satisfied. As one woman pointed out,

> Lots of other people had moved a lot, too, but they seemed to take it better in stride. For one thing, they didn't go up so fast. I think that we couldn't handle being on that fast a track. Although, one part of it was that we loved it; I mean, I was awfully proud of Charlie. People seemed to see us as the Golden Couple. After awhile, I didn't handle it very well. There was a lot of

drinking—it wasn't Hollywood, but it wasn't very stable either. And there was less and less for me to do. At first I edited Charles' reports and all his speeches; and we tended to take part in the community while we were there, because the company liked the impression it made. The next thing I knew, he had a whole technical writing department, and my only role was serving coffee when they came out to work late with him at home, and then, to get out of the way.

The social obligations connected to work readily became stale, and they greatly extended the normal work week, already torn by the degree to which a husband's business life was often conducted while out of town. Sometimes "going up in the world" meant shorter trips, such as days where the husband would fly out in the morning and back at night. One woman said that when her husband assumed this sort of a schedule, it felt to her as though he were just going to and from the office. But in other cases, "doing well" meant extended trips to Europe and elsewhere. Some women began to try to bargain for changes, but without much success:

> Anytime I tried to talk about it, he just said "later." This was supposed to mean that later we'd have a more normal life. I tried to get him to agree to discuss a move with me before we took another promotion or offer from another firm. The fights would be terrible; I knew he thought I was just a hindrance. He'd promise and then the phone would ring and his face would light up. Once he accepted a job over the phone when someone called and woke us at two in the morning—without any gesture in my direction, as I sat in bed and watched him. That time I just said, "It's all over but the crying." He seemed to not even hear me.

To some subjects, the whole edifice of positive meanings attached to "success" began to fall. The "company line" with its metaphors from competitive sports and military life began to pall. One other factor was related to the whole question of self-presentation. Industrial growth had been accompanied by the expansion of occupational specialties such as sales engineering, marketing, and advertising; these career lines became dominant models for a style that was pervasive in much of the business and professional world. One consequence of all of this, according to critics, who sometimes included the subjects' own children, was the need to develop a *marketable personality* [3] People who had functioned effectively as a husband and wife "team" in the pseudosocial corporate roles had, indeed, often done so at the cost of having much of a private life together. This is how one woman described turning what was to her a bitter experience of her husband's continual absences into amusement for his superiors:

> The kids were about six and ten before I really started to give up having any hope at all about our future ever being any better. My husband seemed so elated and stimulated all the time. He "went up" very fast, so the promotions that were crushing blows to me as a family woman wanting to continue to be part of some stable community life—well, they were just another way to be a "star," another dazzling experience for him. His constant absences, on top of the continual moving, simply made a mockery out of any attempts to have a normal family life. I guess I gave up on the couple part of it first, since that seemed to be "over" almost as soon as it began. So he used to come in off the road late at night, and, because he was doing well and was popular, he often brought a regional man with him, or sometimes a higher up from the home office. I used to get the kids up in their pj's to introduce them and I taught them to ask, "Which one is *Daddy*, mother?"

Thus, the problems many subjects faced when trying to launch children and retain their loyalty, and their conflicts about the level of affluence which they were having more and more trouble finding satisfying, considering its drawbacks and the price, suggest some ways in which these people's expectations were being challenged and denied. To some people, reaching this much of a roadblock across their paths was a shock, like walking into a glass door they had not seen. Never before in their adult lives had they met with so much resistance to their plans and hopes—to what their social identities were supposed to stand for.

As mid-life loomed, some of these people had forgotten how to play or be spontaneous or intimate—if they'd ever known. Some decided not to forgo these benefits any longer. Many divorced before children entered college and others before the children finished. Still others feared that divorce would only serve as another wrenching experience. However, as an alternative to divorce, a noncommunicative and nonexpressive marriage carried on into a final move into a retirement enclave did not seem a very attractive fate either. At this juncture, the problem was that many people were without any value system or rationale adequate for understanding what they had done to themselves and each other—what had happened? One decided to

> fall back to the lines of least resistance. I had had dreams of having it all. I really loved the man I married. I knew from the first he was a "winner" and would go far. I saw that the night I met him. On our second date, I decided I wanted to marry him. He asked me to, on the third. But I changed many of my goals, after divorce. I hoped just to be able to support myself, and dropped my hopes for graduate school for the children, and just hoped they'd be alive and not institutionalized in five years.

Another woman spoke of substituting for her hopes gratitude that mother takes such pleasure in her Martinis; Susan finally settled down with that total loss, Roger; and my other child has stopped apologizing for her divorce.

Middle age began to look like an investment that wasn't going to pay off. It looked like the occasion for being shorn of long-anticipated satisfactions. To some people, then, time seemed to be "running out." These facts are inextricably linked to the considerable extent to which long-passage men and women changed many of their views about life. One woman brought a Lawrence Durrell poem to an interview, adding her own emphasis to the last phrase of an opening line, "Find time hanging; *cut it down!*"[4]

3

Brief Passages:

The Immediate (Planned) Remarriers

and the Graduates

SOME PEOPLE move toward postdivorce goals rationally and effectively, but others get bogged down, especially if a divorce is unwelcome or delayed by complicated litigation. Thus, managing one's stock of resolute hopefulness is part of managing the transition, even in many cases of brief passages. A factor I frequently found to be crucial to success in many brief passages is maintaining a rapid pace. This can be, however, difficult or almost impossible to accomplish. Pace is often an important consideration in any form of passage, but it can be an exquisitely painful and alarming factor in some brief passages. Before we look at the first two categories of brief passage, there are a few general points to consider which set the stage for my discussion.

The very fact of being in the *process* of getting a divorce can make the transitional period a very hard time for a person. Learning the role of a separated man or woman, and preparing for the impending role of a divorced individual, can be arduous. For a person who has secretly chosen another mate, appearances must be maintained, since acquaintances will expect one to behave in certain ways, that is, *as if* one is having to deal with a lonely time of separation. There are many details requiring one's attention, such as changing a will to exclude a soon to be ex-spouse. At every step, handling minor business matters can provoke a flood of feelings in the divorcing individual, which may include some very uncomfortable emotions. One subject noted this, saying,

> I have been very happy since my divorce five years ago, but one piece of unfinished business remains, my will. It needs to be redone, as my property is now left between an ex-husband and two children with whom I have little rapport. Until I find someone else or the children straighten out some of their confusion with respect to me, I evidently will not have an answer to this dilemma adequate enough to base a change on. My evasion of this task also illustrates some denial.

The need to make the shifts which result from divorce while simultaneously executing the extra work accompanying the process of divorce can generate much complexity before litigation is concluded. At the same time, one must meet the demands of many other roles as if nothing unusual is happening. For example, a person may have to confer with clients or attempt to secure a contract, *as if* one is not also engaged in crowding into a day other conferences related to ending a marital contract. If professional commitments and all valued social ties are to be retained, they must be honored and protected. In every kind of divorce transition, the stress and workload that accompany securing the divorce can be exhausting for a brief time. It is easy to lose one's entire perspective on Time, when one feels that the divorce process will "never end" or that one will feel overwhelmed "forever." The isolation a divorcing (or newly divorced) person often longs for in periods that test one's equilibrium, can be hard to come by when so many roles must be almost continuously enacted. One subject describes the satisfaction of a brief reprieve:

> The day I was to appear before the judge, I took the day off, got the children off to school, dressed, and drove out to the suburb where we used to live to pick up the neighbor who offered to testify. We went to my attorney's office and followed him downtown to court. When my case was finally called, it was short. I took her home, drove back in from the suburbs, changed my clothes, and the children got home. A man friend had invited me to go out to celebrate that night, but he didn't call, and I was glad. I just wanted to be quiet and be with the children. I fixed some food, and they were kind of subdued. We ate in silence. Then I called my assistant to check on the office, put everything on "overnight hold," and went to bed at seven.

In addition to the likelihood of lacking time to collect oneself and having the extra work related to securing a divorce, one must pick up some of the services a spouse once provided, and, even in mundane matters, this means developing unfamiliar skills. Men no longer able to turn over to wives routine chores like paying bills, become list makers, and women, by necessity, car mechanics and carpenters. Furthermore, as separated or single parents, individuals may be hard pressed to meet their children's needs. Usually some alteration in parenting roles occurs, and this may add to overall role strain. The necessity to make many adjustments can drain one's supply of energy and confidence.

Unexpected complications that add to strain and profoundly

affect the children often arise due to the common tendency of revengeful or overwhelmed parents either to monopolize or virtually abandon children. This can have dramatic effects on former mates as well. Despite the public's impression that there is a national trend toward joint custody and amicable divorce, even among more traditional (older) couples, the fact of a husband repudiating a court judgment and evading most of its provisions still persists. For some time, single mothers in California, for instance, have had difficulty getting loans or in overcoming informal barriers to the extension of their credit even when they are working and have received "good judgments" or ample settlements to augment their earnings. Although it is illegal to take such statistics into consideration when credit is applied for, it is well known (to everyone but these mothers) that immediately following many California divorces ex-husbands get their companies to transfer them out of state and, effectively, out of their obligations to children from a first marriage. A "good judgment" or handsome settlement which proves to be unenforceable is neither.

In other words, it is very common for a mother with custodial rights to take for granted and badly need the co-parenting participation of an ex-husband, who instead withdraws fatherly support of the children and cannot be induced to perform his parental role. This may seem to him the most direct way to punish a woman who left him. The following describes one man's response to not winning custody:

> He said he would continue to love them, and I assumed he would, as he had always seemed to be a most fond father. Instead, after the divorce he gave me two choices: turn them over to me, or I'll ignore them. They didn't *want* to go to their father—so he ignored them.

Nevertheless, in this sort of case, the father who absents himself may appear to be the preferred parent, especially if the children who wish to remain with the mother are, at the same time, angry with her. Here, the possibilities for hostility and punitive action can reverberate endlessly unless some or all of these people tire of these ways of handling their sadness, or work through some of its consequences, by other means.

In the course of this study, I only met five single fathers. Of these, two had received custody of their children by mutual agreement with ex-spouses who had visiting privileges. They had had this arrangement since the children were quite young. Two of the other fathers had gradually assumed care of their children after the mothers encountered difficulties, including illness, and couldn't care for them. These children generally keep in contact with their mothers, who live at some distance from them, by telephone. And, one father, with a twelve-year-old girl—an only child born when he was forty-three—has had sole care of his daughter since the mother left them when she was a two-week-old infant. Since that time, the father and daughter have only received two postcards from the mother. Thus, it is not always clear at the onset of divorce how parenting roles will have to be handled and if a single parent will have to deal with unforeseen, negative consequences of the divorce in an effort to protect the children's welfare and his or her own.

An ex-spouse who has been led to expect to be able to see the children often may be prevented by a former mate from having any access to them, while others (even after they are remarried) may pray for the departure from the scene of a former spouse, who, in the name of parenting, constantly disrupts everyone. The point is simply that unforeseen and extremely difficult circumstances may suddenly arise to complicate what once appeared to be a relatively smooth passage. Such negative developments related to having had children can then expand to undermine one's various other roles and bases of security.

In some cases, on the other hand, an ex-spouse may offer no resistance during proceedings or may be outmaneuvered before the final decree is even obtained. Considering the horrendous possibilities that could otherwise ensue, a good case can be made for outmaneuvering a spouse, from a practical point of view (ethical considerations aside). One woman said, in defense of having asserted herself,

> My attorney was so relieved to represent a woman who wanted a divorce but wasn't so guilty about it that she was ready to give up all her rights, he almost cheered.

Another said,

> My lawyer had represented many women who gave up most of their rights during pretrial negotiations, because they thought it would make things easier in getting along with the former husband and make him want to come back to her. He said usually nothing like this ever happens, and then he has a "hardship case" on his hands, a woman who never gets over the split.

Similarly, a male subject recalled,

> I picked my attorney because of his reputation for being capable and tough. I told him why I wanted him and that I wanted the best terms he could get me, and he couldn't believe me at first. He said almost never does a man walk into his office so unconflicted.

And, describing the reverse experience, another man said,

> My lawyer is a friend, but he couldn't do much for me, because I went back for a reconciliation attempt against his advice. It destroyed the case we had intended to use to protect my interests.

FRESH STARTS

Unexpected setbacks are less apt to occur, however, when two divorcing people put their children's welfare first and plan for it, and also show each other consideration. These people do not convert a divorce into an opportunity to attack each other. The following story containing details I heard from a number of other men as well, describes such an amicable agreement:

> We don't see each other much since the divorce, and that made getting over it easier. We each now have found other people. What we do still do is get together at Christmas (or just before a child's birthday) and spend the day shopping for gifts and having lunch so we can talk over how each of them is doing. The marriage breakup hurt, but we know we are still parents of the same children, and we want to make it clear nothing ever changes that.

Another man whose ex-spouse also valued the cooperation he saw as essential to the children even in their young adulthood told me this:

> When our youngest boy was playing in his band in the next town, I called his mother and asked her if she would like to meet me the next night at the club and hear them play, and she said, "Sure!" We sat at a table together, had several drinks, and talked a lot about a number of things neither of us had been comfortable enough to discuss before. We had a pretty good time. The other kids had come to hear George, too, and they were ecstatic to see the whole family reassembled and sort of impressed with both of us.

An added complication stemming from the presence of children is their tendency to hope for a parental reconciliation long after there is any evidence that either parent would consider this.[1] This desire to reconstitute the original family may surface, in the form of muffled but vigorous objections to a parent's new "friend." Such a reaction may mystify a single parent and, at the same time effectively forestall the new relationship. Although the *parent* may be in transition, children may not have inwardly accepted the changed family status.

On the other hand, children can be of great assistance to a single parent. Getting to know people and making new friends (as well as enjoying old ones) may be facilitated by a child's friendliness or companionship needs, as this woman noted:

> Matt had just started to teach the children chess when we decided to go ahead with the divorce. He left the set with us. I found that everyone who was taking me out liked the game, and most evenings out were thus proceeded by a chess lesson. Several came over just for an evening of chess, which was nice for us all. Later, the man I married, taught young Winton to drive.

One's children may be one's best friends, one's greatest pride, or one's sole concern, and thus a major factor in keeping life going:

> After divorce, my children were the focus of my efforts to go on. I never thought of anything but being there for them. I thought as soon as they were older and OK, I had the choice to "check out," and sometimes I tried to plan by what means. Pills weren't too acceptable as I didn't understand dying by that process, and a gun seemed better (short and sure!) except messy, so I knew I'd want someone else to find me, not the kids. When I tried to decide *when*, that was harder, as I thought them much too young at the time.

> It really got funny—looking back on it. I kept postponing the idea until they got through this or graduated from that, but then I realized it wouldn't *ever* be much help to them to have a suicide for a mother; so I started driving and driving after they went to sleep. I'd go out on the freeway and hold it at 85, trying to decide what to do. Finally I decided on a concrete abutment—I mean, I saw I could drive into one and who could know *why* it had happened? But I kept putting it off until one day somebody at the

car repair shop asked me out, and the next thing I knew, I was having a lot of ideas about things I could do for *me*. That hadn't dawned on me before. I just kept thinking "got to keep going for the kids." Gordon was a painter having his Lotus fixed—he was fun.

Anyone who has not rehearsed what to do if alone, or anyone who is divorced and too depressed to see any grounds for hope, or anyone not recognizing his or her options as an individual, ought to consider using a divorce group or divorce counselor as a tool for managing the transition. A counselor is especially helpful if one can't seem to "get started" rebuilding life very readily, or is new in an area, or finds contacts at work only minimally satisfying. It is often best to avoid sharing personal confidences at work, since confiding can sometimes interfere with one's professional functioning. However, some single parents feel that not only should they not express their feelings at work, but they should also hide any unhappy ones from their children. In so doing, they can prevent the children from expressing their own feelings.

Although both a parent and the children need to discuss together the impact on all of them of the changed family status, very often this does not take place. When the most important feelings and thoughts of everyone go unexpressed, the whole family unit may become emotionally "stuck." An excellent use a newly single parent can make of a counselor is simply to engage the counselor to guide the family members through several appointments during which they can review their feelings together. Doing so in the presence of a counselor means that openness will be facilitated and each person can disclose his or her worst fears about what the future may hold with someone present who is able to offer support to each person while being attentive to the welfare of the family as a unit. Clearing the air in such a manner can free the family to go ahead with building a new life *as a family.* Silence can foster not only unrealistic and unnecessary fears, but a child's private and similarly unrealistic hopes, such as for a parental reconciliation which is not going to take place. Without discussion, a number of hidden agendas can exist on both a parent's or the children's sides which get in the way of the progress of each.

Although I now know that certain conditions are more likely to occur when children are present, and other circumstances to develop when they are not present, and though I continually examined my data watching for clues on how the presence or absence of children influences a person's transition; no clear findings emerged to suggest that presence or absence of children *determines* an outcome. The answer to the question, "Are children decisive as an influence on a postdivorce passage?" would have to be "sometimes" or "to some extent." A divorced parent may be tremendously tenacious in the pursuit of a passage goal despite the requirement of caring for children just as often as because of it. Children may be very visible and appear to be more fateful factors in the transition than they actually are. What turned out to be much more relevant to decision-making than possible effects of a course on children were the *beliefs and values* people brought to the divorce experience to make sense out of it, that is, to understand what happened in order to decide what to do about it. It took me a long time to see that values are the foremost influence on passage. Therefore, the reaction a parent has to the fact of a child's existence when the marriage ends will come out of that person's value system and be only one illustration of the great significance beliefs have on choice-making.

In recruiting subjects for the study, I suggested they omit details of their prior marriage and start telling their stories as they took up life after divorce. Despite this, most began their accounts by summing up both the marriage, and often, salient events that took place before they were out of litigation. This occurred because part of the explanation for the way they viewed passage came from their experiences of marriage and divorce; their values had been confirmed or unconfirmed by these experiences.

The language and the images subjects used to describe their marriages and divorces often served as a "vocabulary of motives"[2] which illuminated their perceptions. Even so simple a thing as a person's choice of a first name had meaning. A "Peggy" in the study asked to be called "Margaret," by which she indicated she wanted to be taken more seriously. A "Bob" became a "Rob." By such means, an individual announces, "Hey, world! new name = new man = new life!"

I did not want to ask directly about values, and it was not necessary to do so. The subjects provided abundant clues. Some were revealed in seemingly minor details of a person's style: details of dress, adornment, demeanor, gestures, choice of car, decoration of a house, or the organization of a person's social life. Others surfaced in subjects' casual asides in talks or interviews, or their reports about *(a)* to which friends their invitations went, *(b)* to whom a prospective mate was introduced, *(c)* from whom advice was sought, and *(d)* from whom knowledge of one's private life was withheld.

Early in the research, I decided that the starting point of passage should be considered the time at which the final divorce decree is granted. Although the initial separation may be more traumatic for many, the time of the final decree seemed the more logical choice, since it marks the official change in marital status and, *formally,* the onset of a postdivorce transition. However, I had barely begun to listen to people's stories when I realized my choice was arbitrary and not an accurate reflection of everyone's experience. In actuality, some people "jump the gun."

The Litigation Process: Problems in Timing

Litigation always takes longer than anyone expects. Furthermore, control of the process has to be entrusted to others, except in the rare cases where everything is mutually agreed upon in states with reformed divorce laws. Many subjects began to feel, and some acted as if, their passage began immediately after the one or several episodes of separation which finally led, as they often do, to litigation to end the marriage. (Divorcing couples sometimes reconcile and remarry; but six years of fieldwork failed to uncover one such case.)

Litigation is time-consuming because of crowded court calendars and the opportunities for delays, when details are contested as they tend to be. Even in states such as California, that have instituted a presumed reform (no-fault dissolution), struggles over property division often become the focus of litigation. The process may also be lengthened when one or both spouses wish to inflict damage on the other by delaying the case's resolution (frequent when there is no agreement on separating or both are angry) or when assets are substantial enough to be worth fighting over (frequent when the contest takes place at mid-life, and particularly if neither party expects the financial picture to improve).

Furthermore, in states with traditional divorce laws, the proceedings are likely to be complicated in several ways. In addition to the usual conflicts over property settlements, the adversary nature of the proceedings sometimes requires evidence to be collected showing a spouse to be negligent in marital duties. Also, custody battles are likely to ensue, since courts in these states are not likely to grant joint custody.

It is also common for a two-income couple to arrive harmoniously at a decision to file, only to end up contending over who made what financial contributions to the marriage, who has how good an economic future, and who holds what sort of retirement benefits (of which, in community-property states, half belongs to the spouse). Actuaries may be brought in by each side to testify as to projected earnings. Other problems involve deciding who will contribute what to the children's education or which insurance or medical coverage will be continued for whom.

These opportunities for conflict often lead to drawn-out struggles between divorcing spouses who become discouraged and confused before they even get into court. Furthermore, one's plans for initially maintaining oneself financially can be seriously disrupted by expensive delays in getting things going legally. It is apparently useful to treat a soon-to-be former spouse civilly during pretrial negotiations; subjects who used this period to be combative frequently had a more difficult time in court and arrived at much less acceptable settlements. For instance, after they had quarreled for months and agreed to divorce, one subject's furious, suspicious husband signed himself into a psychiatric ward, thus effectively delaying a scheduled court hearing on the divorce.

Preliminary Moves Toward Singlehood

People who are not yet officially single but who no longer "feel very married" may explore singlehood in advance. In so doing they may avoid the discouraging "dead periods" that wear them out and make them feel they are only "going backwards." Although they are unable to take major steps before they are officially single and certain of their economic position, they tend to speculate on the future, seek their friends' approval, and end up acquiring new romantic attachments.

New romantic involvements can occur suddenly. Sometimes confiding one's troubles to a colleague may unexpectedly elicit his or her own confidences about a troubled marriage that appeared happy. This event can set the stage for a tentative affair, or thoughts of one. In my study, such disclosures prompted several cases of two divorces and two new pairings. This account describes one such case:

> We both worked in the same branch of city government for several years, and then I was assigned to his staff. We worked together well, but it was never personal, until one day in the parking lot at five o'clock. It was pouring; we were both getting into our cars. I had lost my keys, and things at home were choatic. I found myself standing under his umbrella, pouring my heart out. I was shocked when he said he was lonely and unhappy, too, as I had no idea at the time.

A more common story is that the "new romance" also fails around the time one receives the "final," so a person has two failed relationships to ponder, as this case shows:

> We met quite by accident at a meeting she came up to Boston for. At the cocktail party, my new young partner and I left his wife to buttonhole a client. Barbara was by herself and noticed how uncomfortable my partner's wife was, so she went up and introduced herself. When he and I got back, there was Barbara, being nice to Mrs. Clark. I got her a drink, and we all started talking about this famous restaurant none of us knew. I liked her kindness to the other woman and her sort of "heads-up" look. So, on an

impulse, I suggested we all go together, asking Barb to join us. She said, "Why not!" so off we went in a cab. The Clarks knew vaguely my marriage was on the rocks, but Barbara didn't catch my sudden interest. I wrote her a poem that night in my hotel, and when I ran into her the next day, I gave it to her and asked her out to hear some jazz. We stayed together the rest of the week and met at every chance we had for the next year. It got harder and harder with so much distance between us. When I got my divorce, she was interested in someone else at home, and I never even called her.

Another possible outcome is that the brief experience of a love affair may become a source of increased self-esteem, as in the following case:

It was a brief romance, rather doomed from the start. I was immensely changed afterwards. It was the first serious affair of the heart in which I felt like a beautiful woman! On one of those magical weekends, he said to me, quite abruptly, "Your face is like something from Renoir!" We were crazy about Impressionist painting and saw the best of it all over the country. I lived on those memories throughout the long year after it fell apart. We were a great comfort to each other then, and it helped us later both divorce.

Sometimes an inadvertently begun but failed romance becomes the basis for a long relationship between two people who are important to each other but who do not marry:

We were very happy for a time and went through a lot with each other because of sharing our trials and tribulations. By the time I finally secured my divorce, we'd given up our plans and weren't together, but she was a most important person in my life for a long time.

By summarizing the prior marriage and the insights gained or hardships endured during litigation, subjects gave what they saw as necessary background information. Had these new relationships not overlapped litigation, a few passages would not have been so short; but, conceptually, the same range of outcomes would exist to be charted. (The use of the term, "early exiters," implies no value judgment as to prematurity.) The point is that some passages were longer and more complex than others, often representing conscious efforts on the part of a formerly married to make major life changes. Other divorce transitions were purposively managed so as to be brief, uneventful passages as lacking in impact on the person as was possible.

Immediate (Planned) Remarriers

As the first of the brief-passage subgroups I consider here, the Immediate (Planned) Remarriers characteristically overlap litigation with the process of consolidating a new partnership that cannot become official until the final decree is issued. These people are the first to leave passage, and they do so with dispatch, in order to marry the person whose existence prompted the divorce in the first place. To forestall a spouse's opposition to their plan to divorce so they can remarry, the pair keeps "the big secret," divulging it only to a few intimates.

Since Immediate Remarriers intend to marry again within a few days of the final decree, they do not regard themselves as single at any point after falling in love. Their next potential problem, in addition to detection by a spouse, is retaining confidence in the new partner or in their plans. Many of these couples do not hesitate on either count, as this excerpt from data shows:

How did we meet? Well, it was very uneventful. Carl and I were going in to consult the assistant pastor at the church, Bob. Fortunately we didn't run into each other. There were all kinds of problems, and I didn't know what was going to happen or if we would divorce. I got to know Bob from having to talk to him the summer before when Janie got into trouble at church camp drinking beer. Some of the counselors were kind of rowdy and Janie wasn't going to be asked back. Then Carl moved to take another job in a different part of the state, and Bob and his wife knew I was alone and asked me for dinner. Through them I met someone from Bergen county who had been single a long time and "wasn't ever going to remarry." He played a lot of golf, and I just thought of him as nice and—that was that. But I made an apartment out of the guest house because it was expensive with Carl living elsewhere, and technically, Sam was just renting that; but actually he was the star boarder, and my father and Susan and Sam and I were living together. All we had to do was wait for the divorce! Because Carl didn't suspect, I got a good buy on our house. Maybe the reason was that he had met someone where he was working and wanted to conceal that from me.

Another woman said,

When I met Reid, I knew a divorce was the only thing to do, because I thought, "if there're any more like that out there, I've got to get going." It took a lot of planning not to get wiped out financially as I was the first time around. (That was the classic "he gets the money, she gets the kids.") So I agreed to putting the house on the market which Pete wanted to do, but on the condition that at its sale, the proceeds would be divided into two equal checks made out separately to each of us. Otherwise it would have been to "Mr. and Mrs.," he'd have taken it, and I'd have been up the creek. While our house was being shown, I found one for myself, which required I get my husband's signature on a quit claim deed for it to be mine, since we were still married. I waited to present it until the day we were signing the papers for the sale of our house. Later, I also needed him to sign a document agreeing my house was my own separate property for the same reason, so the deed could be registered that way. I asked for that signature the day we were picking up our checks from the sale, and I said it was "for some run-down income property." It was run down alright, and I saw it as potential income. So he signed, and I had bought my house before litigation was over. It wasn't long before Reid joined me there.

Many plans do not progress so easily, however, since the divorce process can produce many factors that threaten a planned remarriage. These can result from a spouse asking for a continuance (postponement of court hearing), or disrupting a timetable by asking for a series of extra pretrial hearings on spurious issues. Therefore, remarriage is contingent on obtaining the decree without a hitch in plans that could threaten the lovers' solidarity.

One subject's remarriage took place on schedule only because a good friend was able to fly to another state to deliver and return with documents needed for the "final," since concessions were demanded by an angry spouse whose opportunities to bargain were not yet exhausted. The spouse secretly planning to remarry was in no mood to negotiate further, because out-of-town guests were enroute for the nuptials. Many subjects assume extra expense or offer some sort of bribe to a spouse in a position to obstruct the divorce.

Intimates drawn into the conspiracy do not view either one of the new partners as "really single." During this type of passage, there is no need to establish oneself independently as a single individual. Hence these passages are transitional only in the most nominal sense. The barely experienced divorced state is an expedient by which to effect partner change. It was even difficult to locate such cases to study, because these people were "already taken" and tended to remain somewhat hidden until remarriage, when they disappeared back into the world of couples. For this reason, I had to obtain a number of these histories retrospectively. Between the time they decide to remarry and actually do, these people view themselves as part of a new couple.

Reasons for embarking on new relationships during litigation vary. Some people appear to find being alone very painful and stressful, and hence establish a new relationship to avoid loneliness. For others, remarriages result serendipitously from an inadvertent meeting of two unhappily married people who decide to remedy their situations. I observed a number of Immediate Remarriers who emerged from a remarriage by courting their ways into a third or fourth divorce and remarriage. One man described this process:

> I had been separated for awhile when I met Elsie. I had expected to return home, and my wife expected this. But when I'd go by for some clothes or papers, she'd give me a hard time, like "Don't come home until you've shaped up!" I'm stubborn, and that made me mad, so I thought I'd let her worry a little. Elsie was one of the staff assistants when I went to the meetings of the committee planning the new opera house. I talked to her during recess or when a bunch of us went to lunch and later started asking her to dinner. My wife wanted to know what I was doing, but keeping mum made the pretrial settlement easier. We married the day after the final decree. When I left Elsie, for my third wife, that wedding took place two days later after the final decree.

Another male said,

> I've been in two long marriages and am now in my second of two long-term "relationships." At each of the three breakups, there had been a huge row after which I took off and presumably was "taking time for myself and sorting things out." Usually I went back to some extent, as if reconciling, since I rather wanted to. But at the same time, I was establishing the next relationship. When my "mate" pressed me for a decision or indicated she wanted us

to stay together, I just said "this isn't going to work," and took off for the other woman.

In some cases I studied, the plans for remarriage went awry. These situations can have a built-in inclination toward instability, because, during the courtship and while awaiting the divorce, the secret lovers put their entire focus on *securing the divorce* rather than into planning for their future as a couple, making sure these hopes are well founded. I observed some failures that seemed to rest on lack of attention to meeting the tests that generally do take place in a tentative match. Here, working together as a couple was sometimes secondary to an emphasis on problems in the first marriage of one of them and to the threat presumed to exist in the form of the spouse of one. Thus the cement that bonds some couples while they await the divorce of one or both can be that they take the spouse of one as their common enemy. When the enemy is removed through divorce (and particularly if the ex-spouse then goes about his or her own life), a pair may have lost one of the main things holding them together. For this reason, some people institute the following rule:

> I have made it a practice not to go out with anyone unless two years or more have elapsed since the divorce. I've had mine for four. I only got caught once on being a "rescuer" to someone very upset about having been "victimized" by a spouse, but once is enough! It can be very exhausting to devote a lot of time and energy to someone who is all up in the air and fighting with a soon-to-be ex-spouse and then, recovering from battle. I know it sounds cynical, but I think that some people go crazy when a divorce is pending and are, for some time afterwards. Three people in a romance is one too many!

Many Immediate (Planned) Remarriages reach a happily married conclusion fairly smoothly because the new relationship is given a priority over all other considerations. In fact, of those I studied that took place without delays or interruptions, all seem highly successful remarriages. Nevertheless, failing to build a partnership gradually and with much care differentiates unsuccessful lovers who were covert pairs from those involved in longer, more sociable passages such as Steadies, who plan to take longer to remarry, seem able to tolerate irresolution better, and involve many more people in their plans. In spite of this, the only cases I saw in which the immediate remarriage plan was not carried out was when there was some inattention to passage-management tasks or some indecision on the parts of one or both lovers, who then later settled on a second pairing. Hence the potential problem for these people is not simply securing the divorce but of sufficiently anchoring the new pairing during litigation so that they do not lose one another.

Graduates

Graduates, who constitute the second brief-passage subgroup, also make a very early decision about their futures during passage. But because of the failure of their previous marriages, they are disillusioned with marriage in general, and decide to establish themselves as confirmed singles (which, had they been wiser, they would have been much earlier). Graduates set up relatively stable same-sex (and a few cross-sex) friendships, usually retained from earlier times, through which they carry on a limited but continuous form of social life. However, these relationships are subordinated but complementary to their extended family allegiances. Graduates have no quarrel whatsoever with traditional values such as the importance put on marriage and the family, but it is one's blood ties, not marital

—the family of one's childhood and one's own children—that are central to Graduates' interests.

What unites these men and women is their flight from remarriage. It is their distinguishing feature, as it also is for Runners, who will be discussed later. Their prior marriages were much too penalizing for them ever again to consider remarriage. Because many people depart from marriage heatedly declaring, "I will never marry again!", almost everyone leaving divorce courts might initially seem to be a Graduate. I heard many of these declarations from my subjects. Generally, the resolve "never to mate again" breaks down before too long. However, this was not true of the Graduates in my study, not one of them.

The reason that Graduates cannot be successfully wooed is that they simply do not change their minds. This transition can be differentiated from all the others, except those of Runners, by the emphasis both put on the very high costs of the first marriage in contrast to its very low yield, as far as satisfactions go. The only positive yield of marriage for Graduates is the children.

People in other kinds of passages tend to forget what an awful experience the first marriage was, and they stop referring to it. But Graduates feel that they paid too dearly for honoring what was a "very bad marriage" for a very long time, and that they had few defenses against incurring these costs while they were married. Thus, they do not spend much time talking about the difficulties of being divorced, nor do they report any present regrets. Over and over again, they point to the advantages of singlehood, as did this subject, whom I encountered early in the study:

Marriage? Well, it started out looking very nice indeed. He was a Naval officer I met at church when I was first living in Manhattan and attending services at a church with a very nice congregation. We were introduced by the rector, and I thought Henry was most impressive. He was good-looking, well educated, and certainly well mannered. He shortly introduced me to his sister and brother-in-law who were in town on a visit. He expected to spend little time out of the country; he was a career officer in the legal division of the Navy. We were married within three months and found a very nice larger apartment near Gramercy Park. It was a terrible mistake! I saw that immediately once we were married. He was autocratic, patronizing, and distant. He expected me to wait on him and have no opinions of my own. I was appalled at his expectations. I packed my personal things and left the apartment fully stocked down to each pot and pan. I was absolutely delighted to get rid of him.

This subject was a good-looking, cosmopolitan woman. After her divorce, she continued her work and found many diversions, among them the Alliance Française and an opera study group in which she was very active. She dressed modishly and traveled widely. Occasionally she had a glass of wine with a male friend or invited one to lunch, but she stated that such activities involved men who were very old friends; that is, none was in any sense a boyfriend.

Immediately following divorce, Graduates establish themselves as "not interested" in another mate. Even in conversations long after the divorce, they leave no room for anyone's drawing the wrong conclusion about their availability. It is a point of honor never to mislead, and it is also a practical measure. During passage, or afterwards a potential problem can arise when newcomers who become tenacious admirers refuse to accept a dismissal; then, Graduates can be quite brusque. Well-meaning friends do not pressure them to remarry, because, metaphorically, Graduates carry placards reading, "Marriage isn't for me—thanks anyway!" These men and women simply brush aside any gesture that might be construed as romantic interest in them.

Graduates' conversations tend to be liberally sprinkled with references to their resolve not to get cornered into pairing. At public events such as singles dances, Graduates sometimes rebuff new people in advance of their showing much interest in them. In other words, they rush to make the point, and this functions to convince others they really have taken themselves off the marriage market and are "out of play" as far as pairing is concerned.

Two reasons Graduates must deal with the situation fairly often, are that they are attractive people and they tend to use singles clubs as a means to structure their recreational time. When they join these clubs, they often form the nucleus of club officers or of a clique who turn out to be among the few long-term members of the club. In contrast, people eager to pair usually at some point desert club functions with someone who interests them, or they decide that singles clubs are not promising locales for meeting anyone.

Social life for Graduates tends to follow habitual patterns. Women go out to dinner, perhaps on Friday night, with one or more women friends. Men stay in touch with several male friends (also trusted confidants) by means of weekday lunching. On weekends, both may also go to singles dances, but as two separate groups. Although they may enjoy dancing a great deal, they make their disinterest in pairing known to anyone new they dance with. Thus, on Saturday nights, the same male Graduates might dance with the same women Graduates whom they know well, and who are there for similar reasons: they want to "get out," and they like to dance. This enables these singles who are not interested in or open to partnering, to attend such functions—and this situation removes the stigma of going repeatedly. Furthermore, their willingness to run the singles' clubs is appreciated, since they do most of the work. Volunteering their time and services thus justifies their continual presence. The following excerpt illustrates one female subject's reaction to a male Graduate:

> Before I met John, I went to that club's singles dances. Two men who were fantastic dancers always came and left together. I was there four or five times before one of them asked me to dance. The next night he did again. All he talked about was his daughter and her kids—*that* came as a surprise! I'd figured out the message just before he said "he'd never marry again." Then I saw that they were "regulars" who never spent much time with any one woman. After that, we just waved at each other; he knew I wanted to meet someone, I guess. You know—have something *happening!*

Graduates use singles clubs in the ways they are advertised, to "get together with nice people and have a good time." But at first, no one believes them, since everybody else is hunting for new partners. While others pretend they are interested in belonging to a club for its own sake—and may in fact be dance addicts—it is only the Graduates who are not pretending about why they are there. Hence, Graduates must continually explain —or dodge hopefuls.

Bowling is another favorite get-together activity. The women bowl weekly with the same men; they are all old friends who enjoy each other. Transportation arrangements reveal the consensus from which everyone is operating. The women arrive in one car—as do the men—and they meet at the bowling alley. After either dancing or bowling, both groups (in two cars) go out for a late snack where everyone goes Dutch. Despite their strident, flirtatious joking with each other and the waitress, they are only *appearing* to be trying to engage each other. The proof lies in the fact that they depart in the same groups —usually to get to bed early.

The Immediate Remarriers and the Graduates

During my fieldwork, I never observed any woman Graduate leaving her group to go home with a male escort, nor any male Graduate taking a woman's phone number. Graduates keep each other at a *proper* distance. These are the only men on whom a single woman can depend if all she actually would like is some one *just* to drop in to fix her washer. In short, all the interaction of these attractive people is determinedly nonerotic. An offer of help which among other people would be a pretext for trying to get better acquainted with courtship in mind, such as giving a woman a ride to pick up her car at the repair garage, has for these people only an instrumental function—getting the car. In short, for them, sex means marriage.

Additionally, Graduates maintain a round of ceremonious calls on older relatives, especially on Sunday. The men also call assiduously on married friends, and are standby friends, for instance, tending bar at their parties. Graduate women ask Graduate men and other women from the office for party meals.

Among their several roles, the familial role is given first priority, because it is so fundamental to identity ratification. Work is important, but these people are not ambitious career people. For them, occupational niches only structure time and ensure retirement benefits; it is the family circle that really counts. The sexual role is nonexistent or muted, and the interpersonal role is not a dynamic one, because Graduates regard mid-life as a time to settle into a satisfying, low-risk quiet kind of life. Nevertheless, Graduates may want more distant friends (acquaintances) to interpret the bowling and dancing in an "as if" way—as if both were the occasions for bona fide mating possibilities.

Graduates have little interest in making personality or lifestyle changes; and they encourage children to live "safe," conventional lives. They are attractive, carefully controlled people who tend to change little and seem to be quite content and relatively insulated from modern trends of thinking.

Among the women in this category, some of whom I followed for the entire study, I found no one who ever risked even one dinner engagement being construed as preliminary to courtship. However, Graduate women do not stop thinking, at least privately, about the courtship option, despite their denials. One subject, sometimes a bit wistful about remarriage, decided to attend an outdoor convocation of country Western music lovers "to look for a comfortable widower—*just this once.*" Instead, she met a raucous bunch who called each other by outrageous names and whose jocular familiarities repelled her. This disaster was her one reported postdivorce venture toward the opposite sex.

When married, this woman had traveled the state as an avid supporter of her son's competitive swimming. She was a popular part of a nucleus of enthusiasts who followed the meets after their children outgrew competition. But when she divorced, she dropped this activity, forfeiting ties with many buddies who offered comradeship and might have become her allies in a search for a new mate. At the conclusion of a follow-up interview, she declared, "At retirement, I'll go *home* and look for somebody." This statement, characteristic of a Graduate, functioned as a socially acceptable way to prevent unwelcome advice, as it closed off comments beginning with "Why don't you . . . ?"

Graduates have highly stable existences. They depict the marriage-cum-divorce as "ancient history." They face old age with equanimity but rehearse it. For instance, one male subject said he lied about his age to join the American Association of Retired Persons, because he wanted to secure the insurance plan and other benefits he knew about from his mother.

Graduates are stoutly loyal to their children. If childless, they make other people's children into adopted nieces and nephews. Few, among my subjects, however, were childless. One subject who telephoned on an autumn follow-up commented happily, "I guess we'll be having a big bash here Thanksgiving and Christmas." Women in particular take very active roles in family celebrations, office parties, and gift giving.

A major source of recreation for women Graduates is joint shopping expeditions, after work in the evening or on weekends. Men are good hosts and like to entertain relatives or friends from work, especially at barbecues or spaghetti dinners. It is common for them to have a supply of household hints and to be as hospitable as this subject was:

> When are you coming over to my house for dinner? How about Wednesday—could you? I have my sons several nights a week, and I let them ask two girls. I ask a woman. That way they learn party manners, and I can watch over them while they learn to date. You have to stay on top of teen-agers! It's been eight years since the divorce. They live nearby with their mother. I'm a great cook and I have a lot of nice plants—I give them away. When we have company, I buy a big bunch of flowers for the table, and after dinner, we divide them, so each lady has flowers to take home.

Singlehood is not romanticized or discussed constantly by the Graduates as it is by people trying to make extensive changes in their life patterns or by those looking for dating partners. Graduates are careful with money, worried about retirement finances, and content to view themselves as "sensible" at mid-life. If sixties' activitism or social movements had any impact on them, it was a disturbing one that came through their children in the main. One subject reported,

> Marty was here all last year. I guess I told you I don't see my daughter. She hitchhiked around the country and never did finish school. Well, she's grown; I hope she's alright. I tried hard when

they were little. She had a lot of advantages when her father and I were married and living in that big house. I don't think she ever forgave me for all of that ending! Marty was younger; I thought he needed me. But all he did was lie around smoking pot and watching TV. When I got home, he wanted me to cook a big dinner. He'd move out—but he always came back. Finally, I told him, "Look—I've had my condo for five years and I'd like to do it over with a guest room. Can't you go 'do your thing,' or whatever you call it?" I wouldn't let him move in again. I think he respects me a lot more now. He comes for dinner about twice a week. He's OK. You win some—sometimes you lose!

Graduates carefully protect the work role on which their independence is based because of its value for later security and the extent to which it secondarily sustains identity. Juggling the dual roles in the worlds of the family and work is quite easy for them, because these roles are mutually supportive and not allowed to become competitive. For example, the women have modest career goals, do not vigorously seek advancement, and are neither attracted to nor exhilarated by feminism. The men tend to stay on the same occupational track for which they originally left home towns and went to college. As one man nearing retirement put it, "My father never got to college, but my B.S. in engineering will take me through retirement." At the time this study was written up, not a single Graduate had deviated from the solo path chosen at the time of the final decree.

Chapter 4 describes the most "active" and interesting group of brief-passage subjects, the Comfortable Courters. It discusses how they use their social ties to effect their goals, and how their beliefs and strategies for goal attainment compare with other people who also leave the transitional state quite quickly.

4

The Comfortable Courters

and Brief-Passage

Subgroups Compared

WHILE Graduates proved less mobile and less adventurous than some other groups of subjects, the equally conservative Comfortable Courters were determined to entertain the risks of entering another partnership. A surprising number of subjects turned out to be Courters.

Comfortable Courters tend to be unhappy when they are not part of a pair. The theme uniting and animating this group of brief-passage subjects is the drive to remarry. Courters always consider themselves just "temporarily divorced" and headed for marriage. However, until such time as they find a new partner who is receptive to them (and finally, chosen by them), they tend to act as if they had not already decided on this kind of an exit from passage. In so doing, they are able to mask their intentions while making their future selections.

This ambiguity serves them well while the selection negotiations are underway. If one is being wooed by a Courter, his or her intentions are more obliquely than fully manifested.

Many Courters remarry almost as quickly as do Immediate Remarriers, but they tend to marry people whom they neither selected nor knew well at the time their divorce suit was filed. Nevertheless, they may drag out the prior marriage so that under its protection, a new pairing can be found, set up, and tested. Courters view mid-life as a time for caution—not for the risky adventure that may accompany singlehood. Like Graduates, they worry about retirement security, but they define it as having the financial means to live moderately well —and *having a partner*. They view long-term divorce as a highly stigmatizing and isolating state of affairs and they certainly do not relish being labeled "single." They regard being "temporarily divorced" as "alright" and talk a lot about "how times have changed" on this point. Otherwise, they seem neither interested in nor approving of the cultural changes that came out of the social movements of the sixties. They regard social innovators of their own age as "not our kind of people." A Courter named Claude had this to say:

> Social movements? Sure, I know plenty about them. I had the misfortune to have a feminist for a second wife. It lasted eight years. I was damn glad to get out of it. Well, I thought she was "interesting" when we met. I married two days after our divorce. A nice widow who's a perfectionist—she always looks like she took three days to get dressed, you know, every hair in place. She's got a nice house in Westin Park, and with my retirement plan, we'll be nicely fixed. Ann is like my first wife—knows her place. When I used to kid Ellie that way, boy, did she blow up.

Being *comfortably* repartnered is more important than any specific set of partner characteristics. Courters do not romanticize pairing. For them, conventional marriage is so desirable a state that it is simply a "given." They are eager to terminate passage. Once safely remarried, they announce the fact with jubilation, even to business associates who are merely acquaintances, and try to shift into a sedate, predictable married life. They are openly eager for everyone to ratify them as a "once-again married person."

One phenomenon observed among Courters is that, early in the new courtship, some of them and their old friends may slip and call the potential mate by the former spouse's name. This occurs without self-consciousness or apologies, and in a group situation, it is apt to be the cause of merriment. The goal is to reenter the Noah's ark world of pairs, not to find someone who possesses long-admired personal qualities. For example, one subject described his handsome, rather stately new spouse merely as "someone I met fifty-two years ago," by which he conveyed that their parents were once acquainted and they had played together as children, a fact he saw as indicating the rightness of the match. Effecting a rapid remarriage is a triumph in itself; one subject observed with satisfaction, "Some of us have a talent for remarriage."

Courters have many friends and associates who are also preoccupied with planning for retirement. They, too, take a conservative view of aging. In their judgments, middle age is something of a relief, because one can "slow down." During passage one is actively focused on its termination. One of the rewards of completing passage is being able to "take things easy" once again. One's full attention is directed to "slowing down" with the new partner, not in evaluating options or looking to fill out one's experience of life.

Courters deplore the sixties and regard growth-movement ideas about transforming the Self as quite funny. They assume, for instance, that no one would be in an encounter group because of being serious about making personality changes; rather, one would merely be using it as a mechanism for finding a partner. Since Courters are persistent and rational in partner searching, they are not above using all manner of singles activities; but more often, they tend to find new partners through co-workers, married friends, or relatives. A typical pairing would consist of a woman who kept the house after divorce and a man who took from his own home only a few pieces of furniture once belonging to his family—perhaps the wedding presents sent by his relatives, a few keepsakes (particularly from his college years), his clothes and papers, and his car. Remarried Courters quickly settle into the very married routines which reflect longterm interests, such as playing golf. Thus remarriage is achieved with a minimum of change in daily habits. Courters neither romanticize the new partner nor the new marriage, and they are not too enthusiastic about becoming middle aged. On the whole, they deemphasize their solo period as soon as it is behind them, although they may portray themselves as glamorous and footloose while jockeying for a remarriage position.

A favorite Courter mechanism that often "tides one over" early in passage is calling on old friends between five o'clock and dinnertime. Before a potential partner is located, and when courtship begins, men tend to drop in to chat with stay-at-home wives of their men friends, often remaining long enough to exchange pleasantries with a husband returning from his office. Male Courters let these couple friends know they are available in any emergency that might occur when the husband/father is unavailable or in a situation where the wife might need an escort. This permits the Courter to maintain some vestige of the husband role as a surrogate. In return for this, couple friends will assist the Courter in partner selection. Women Courters tend to drop in on married friends (also on the way home from their offices) and may be asked to stay for dinner. For all Courters, these "pop calls" function as opportunities; the males feel "needed" when they are able to assist their friends (for instance, being available to help when the husband is out of town), and the women have a chance to ask someone else's husband for advice (in the presence of his wife). Couples used in this manner by Courters are friends to whom a potential new partner is introduced. Thus friends share some of the responsibility for ultimately contracting an "appropriate partnership," and they vicariously experience some of the excitement and "inside information" about efforts to repartner to which less intimate friends are not privy.

A Courter's "new friend" realizes very quickly that one or two married couples who are old buddies may hold virtual veto power over a courtship and so adjusts his or her demands and conduct accordingly, at least until the coupleship is approved and established. If the new friend is relatively new in town and being introduced to a Courter's circle of very old friends, it is imperative to the courtship that the new friend make concessions to the stronger position of the person on familiar ground, surrounded by supportive and highly interested longtime friends. Because these intimates prefer that the group's equilibrium remain undisturbed, the new friend must carefully determine not only what roles have customarily been assigned by the group to the Courter in question, but also what relationships exist among the people making up the circle, and what is "meant" by extremely subtle interactional nuances in even apparently spontaneous get-togethers. At the same time, the new friend must also decide fairly early in the courtship (usually before the Courter has made an overt commitment) just how important the pairing might prove to be. This involves estimates about what is at stake, and, in particular, what "bottom line" can and must be maintained in order for "the new friend's limits" to be honored. One subject said,

> My friend has a very close circle of people he went to college with or knew in general since his first marriage. He always wants to go places with them, and we pay little attention to my (fewer) friends. At first I was very uncomfortable with this because we have little privacy, and they make unstated demands on me to appreciate their jokes and be enthused about what is going on in their lives. I hit on asking if we could be active in the symphony advisory committee, and he liked that idea and it meant we could go about on our own.

At the same time, a Courter who wants to forge ahead with a remarriage will try to gauge how far to insist on a potential partner's fitting into his or her habitual rounds or circle, since it would be essentially a closed circle, were intimates not so concerned about and eager for a Courter's remarriage. In addition, sociability patterns set down early in courtship are difficult to overturn later. Another important point is that these pairings are not experienced by the new partners as "love matches." Hence, a new friend, who is presumably only "being treated well," has ample opportunity to recognize that subsequent rounds of sociability can be in reality fateful dress rehearsals for their possible remarried life together.

Reactions to the proposed new pairing are very important to Courters, who hope their friends' encouragement of the match will be forthcoming and will symbolize their readiness to incorporate the new person into the group, if the pairing remains stable. Therefore, introductions to the circle are much more important than presentation to children or parents, because the pair's life *as a married couple* will be their most valued roles, and, hence, are central to their identity maintenance. This social, or interpersonal, role is of enormous significance before, during, and after passage. One problem for a Courter lies in the ever-present possibility that the married couples who are valued old friends may be very cordial to a new friend who may not feel similarly disposed toward them. Courters focus on the hoped for approval of old friends in order to protect cherished social networks, but the courtship can abort if revealing these old ties and their importance causes a new friend to cool off. Thus a Courter valued by both these old friends and a potential mate may be pulled in two directions.

For example, while the goal of Courters is to effect remarriage expressly for the purpose of resuming married life with the same set of people enjoyed in the prior marriage, both old pals and potential mate can make claims on the Courter's time and loyalty. The ensuing personal conflict may resemble that produced when balancing the demands of a family and a lover. Generally, Courters not only attempt to control the bargaining that goes on among all of these people, but they may also have to offer some compromises by which both the courtship and prospects of resuming married life within the circle are protected. It may be necessary for a Courter to change emphasis among old friends to satisfy the new lover sufficiently to accomplish remarriage. Therefore one's "best friends" may be demoted in favor of another couple with whom a potential mate feels more comfortable or has "hit it off" extremely well.

At the same time that the Courter and potential mate are working their way *as a couple* (and privately, between themselves) through a series of sensitive negotiations, people in the intact social circle also have a considerable stake in reading cues carefully. It is important that they, too, maintain their own influence, popularity, or sense of belonging within the circle and in their relationship with the Courter. When the courtship continues to the point of setting a wedding date and choosing where to live, the new couple's decisions as to who will be in the wedding party, where the reception will take place, and what will be the neighborhood of new residence can reveal which set of friends "won."

Because married life, not family life, is seen as the ultimate good, the integration of one's lover into one's circle, or among two sets of one's married friends (which is more problematic), is the primary hurdle to overcome. Potential mates view such acceptance as critical to their future as a well-received, socially secure couple. The Courter's children tend to pose less of a problem in terms of accepting the new friend. By mid-life, his or her children are generally of college age or out on their own; their interests may vary greatly from one another's and from the parent's, and the parental role may already have become substantially diminished. Furthermore, the children may not be particularily interested in the prospective pairing. Nevertheless, it is common for some children to attend the wedding.

In general, couples who are a Courter's old friends will go to heroic lengths to assist a Courter's efforts towards remarriage. Sometimes friends "stand in" as would brothers or sisters. For instance, they may take a Courter's new woman friend's teen-agers to a sports event so the male suitor can take the woman on a short trip. Or, when a Courter tends the lover's house, children, and pets, because the lover must go out of town on business, friends may entertain those remaining at supper or for Sunday at poolside. In so doing, they help portray the Courter's social assets as quite ample.

A potential problem lies in being able to determine fairly early in passage which pairs of married couples will be retained as friends by which divorcing spouse after the divorce. If home ownership exists after the property settlement, and it is important to at least one of the pair to stay in touch with neighbors, deciding which neighbors are still loyal to the Courter (rather than the other ex-spouse) can be a touchy matter. If a Courter wants to return every summer to a particular resort, another set of people will have to meet and appraise a new prospect, while the Courter must hope for sufficient acceptance and a "good fit" all the way around. The following illustrates how a Courter in an unusually troubled passage located a way to bring some of this kind of continuity to his courtships:

> My friend was very upset after filing the papers, because his stormy last few years of marriage had cost him his job, and his wife was trying to find him to harass him. At an especially trying point, before he took up different work, he suddenly decided we should go up to a remote part of Maine he'd loved for years. So we packed in a hurry and left town. It was spectacularly beautiful when we got there, but cold. We found a guest house at a beautiful farm and rented it for a week and liked the owners. The week was mainly spent driving and driving all through the area, which was really tiring considering the trip up. After a couple of days, he explained that he'd summered there for 24 years with two different wives and two sets of children, and he set out to find every house he'd rented for all these years. I was simply dumbfounded and finally, exhausted. On the return, he just collapsed, and I drove us in. When he took his next romantic interest there, several years later, I said, "Why there?" He said, "I've always liked it."

If one's circle is intact, attending civic or charity events together is a mechanism frequently used to find out how a pair is received and handles being together. A major problem may be either fitting two people with two sets of friends into one congenial life round, or constructing a new one. Courters usually have so many friends that a likely bonus may accrue to the pair when one partner's friends prove to be acquaintances of the other person's friends, comparable to being able to declare, "Bingo!"

Throughout this period of testing a new couplehood against the backdrop of valued, long-term relationships and social rounds, many new combinations of married friends can result, as old and new friends are reshuffled into new friendship configurations. Courters quickly get down to the serious business of checking potential fit. They may not be very receptive to other singles, unless encountering another tentative couple likely also to be altar-bound, who are socially connected in a manner that ratifies the old crowd's social investments and customs. If there is a commonality such as the second pair summering in the same Vermont village, the Courter pair might include the other couple in some of the circle's partying, particularly to indicate to old friends that one is "very much in the social swim."

Another tactic common to sociable Courters is their use of social life for all kinds of problem solving. One way Courters can maximize chances to court successfully is to take turns entertaining together. An easy event to host, such as holding open house, presumably to entertain for someone else (for example, a bon voyage party for old friends going on a cruise), creates an opportunity to invite almost everyone important to the social success of the potential remarrieds. The honorees, in turn, are indebted to the pair, and the hopeful couple has only to sit back and count acceptances (or, eventually, return invitations) to assess the likelihood of being sought after as newlyweds. While awkward incidents can occur (such as one being disappointed in the other's mode of entertaining), much of the data the Courter couple needs can be readily and rationally assembled in this manner.

The most devoted among the married couples, who are old friends and understand what the Courter is up to, may themselves lend a hand by also giving a party on some pretext, which permits them to signal their sponsorship of the match and advance it. Thus they help Courters acquire more responses, rehearse their joint roles, and meet other people. If unexpected support comes from some quarter not counted on, that sympathetic person or couple may then be cultivated and thereafter assume a newly central place in the pair's life.

During the period in which the pairing is only tentative, many other courtesies may be extended by married couples to appreciative Courters. For instance, the husband of a woman Courter's close friend may invite her suitor to a sporting event; or the wife of a male Courter's longtime business associate might ask the Courter's prospect to play bridge. A form of pressure often encountered is an old friend's taking a Courter's "friend" aside to make an "off-the-record" report on the Courter's character or former marriage, or provide some other "inside information." In these tête à têtes, the Courter's virtues are extolled with an eye to improving the Courter's chances; and the prospect is invited to inquire discreetly about details of the Courter's life that require more interpretation than the Courter provided. Once this dialogue is underway, an old friend may repeatedly vouch for the Courter. This can result in a form of support, if the couple accepts the "behind-the-scenes" coach. Informal coaching tends to increase old friends' investments in the match, reassure the prospect, and supply a referee determined to keep the courtship going.

At any subsequent point, if a couple hesitates, friends may come forward to encourage them. But this matchmaking generally occurs only when old friends have adjusted to the person chosen, and only if they see the twosome as a promising pair that needs to be nudged along. In addition, a Courter who fears that a new friend is having second thoughts may decide to "call in" all outstanding social debts and thereby generate an array of invitations designed to create a flurry of attention around a reluctant prospect. The purpose of the maneuver seems to be clear to the friends or business contacts put on notice that their help is needed, even if the reasons for their hospitality are not understood by the prospect.

By the time a wedding date is set, a major clue to the realignments that occurred among the old crowd because of the pairing is evident in the ways old friends rally around the Courter and mate-to-be. They may allot among themselves various featured roles in the remarriage drama. This is the story of one such wedding:

> Marcel and I wanted to host our own wedding, but a number of people who were his friends more than mine, made things much nicer for us. His business partner and his wife gave a beautiful rehearsal dinner for our quite elderly parents and all the wedding party. Then his stockbroker, who was also an old pal, and his wife, lent us their home for the reception. It was a pretty house with a lovely terrace, and they even planted the garden for it, insisting we pick colors. My best friend couldn't stand up with me, because we were divorced and she was Catholic; but she and I asked another friend I'd met through work. I was new there.

By this shared participation arrangement, the bride and groom's parents had only to attend; the couple controlled their mode of marrying, relieved of much preparation and expense; and the groom did not have to choose between two "best friend" married couples of whom he was very fond. The two supporting couples enacted their best wishes by each ratifying the marriage.

Thus, among the old friends, there may be a division of labor, and a sharing of the limelight and rituals that legitimate the marriage. Furthermore, both members of the marrying couple chose someone special to "stand with" them at the ceremony. This is usually a married person who is an old friend, which means another couple is involved in the wedding. Since Courters tend not to compartmentalize business and social life, business acquaintances who do not know the partner, the circle, or the Courter very well may be invited.

The pair's college-aged or older children may attend the ceremony, sometimes accompanied by significant others. An offspring may bring home a new romantic interest, whose unexpected presence leads to rearrangements designed to acknowledge another possibly significant pairing. At the least, children tend to bring home from school one or two staunch friends, whose presence mystifies most guests. The function of trying to explain who everybody is to as many people as possible may be assigned to another intimate whose part in the festivities then reflects his or her close relationship with the marrying pair.

Orchestrating a courtship to so complex a wedding finale can be complicated. One woman subject was so exhausted that her new husband had to stop at a shopping center coffee shop a few blocks from where they drove off in a shower of rice, so she could recover and begin the wedding trip. Courter weddings demonstrate the importance a couple puts on an active social life and community participation, in contrast to the weddings of couples who define marriage as a means to what is essentially a *private* life together.

Further evidence of the rather public character of Courter passages and remarriages lies in the fact that before the wedding, the couple may already have accepted (or issued) invitations to parties that will take place on their return from their marriage trip. Because the meaning attached to a social life as couples is shared by the new couple and their friends, once the honeymoon is out of the way network activities resume with hardly an interruption. They may expand from whatever alliances were struck up between various couples involved in the pairing. A strengthened social circle and enhanced social status are paramount concerns of both Courters and their friends, and although no one may openly comment on this everyone knows that these basic commitments are at the heart of one's life as *part of a couple.*

Because of this underlying agreement, Courters and their friends understand their roles during passage. The more quickly a consensus can be built around a pairing, the briefer a passage is likely to be, which is exactly what Courters want. Many Courters are very skillful at reconstituting a social life marked by one major change, a new partner. This might seem to amount to a "salvage" operation after divorce. However, at these professional, upper-middle-class levels, men tend to retain the same business associates and pals into middle age, when taking a transfer is less likely; and women tend to keep friends from college or young matron days, using them to make additional new friends. Thus, for each, a relatively high degree of social continuity is possible.

Lastly, Courter passages tend to be chosen by people who were occupationally mobile but stayed near their home areas (by moving to nearby cities) or who made only one move after taking their college degrees. Hence, they are able to hold constant many factors that forced other subjects into constant readjustments. At any rate, the replacement of one spouse by another does not seem to be a disruptive experience. Some Courters (particularly males) went into fourth marriages when studied.

Brief-Passage Subgroups Compared

For all early exiters from passage, divorce is viewed as a step to use as expeditiously as possible as a means to an end—stabilizing one's life again. For Immediate Remarriers and

Courters, being divorced temporarily is no cause for alarm. As for Graduates, while a great deal of denial may go into their accounts, singlehood appears to be a positive adaptation, and the stigma of being formerly marrieds is mitigated or removed by being divorced men and women who are *not* interested in "looking."

In each of these groups, divorce is associated more with the termination of a marriage than it is with the prospect of singlehood. Conventional marriage is defined as a social benefit, not just by Courters and Immediate Remarriers who race toward the prize of remarriage, but by Graduates also. They acknowledge the satisfactions of marriage (in other people's lives), invoking their previously married status as legitimation for their present lack of interest. No one in these groups questions the desirability of marriage, at least, as a concept. Graduates simply point out, "I *was* married," by which they reveal that the status of a formerly married is, in their opinions, more desirable than being a "never married."

Indeed, most women Graduates retain an ex-husband's surname, generally using "Mrs." before it. This contrasts with younger women, or those in long passages, who may resume use of a maiden name or keep a name from a prior marriage by which they are known professionally. Former in-law relationships are often maintained by Graduates. One Graduate called on his long-dead wife's sister and her fourth husband whenever he was in her vicinity while visiting his cousin. It is not unusual for a male to continue to drop in on a former mother-in-law. The vehicle through which a woman stays in touch with former in-laws may be her children, because grandmothers tend to correspond with former daughters-in-law. One male Graduate acted as the designer for his ex-wife and her next husband when they built a sloop, stipulating, however, "I'll do it as long as she doesn't change her mind about anything; I've had enough of that already!" Thus Graduates may continue contacts from the prior marriage while defining themselves as not needing another; these contacts are part of the reason they don't.

With respect to the aging process, Courters seem haunted by the prospect of facing old age. Thus they are oriented to the retirement years well in advance of their arrival in terms of their anticipation of possible problems, such as being poor or mateless when old. One male Courter expressed his attitude in recounting the following exchange:

> Middle age is the point at which we ought to look for security. My neighbor's my age and she isn't remarried. I told her the other day, she shouldn't look for romance or a lot more fun. She looked surprised. I said, "When are you going to retire?" Then she looked more surprised, and she said, "Well, I don't think I'll *want* to. I mean, I'm self-employed and I certainly think I want to work for at least ten more years." I said, "You shouldn't work for much longer and you ought to get someone to take care of you."

How Immediate Remarriers view aging was difficult to study as my subjects tended to focus continually on the problems they were encountering in litigation and the temporary measures they were instituting to organize life while they were awaiting divorce. After remarriage, they tended to focus on the advantages of their present match, detailing its delights. None of my subjects in this category ever made any of the negative references to aging that Courters tended to make, revealing Courter's concerns about aging and the retirement years.

Immediate Remarriers seem less concerned about retirement, looking forward instead to a new life with new possibilities. One of these couples moved to another state after marriage, and, in the next three years, built two large houses in the country at the same time as they were each active in professional careers. They sold the first house and moved into the second. During my follow-up telephone conversations with them, they discussed their current wish to move into a city residential pattern when they can sell the second house to good advantage, and also recounted the activities of their grown children and events in both of their careers. The wife described her new hobby, sculpture, and her interest in going into business with two other sculptors.

The following concept of aging, from case material on Immediate Remarriers, emerged in my follow-up of a woman now remarried several years:

> I'm loving being an interior designer for Sloane's, and I met a darling graphic designer I introduced to one of my sons. He needed some work for his business, and I knew she could do it. I wasn't matchmaking, but they married. After my daughter married, and I heard I'd be a grandmother, I stopped saying "Shit!" and changed to "Shoot!" By the time the baby came, I was using phrases like, "Oh, my stars!" but nobody around here seemed to like the change in my personality all that much, so I went back to using "Shit!"

Graduates accentuate retirement planning and, to this end, are attentive to their expectations of their extended family and to their terms of employment, which must be met to ensure pensions and other benefits at retirement.

Courters consider mid-life singlehood so undesirable that they will make concessions in partner choice. One woman gives this account:

> He said he cared a lot about me, but he was without very much money and he'd found a younger woman he liked with an interesting job. He called her a "young lady," so I thought she must be in her thirties or maybe, thirty. So I asked him, and he said, "forty-five."

For Graduates, on the other hand, singlehood is regarded as a direct, positive yield of divorce. Hence, they value mid-life as the point at which they might reclaim the freedom they forfeited in marriage. Having been a responsible parent despite the "bad marriage" is almost always cited in Graduate accounts as a reason for making mid-life the occasion for independence, privacy, and the right to do as one wishes. This is in direct opposition to the Courters' view of mid-life as the worst possible time "to go it alone," because they dread old age and want to shore it up with a partnership.

Despite these differences, examining some characteristics of the groups who engage in brief passages reveals a number of similarities among them in the ways they handle their transitions. The successful transitions of people choosing to exit passage fairly early depend on their resourceful manipulation of these transitional factors. The intelligent, effective ways by which people develop winning strategies are highly individualistic. Tactics are determined by *selectively* making use of specific aspects of some passage characteristics, which produces the results people want.

Timing and control are factors essential to the brief passage. To be short, it must be very tightly controlled. People hope to go in a direct line to a chosen outcome. And, because people choosing these kinds of passages *know exactly what they want,* they are free to be decisive and goal-directed throughout transition. Although they have different goals (depending on the subgroup in question), they are alike in letting nothing distract them from their course, carrying out their plan with disciplined effort. Limiting passages to somewhat narrow goals makes them more manageable. The extent of their purposefulness reflects their conviction that they must avoid ambiguity and risk-taking above all, in order to give first priority to stability and security.

The Courters and Brief-Passage Subgroups

Another way in which they manipulate passage so as to minimize risk and optimize security is by controlling the degree to which they disclose their intentions. Regardless of which of the three outcomes people in brief passage seek, the kind and degree of disclosure is one criterion for examining their management strategies. People's decisions about divulging or concealing intentions (plans for passage aftermaths) range from complete frankness to a willingness to mislead someone deliberately. Their approach may be ascertained by examining the amount of information about their intentions they reveal to whom and when.

Immediate Remarriers are veritable entrepreneurs, operating as conspirators with a hidden agenda: the secret plan to divorce and remarry. This secrecy they rightly deem vital to executing a plan without disruption, given the objective of prompt remarriage on the most advantageous terms. However, to see how their handling of the disclosure factor actually works, one must realize that their efforts to forestall premature (public) disclosure of their relationship are conditional on their making open, full, and quite early declarations of commitment to one another. Strategically, immediate remarriage depends on a high degree of disclosure between the lovers, but a very low degree of it as a couple vis à vis each individual's social world. During passage, they veil both true motives and intentions from almost everybody—except attorneys—until the plan is a fait accompli. In other words, if their plan is not hidden, it may be impossible to execute it, especially in states with restrictive (adversary) divorce laws. The lack of uniformity in divorce statutes among states leads many people, whose own state's laws pose obstacles for them, to feel justified in seeking to equalize matters by deceiving the soon-to-be ex-spouse. They may have little choice, since the only other alternative may be to move to another state, and at mid-life, it is often next to impossible to relocate an established professional practice. However, one such pair of subjects did relocate in order to marry.

The longer passage takes, the less smoothly it may go; so attention to timing and control are imperative to the Immediate Remarrier. A long-drawn-out passage may make it more difficult to prevent an inadvertent disclosure—and the more the plan is exposed, the more it could cost the lovers. Therefore, it is not unusual for the married lover to encourage a spouse to assume his or her frequent absences or preoccupied manner result from "problems at work," or to hold out to the spouse hope that repeated marital breaches will be met with repeated reconciliations. Such deceptions may prevent the spouse from recognizing that it would be prudent to get legal advice; this is their purpose. Because no resources have to go into a partner hunt, Immediate Remarriers are free to invest their efforts in formulating plans and making time for one another. However, the necessity for discretion about their hopes may inhibit their performance in some of their other roles.

Another motive for secrecy is the lovers' sense that the community expects people to "suffer" or wait a "decent interval" before replacing a spouse after a breakup. Therefore, a lover heading for the earliest possible remarriage on the most desirable terms (his or hers) must not risk exposing the happy new relationship to a relative or an acquaintance. Because it is hard to conceal from friends one's uneasiness or elation, a lover may try to prepare associates by hinting that something is painfully "out of kilter" in his or her marriage. But it is more common for the lover to withdraw to some extent and avoid people with whom the news is not yet to be shared. The lover's floating a rumor about his or her unhappiness may only add to the need to dissemble, by causing unwelcome inquiries. Further, if a lover becomes distracted by questions of credibility or fairness to a present mate, the plan may be ruined.

One consequence of declarations of intentions can be their being taken by others as guilty confessions, as the following case shows: A subject planning immediate remarriage gave up all control over his intended passage by advising his wife, his parents, and his children of his decision to divorce and remarry someone he was seeing. This degree of disclosure was honorable, but it opened the way for his wife to call on others for assistance. She availed herself of the services of a psychiatrist who repeatedly urged the husband to delay his plans in order to give his wife time to adjust, and the projected wedding was delayed out of existence. The wedding which followed on the lover's inability to keep his own counsel was contracted happily between the woman he was seeing and yet another suitor whose commitment was neither provisional nor jeopardized.

Manipulating disclosure covers up key indications that could lead a spouse to conclude that only by hiring a private investigator can the meaning of the other spouse's behavior be clarified. However, hopeful or complacent spouses often participate in the plan, by accepting explanations, that should be seen as only partially satisfying. One subject's despair over her husband's evasions of their marital problems led her into several affairs, one resulting in the romance which prompted her secret plan to leave him for another man. When her mate finally confronted her with an irate demand to know if she were "seeing someone else," she was so furious the question came so late that she replied, "How do you want the list—*alphabetized?*"

Nevertheless, the foregoing should not be taken to suggest that the study only turned up few instances of concern for a spouse's welfare. One subject held the news of his impending departure until his wife's sister weathered a medical crisis. Male subjects tended to resolve guilt by being more generous about financial settlements than they had to be, so a spouse's situation would be less disadvantaged later on. One subject who went into two planned remarriages explained he wanted to "leave every woman I have been with better off for that fact"; hence, he relinquished claims to many jointly held assets. Sex therapists William Hartman and Marilyn Fithian told me about treating a married couple in which the husband's motive for their entering treatment (to help his wife become "more marriageable" before he left her) had escaped their screening.

Although passage into immediate remarriage may seem to involve the calculated unfolding of a cold plan, most subjects reported months or years of soul-searching before reaching a private decision to divorce. A typical report from these male subjects was, "I simply was not in a financial position to take the step earlier, much as I longed to." Women often reported delaying because of their belief that growing children need a stable family unit. A decision to depart is often unexpectedly put in motion by meeting someone appealing to or appreciative of one, at the time when homefront obligations begin to decrease. Hence, while the partner switch may seem to onlookers to occur with stunning rapidity, the buildup to it may have taken a very long time and involved reaching a decision quite reluctantly.

Although maintaining secrecy may facilitate plans, it may also create problems. While covert lovers rarely throw caution to the winds, one major problem for them is struggling with their consciences. Their sense of guilt is heightened by the secrecy requirement; and the pull of attachment (even in a long, unhappy marriage) functions to weed out the less resolute, who cannot advance the plan without faltering. One subject experienced a great deal of ambivalence about his own hidden agenda, only to be savaged throughout the extended litigation forced on him by his wife who, rather than being victimized, turned out also to have had a lover, and she put into action a much more brutal covert plan than his. The subject's career was wrecked, and his romance was not consolidated.

Another important way in which outcome may be affected by such secrecy is that *the covert nature of the plan may cut the couple off from all kinds of social ratification and affirmation of the pairing.* This rarely troubles the lovers at the time, because secrecy heightens romantic intensity; but the *effects* of lack of social support can be much more serious than they initially realize. In contrast, the courtships of Courter take place so openly that time alone together is far more limited. The price they pay for their friends' support is that they relate less to each other than they do to the circle. Since Courters want security and couple life, more than they want romantic intimacy, their courtships are structured positively.

For Immediate Remarriers, on the other hand, the failure to take into account the importance of external support makes them more vulnerable, and the success of their courtships depends heavily on timing. If passage duration is not held to a minimum, the intimacy inherent in this secret romance, which originally made the romance seem so delicious may swamp passage, because the couple fails to recognize and take care of their need for affiliation and support. This can pave the way for the emergence of reservations about the pairing. Therefore, the time period a Courter puts to good use to assure a stable coupleship may sink the Immediate Remarrier's covert plan and the lovers along with it. Being goal-directed is a prerequisite for individuals seeking immediate remarriage, because "time is not on their side."

For Graduates, the disclosure factor is much easier to manage. Although they publicize their resistance to remarriage, these pronouncements also preserve their security. Being frank about a refusal to remarry yields another benefit: individuals are rewarded for their candor. Ambiguity about one's position is avoided and stable routines ensured. Unlike Courters, Graduates do not need sponsors or mentors, since they do not intend to make personal changes in passage. The divorce which begins passage is the desired change; the prior marriage is defined as the last traumatic adventure one enters voluntarily. The resources required for hunting a partner, were this an acceptable alternative, go into enhancement of a status quo, which is accomplished early in passage. One subject bought a condominium in a pretty, wooded area and furnished it luxuriously. She did not plan to marry again, and thus, she did not plan to move. She was so proud of her new home that she invited her former spouse and his new mate to brunch and began entertaining friends from her former married life.

Along with the bowling and dancing that are pleasant pastimes and allow one to point out, "But I *do* go out!" many Graduates check out dating possibilities as they are settling into singlehood. One subject summed up her reaction to her opportunities this way:

> City government is very active here, and there are plenty of committees I could be on. Our recreational facilities are extensive. I could meet lots of men; but I have changed jobs and started to take expensive vacations. I just don't feel I have the time.

Men in this passage subgroup readily master the tasks necessary to entertaining and running a home. They speak most often of having "no *need* for a wife." One man referred to a longtime marital annoyance by explaining that, since he divorced, he saw to it that "all of my socks are matched up after I finish the laundry." Males tend to stock larders with expensive convenience food or budget to eat at restaurants. In addition, since presentable, older single men are at a premium by mid-life, men receive a steady stream of invitations. Women Graduates, too, find they no longer need a husband. A typical comment from a woman Graduate is, "I like my independence, and the men I meet really don't interest me." Reversals are not relevant to the passages of this subgroup, as they can be in the other two, because a change of heart or plans is not a possibility they elect. As one woman noted in a last follow-up interview,

> I suppose a companion might be nice, but I really doubt I would be willing to adjust to one. Haven't you noticed how people who remarry just seem to take care of each other's needs and sort of "go into a cocoon together"?

A minor problem for Graduates is the disinclination of others (who meet them at the onset of their passages) to take the stated refusal to pair seriously. However, Graduates handle disbelief patiently and express their resolve by acting it out. They give no time to courtship activities and effectively remove themselves from the reach of admirers, unlike the subjects who begin passage with avowals they will "never remarry" or "fall in love again" but then move fairly soon into dating patterns.

In contrast, careful control of the disclosure factor and the choice and management of agency (sponsorship) are tasks important to Courters. Using old friends' willingness to advise, entertain, and support one's plans to remarry is an effective mechanism of disclosure. One thus acquires agents who help one secure "a proper mate" (much as other agents find people jobs or guide professional careers). Graduates take comfort in locating opportunities to date but then dismiss them, whereas hyperactive Courters will exchange one prospect for a better one or keep quiet about who is the "favorite," while dashing all over trying to maximize all potentialities for pairing.

For example, Courters are clear about wanting to limit passage to a straight-arrow course into mating, but a problem may rest in determining a prospect's receptivity to them. Courters enjoy dating and may use a particular person or be used just to "look around" or "keep active and meeting people." Getting safely repartnered well before the upper ranges of middle age can demand concentrated effort. Sometimes remarriage is facilitated by finding someone who wants to be rescued from singlehood, perhaps a widow not aggressive in partner search, or a widower whose children are just old enough not to be threatened if he remarries. A daughter who once joined her siblings to sabotage each candidate their father found later became his agent, reporting, "Dad's still looking—but he's not *taken!*" Other likely prospects exist among widows who do not care to go out unescorted and, have hence, inhibited their chances of meeting someone, or among the men and women for whom multiple role management has begun to assume the character of not just a dilemma, but a disaster.

Courters become clever at sizing up marital prospects, but they want a *safe* as well as swift courtship. A number of Courter men repeated marriage proposals at intervals, despite having already been accepted by the woman in question. Because of the centrality of pairing to Courter passages, they ignore the opportunities for travel and fixing up a home which Graduates so enjoy. In fact, housing provides the best clue to identifying someone as a Courter. Most Courters live in small, messy, hastily chosen apartments which are no more than staging areas from which to set forth—and they are rarely home. Though women Courters make some effort to spruce up part of a room, they also tend to pay little attention to their surroundings. Courters are immensely practical. They know they cannot advance their goals by staying at home and that little of significance will take place there. Once a Courter male finds a prospect, he usually spends time at her place.

The Courters and Brief-Passage Subgroups

Since timing (rate of activity) is vital to Courter transitions, and so well understood by them, they rarely devote any time to regretting the breakup of their former marriages; rather, they immediately scout around for a prospect. Courters adhere to their timetables and cannot afford the leisurely pace at which Graduates begin to organize what one called "a most self-centered life." Thus Courters will use money to facilitate exit, sinking most of their disposable income into courting; whereas the critical issue of money management is never ignored by Graduates, who may know they must be extremely careful with money, especially since they are not counting on the assets, talent, or financial astuteness of a new spouse.

Courters were very easy to study, because they date assiduously and are very visible. The reason that they can reach exit so easily lies in their handling of disclosure so as to combine elements of secrecy with openness. While friends who participate in a Courter scenario are well aware of the Courter's wish to repartner, and may be directly asked to be sponsors, Courters nevertheless remain closemouthed about how a courtship is going and are very guarded with prospects as well. Friends may advise and consent, but they rarely "interfere" except in subtle, indirect ways. Since the old crowd and the Courter know each other so well, direct objections are not necessary anyway. Further, keeping some information quiet tends to increase the old crowd's interest in the Courter's direction.

A person being wooed by a Courter rarely knows how many other people may also be receiving the Courter's attentions. Courters mix business with pleasure and give few accounts of how they use their time. For example, many protect their privacy by using answering services to enable them to return telephone calls selectively without acknowledging all of them. Another popular (male) strategy is using a post office box. The most wary men in the study used this to conceal their home addresses. As a result, equally shrewd women discourage the attentions of men who do not produce home telephone numbers and don't entertain at home. They realize such secrecy may mean that a man may be temporarily living in a common-law union he is not openly acknowledging, or has well-established "outside" alliances. Other men understand this, too. Therefore, an interested man usually promptly produces a business card, home telephone number, driver's license, or introductions to a friend, to make clear to a woman the fact he is available and not misrepresenting himself.

The self-presentation of Courters is enhanced when a Courter entertains a new friend with old friends present, if they are attractive. Also, if a Courter's interest wanes, what was actually the serious work of checking fit can be passed off as merely genial sociability. In this regard, seeing an interested Courter or two may remind a woman of sorority rush week. Whether the Courter is a man or woman, the Courter's active social calendar assures that prospects get attention, but this rarely includes an early commitment.

While Immediate Remarriers try to ensure a pairing by means of clearly declaring for one another, Courters protect themselves by withholding declarations or by hinting they will be forthcoming. They value the respect of the old crowd and business associates who play major roles in social life; hence, saving face with both of these audiences is important to them. They court obliquely throughout much of the selection process, and what may be genuine hope for a pairing with a certain person can be expediently covered by their obvious enjoyment in "getting around a lot."

Exploiting the old-crowd network is perhaps the most valuable mechanism Courters use. It permits them to manipulate disclosure on their own terms. Enlisting the old crowd's interest puts their resources at the Courter's disposal, supplying a host of people who have an investment in portraying the Courter in a good light (since to do otherwise would reflect poorly on their joint histories), and gives a Courter the judgments of trusted intimates, who can scrutinize prospects at close range but with detachment and tact. Most importantly, this circle provides a home base where Courters feel not at risk, but at ease. It facilitates putting a prospect through a series of tests under the guise of hospitality; and, group solidarity means that neither the Courter nor the friends stand to lose much from a rejection. Displaced Courters, who have lost access to the circle because of moving or an ex-spouse's influence, may use a circle of housemates or new friends they work with to control and evaluate the prospect.

Courters distrust romantic love and strong attraction. They know what they value is an uncomplicated life with an acquiescent mate. Locating courtship in "homey" paired routines, and/or the circle, allows Courters to conceal their intentions about selection but indicate what would be expected of (and offered to) a mate. Foremost among the data so evoked are also many clues as to how the prospect views the Courter. The more a Courter can extract this kind of information about a prospect's reaction, without divulging in return, the more a Courter can court comfortably from a position of strength. Thus, Courters are extremely realistic about manipulation of disclosure and use it well for their own ends.

When a Courter is ready to make a commitment, he (or less often, she) is not acting on impulse, that is, plunging into the unknown, as this case material shows:

Although my suitor has been separated for two years, he has neither filed the papers or proposed. But for the whole two years, he has tried to get a pledge from me or get me to urge him to file. I keep pretending that I don't know we are bargaining, so I always answer him with "you're not in a position to get serious."

Shortly, this subject's suspicions were confirmed; the man told her he had gone to his wife and announced he would file, if she did not do so at once.

If the usual old circle is a resource, the Courter is also not "going it alone" in making a commitment and proposing marriage. The old crowd is also trying to "sell" a prospect and offers a fallback position if one is needed. Indeed, the likelihood of a rejection, tends to increase the loyalties of old friends. Thus they are a valuable resource, as is the extended family of blood ties to any accepted member. The manner in which Courters use old friends as if the circle were a family shows how creatively a person can build dependable, sustaining social worlds. In the absence of an old crowd, a Courter might make use of a therapy or encounter group or social club in an instrumental fashion to effect a pairing with a prospect who has been encountered there and who also continues to attend.

Therefore, while all brief passages give people a chance to exit early, everyone also has the same general goal: restoration to a gratifying social identity and stable life according to individual preferences. Within this framework, people choosing brief passages make choices that appear unique. However, the social processes by which they become winners are only different forms of "normalizing," which individuals construct socially out of their definitions of their own situation. These evaluations always take into consideration what middle age means to each of them.

People manage passage well enough to take possession of futures they perceive as entirely desirable—"normal." But, the most significant fact to bear in mind is that all these men and

women were convinced throughout passage that the aftermaths they chose were possible for them to achieve. This
belief, coming out of extremely diverse personal values, has
inestimable power in determining one's success in happily concluding a passage. It operates as a self-fulfilling prophecy.

5

Mid-length Passages:

The Steadies and

the Enforced Remarriers

$\mathbf{M}$ID-LENGTH PASSAGES involve pairing to exit and are more complex than shorter transitions, thereby requiring more time. This is true because there are sometimes more people directly involved in the potential new pairings of people in this type of passage or the people involved had many more problems after their divorces.

For example, Immediate (Planned) Remarriers *begin* transition with a partner substitution already achieved. Though this is a major and perhaps, dramatic shift; it occurs swiftly. Courtship takes place in private, with only the two lovers, or principals, having to be satisfied with the match. They move toward divorce as quickly as they can. As they await it, their social networks are partially and quietly rearranged by their advising in confidence several intimates who then become confederates in the secret plan. Graduates have only to drop back into the familial embrace of relatives and buddies from work who already exist as their main ties and who continue to sustain them throughout the divorce process, closing ranks around them afterward for the rest of a Graduate's life.

Courters both subordinate other roles to partnering, and, at the same time, convert these secondary roles and their social groups into resources for remarriage. But the boundaries between their groups, like the lines between the worlds of work and friendship, have already been crossed so frequently that these lines are blurred and without the meaning they may hold in many other people's lives. Thus, when they invite business friends to their weddings it reveals the reciprocal character that already prevails or is expected of these people. That is, someone who is now only a business associate is expected to become an intimate or substitute for an intimate. But it is not uncommon that a Courter's attorney or a customer (who is a "good account," and "gets a good deal" over the years) may stand by a person through three or four decades—and three or four successive weddings.

My depiction of brief passages in chapters 3 and 4 emphasizes that brief passages contrast with all longer ones in terms of the passage *content* a person has to (or wishes to) handle. Such content includes one's roles and personal identity. In brief passages, people try to maintain the balance among their roles (that are naturally, or have already become, reciprocal) and to maintain their personal identities without alteration. This is less the case in some longer passages where the content may include potentially or already competing roles which must be integrated or ruthlessly separated into distinct worlds. Mid-length passages also involve both more ambitions for situational or personal change and a larger cast of characters who are active participants in the transition—for example, the children, whose needs must be satisfied by the outcome.

In addition, another element present in many longer passages, and certainly in those of Enforced Remarriers, is the proliferation of problems of all types that bear on the conduct of a passage and cannot be held to one side, because they may fundamentally influence outcome. Brief passages may involve single mothers with children who define themselves as courting women who also happen to have children, but mid-length passages involve women with children who go through the transition *as a familial unit*, or men or women with seriously disarranged transitions. I discovered two subgroups who undergo mid-length passages, the Steadies, whose goal is to construct a stepfamily, and the Enforced Remarriers (who are usually either women with children or men who are going solo), who need to be and succeed in being rescued by virtue of another pairing into remarriage.

My mid-length passage subjects tended to be a bit younger than say, Courters, and to have both children and careers with which they needed help. In the Enforced Remarrier cases, the difficulties they had to overcome while in passage prevented them from executing their original plans for passage under the current circumstances, or in the time they had anticipated, or with as much success as they sought. Some of their problems were a matter of degree, however; they had hoped for more money, more occupational stability, and/or a happier pairing than they had thus far had a chance to obtain. At the same time, they perceived their positions as becoming more precarious from day to day. As one put it, "I'd been out there on the front lines by myself too long!" She added,

> I just went to a session and told my therapist I was marrying John Martin. He was startled and angry that I had made a decision

without further discussing it with him. "You'll never know love," he said. That angered me. "I don't think we can say that, for sure, at least not yet. What's so wrong about marrying a good man I respect? He is good to the children, too, and we're already feeling like a family. Besides, how about being able to sleep at night and having some sense that we're safe? Who knows what it might be like later?" He softened at that and said, "It's true that you need somebody."

It was often this kind of retrospective observation that finally enabled me to identify the subjects who were people who entered into marriages that they saw as enforced; this was belatedly seen and it took me a time to have enough confirmation of my hunch to be satisfied with classifying them as I did.

Another factor in the Enforced Remarrier cases is related to the "locus of control" theory, that states that the person in control of the decision to divorce (or of the terms of the divorce) feels better about divorcing than the person who has little control. One of my research subjects mentioned this theory, because he knew about it and felt that he had been the one who controlled his divorce. He took issue with the point because it overlooked what he believed was an important aspect:

> Initially, people who do the "dumping" feel better than their spouses, because it is their decision to divorce that ends the marriage. On the other hand, dumpees are usually devastated and just want to recover what they lost—a husband or wife. But the dumper, who knows only that he didn't want any more of that marriage, has no idea of with what to replace it. After awhile, the dumped partner *does* find someone, and about that time, some of what the dumper has tried, has failed to work out. It's then that the person who left the marriage starts to experience some of the confusion the spouse felt on hearing the original announcement. By the time the dumped spouse starts to have something to feel better about, the dumper has had time to start feeling badly.

Many Enforced Remarriers among my subjects had not been the person in control of the divorce decision or process, (child support or custody were often issues here). My research yielded no clear conclusions on this point; however, the subject quoted here was an astute informant and the situation he describes may have influenced the course of enforced remarriages.

I also found some subjects who did not want to choose singlehood as a goal, as did Graduates, but who were also not as convinced as the Courters were of the worth of conventional marriage. Among these were often the Enforced Remarriers, who were quite interested in at least a tentative exploration of singlehood, but, just as passage looked promising, circumstances pushed some of them into seriously considering marrying again, leaving them with only a taste of singlehood's pleasures. They had expected passage to yield highly positive developments; instead, they got negative ones, rather like the story of counting on chickens that hadn't hatched.

Problems Complicating Passage

Some subjects seemed to be "late starters" as far as recovery was concerned, or "late bloomers" who were using the first part of passage temporarily as a "holding pattern." Some used it to shore up roles separate from but related to their "careers" as a man or a woman. In so doing, they were "playing catch up," designed to create a more advantageous set of circumstances from which to launch a partner search. For instance, some people made efforts to upgrade their occupational roles, increase their incomes, or stabilize their children's situations, especially when divorce appeared to have seriously interfered with a child's course of development. Thus, while doing so, they had little free time, energy, or money. Others seemed to start passage by *taking refuge* in doing more parenting or getting further training, as if they were simply not prepared to muster their forces for mating. All of these reasons were cited by subjects who postponed what they saw as the "real" start of passage: beginning to "see someone."

While the inner psychological states of my research subjects were not the direct focus of my study, it seemed to me that some men and women just "took the divorce harder" than others and were slower to move onto partnering possibilities. Their approaches to passage seemed to reflect the overall way in which they went about the business of life; that is, it was a matter of an individual style, or pace. However, for many others, the problems of getting a passage into a desired shape were structural in origin. While many people had expected (understood in advance) that a slow start might be a consequence of divorce, and while they nevertheless saw the divorce as an improvement over the marriage, they reported starting passage with a large number of practical difficulties which increased, weighing them down. Many experienced severe (if sometimes, only brief) downward social mobility as a result of divorce. One said,

> We were in a new community when we divorced, and I had no old friends in Dallas. I got a job right away and rented a duplex near the girls' school so they didn't have to move. But I did poorly on the sale of the house, and financially, there was one emergency after another. The worst part was that we had no place in the order of things, though I kept going to church, because the minister fell ill and left. Then I moved closer to work.

Because of needing time to adapt to changed circumstances, some people did not yet feel ready to enter the marriage market. In other cases, people deliberately slowed the pace of passage, postponing an intended partner search they had great hopes for, because they first needed a year or two of solitude—except for work and family—to get their bearings. One subject declared, "I just overdosed on marriage!"

With respect to pairing, many subjects reported resenting people's well-intentioned matchmaking. One commented, "I can make my *own* plans!" It seemed to inhibit their progress back into matehood if long distance calls to parents in other locales elicited persistent inquiries like, "Are you dating yet?" Sometimes they perceived that new friends were pushing, not helping, in this regard. They were adamant, if not vehement, about not wanting to alter their private lives to suit the expectations, needs, or wishes of anyone else, except perhaps the children. A woman reflected,

> I just had to have a long period of being alone. For a time, my daughter stayed with her father in the house, and I had an apartment without a TV or radio. I'd never known what it was to be alone, and I couldn't get enough of the silence.

Subjects in all types of passage except the Immediate Remarriers were apt to express such sentiments. The value some men and women put on privacy was very high. Their strong feelings about this were repeatedly reported to me in interviews and during my fieldwork, and were cited by subjects as a sufficient gain for justifying a divorce. One man explained his retreat from pairing after a stormy marriage by saying, "I went into cold storage for a while." A woman reported,

> All I was sure I wanted was to keep my job and have my own place. For months, I never invited anybody up, even though I worked to get a guest room ready. My greatest pleasure then was being able to lock the front door, knowing no one could come

through it without my permission. That alone made divorce worth-while!

Another factor prolonging passage was that complicated postdivorce romances, particularly the first attempted, tended to mislead many subjects, who took them for serious affairs that would lead to remarriage. The phenomenon of the "rebound romance" captured many subjects for the first several months or, sometimes, years of passage. Some subjects who thought they were unmistakably on the way to being repartnered, served almost as transition "guides" or "nurses" to a "new friend" by virtue of their having been through the divorce process much earlier than the new friend, who was just getting into position to file for divorce and was in need of support. People conflicted about divorcing and making a new commitment, but very shaken by the prospect of facing the divorce process alone, seemed to try to scout up someone who had been through the experience recently and who had handled it fairly well. This sometimes provided grounds for a tentative pairing that appeared both a promising and fairly stable one until the "new friend's" divorce became final. At that point the prospect of actually going through with plans for another partnership sometimes rekindled in the newly divorced person a fundamental ambivalence about the paired state or a realization that he or she was not ready for this.

Thus, after the "new friend" emerged from the initial, most difficult part of the divorce process and became increasingly able to cope (which may have been facilitated by the subject as a guide or nurse), the subject would sometimes then hear that he or she was finding the present romance as confining as the marriage had been. In other words, the person finally past the final decree (which was "ancient history" to the subject who was the lover ready to pair) might announce a sudden awareness of a need for "more time to myself." One male subject spoke of a relationship like this in which he was the one to see that immediate progress in being paired was unlikely:

> I think I really loved her and that she cared for me, but she had a lot of developing to do for herself and this wasn't going to combine very well with our being together; so I gave up on it.

In instances where a "guide" or "nurse" was told that his or her previously appreciated acceptance was now seen by the lover as "threatening," the subjects may have been manipulated into providing all manner of help on an "as if" basis— as if a stable pairing would then result. Some subjects had lovers who changed their minds about the pairing and then had easily located new guides or nurses who became the next helpers. One subject said, "Everybody probably uses everybody else to some extent, but the business of being a 'rescuer' is complicated!"

Frequently the abrupt termination of an exciting rebound romance left the first person so perplexed and disappointed that further dating had to be shelved in favor of a year of psychotherapy. This often took place if the affair had developed so rapidly that no realistic postdivorce reassessment had been explored and accomplished. Subjects then had to fall back and delay things for a time, to "get my life in shape," as one put it. Another common remark was, "I've got to get my act together." By this subjects meant that it had proved necessary to have a well-organized base from which to develop options.

Two fundamental structural problems were common. First, there was the struggle to assume total responsibility for running a household and caring for children. Second, there was often the race to take care to retain (for men), or to carefully build (for women), sufficiently coherent occupational careers to earn the financial rewards that would lend a measure of stability to life. Singles with these concerns had to, at least partially, resolve these difficulties before they could begin to meet new people and build new social worlds. Some perceived these two structural problems together, and, in many cases, this combination of stresses was so severe that it cannot be overemphasized. One twice-divorced subject reported a conversation with the man who had been her first husband, who related to her that he had just finished devoting a weekend to giving their younger daughter a party complete with an orchestra in honor of her birthday. He said that he had

> made a mistake not hiring more help but that Janice had had a good time. Then he mentioned that it had been a job even getting the house cleaned up afterwards, and he asked me, "Have you ever been so tired you were *shaking?*" and I told him, "Sure —remember those years when you'd left and the kids were still all under five and I was doing my graduate work and working at the same time?"

Day-to-day or week-to-week crises tended to submerge long-range concerns. Subjects often felt as if they were battling a many-headed Hydra, because as soon as one set of tasks was mastered, a whole new set requiring more capable role performance cropped up. In this way, many disruptions in plans resulted, and difficulties in coping became a basis for role discontinuity in the interpersonal sphere. Many people therefore found themselves continually pushing into the future, projected timetables for the long-hoped-for sallies into cross-sex exploration. In these cases it was *life,* not just seeing someone that subjects perceived themselves as having to wait to start. In such passages, one's "career" as a man or woman would thus be effectively blocked for what subjects saw as a critically long time. Their futures as somebody's potential mate were being repeatedly forestalled.

Subjects in this situation tended to be single mothers whose former husbands quickly entered new marriages in which they served as fathers to the new wife's children or had more children with her, thus relinquishing responsibility for his own children. Or, such subjects tended to be fathers who discovered, to their distress, that for them divorce meant loss of children. The extent to which many men were devastated by virtual loss of children was an unequivocal, unexpected finding. Of these men, those who were unprepared to relinquish the father role and unable to parent, or disinterested in parenting, another man's children (or having more children) found the single state to be what is best described as "chilling." One man said,

> I was *always* asking my wife to keep the children out of my study and they were *always* nuzzling around me, demanding my time. I had just not thought about how terrible it would be *if they were just not around at all.*

Thus, two serious miscalculations, usually contrasted by gender, were women's failure to appreciate the loads they might have to carry in assuming complete responsibility for a family and men's belated recognition of the degree to which divorce effectively means forfeiting access to one's natural children. The worst part was that neither of these possibilities had been factored into the divorce decision, and overlooking them proved to be a significant mistake. In particular, women reported having no idea of the extent to which they needed the contributions of the father-husband role. Men confided during interviews that they had never before appreciated the degree to which they had depended on family life for emotional satisfaction and a sense of being "whole men." One male subject commented, "At divorce, I just thought I didn't want the responsibility of raising a daughter. Much later on, I saw that I had missed a lot."

These dilemmas—of having former husbands who refused to co-parent or former wives who withdrew children—seemed present in cases where the "overloaded mother" or "discarded father" had been the person who initiated what proved to be a bitter divorce. That is, these individuals may have been targets of highly successful punitive strategies employed by former spouses bent on retaliation. At any rate, these subjects' expectations during passage onset were later unconfirmed. Thus, down the road, some subjects saw that they had been mistaken to assume that divorce was a matter between spouses alone. One repercussion was a discontinuity in parental roles with implications for which they had not bargained.

Accordingly, many subjects reported a period of emotional turmoil while they tried to deal with a sense of their being "permanently out of things." One woman reported,

> When we divorced, we were new in that city. Chad immediately remarried and left the state. I discovered that the children and I simply had no place, socially. It took me a long time to get going and I never will know just what it cost the children.

Another phenomenon that initially complicated some passages was trouble dealing with the resumption of a sexual life. Many men and women took up a course of sexual promiscuity with highly positive expectations of enjoyment and increased self-esteem. They were ultimately disappointed, however, as they failed to establish or sustain satisfying relationships. Women reported feeling that they had been pushed into a series of "one-night stands" with no understanding at the time of what it might take to recover from what they perceived as the cost of this. Although they were initially pleased by the degree of sexual interest in them, many subjects later pulled back from what they had thought would be a rewarding activity to insist instead on establishing their *own* standards of control. "For a long time, I just went erotically crazy!" one man reflected. A woman subject explained,

> At first, I had no defenses at all against continual sexual invitations. Finally I was able to take control of my life enough to refuse a new lover, because I just didn't like him as a person. He said, "But everybody *wants* me for my body; I've *never been turned down* after just one encounter." And I said, "Well, you have been *now;* you'll have to get used to it!" That was a real milestone for me!

Turning to indiscriminate sexuality seemed to be a prominent feature in the passages of subjects who had originally married very early and without much sexual experience. This included as many men as women, interestingly enough. At first, both men and women assumed that simply reversing the situation ought to be a corrective. Later, they decided on more moderate courses, such as holding out for sex with affection. In the meantime, then, some subjects had to reevaluate the place of sexuality in their lives, since they began to perceive the sexual role as something they had reinstituted before sufficiently thinking it through. For others, however, resumption of sexual activity took place with unmixed consequences and was a sustaining and enhancing aspect of life from the beginning of passage. Nevertheless, actively pursuing this role potentially complicated for many people the task of multiple-role management.

The Steadies and the Enforced Remarriers

Steadies

Of the two subgroups involved in mid-length passages, I shall first examine the Steadies. The courtships of these subjects were reminiscent of old-fashioned ones; they seemed almost enactments of their idealized dreams about being old-style sweethearts. Although, as with Courters, their first pairing effort usually led to a remarriage, subjects going steady after divorce tended to be much slower to pair, setting themselves a more deliberate pace. They controlled the timing factor to enable them to go through a much longer, more cautious passage since their goal was to form a step family. The passages of Courter and Steady subjects also differed in that the going-steady pattern is a more privatized bonding.

As with the Comfortable Courters, the primary interest of Steadies is remarriage, not experimentation with a variety of partners. This value is combined with a strong conviction that the married state is the "natural," desired, *adult* condition. Thus, going-steady singles are noticeably traditional in values, family-centered, and relatively conventional—with one exception. Gradually and discreetly, some going-steady couples turn this mode of relationship into a living-together arrangement as a prelude to remarriage. In the passages of Steadies, there can be much self-consciousness about living together as a transition because of a concern about "respectability." Therefore, some of the aspects of going steady may be covert and somewhat uncomfortable to participants, such as their perceived necessity to dissemble to children. For instance, one subject, when sufficiently satisfied with her new partner to plan remarriage, agreed to a living-together stage of courtship in the passage, but before her new partner moved into the family home, she told

her children they had gotten married. When they were ready
for this step a year later, they went out of town with her sister
and the sister's husband, who were privy to the secret and acted
as witnesses at the wedding. The actual wedding date was not
divulged to the children.

Another subject who went steady to remarriage reported
that after two years of cohabitation, "we left the children at
home and went up to the mountains, and got married, by
ourselves." Without cohabitation, Steadies tend to "stay over"
together—as staying overnight is routinely called among these
singles. The man is more apt than the woman to be the one
to stay over at the other's residence, and he may park his car
out of sight and leave before dawn.

Subjects studied throughout a going-steady passage took
quite a bit of time to introduce the new partner to friends and
relatives, and, from the very first, most of their interaction was
home centered. Their familial role received first priority, because subjects focused on protecting ties with children and
significant relatives. Indeed, much of their early interaction
consisted of taking his, her or their children on outings. Later,
they went to his or her siblings' and friends' homes for Sunday
and holiday visits.

Steadies are thus careful to integrate the new partner into
an ongoing situation and to give everyone involved "time to get
to know" the new partner. They tend to review the prior
marriage for the purpose of comparing it (negatively) with the
new pairing. They do a lot of partner testing and tentative
family-unit exploring. A stable, reconstituted family is the primary goal, and this takes time to accomplish. Together Steady
couples grocery shop, cook dinner, take children shopping, and
pick up teen-agers at the movies. They worry about children
being on drugs and are interested in discussing their concerns
about their children's welfare and futures.

The Steadies and the Enforced Remarriers

Steadies' interaction with each other and with their friends is somewhat formal, especially because of their concern about appearances. They may be church goers; at least they faithfully attend the church weddings of their older friends' children, utilizing these as occasions for presenting the new partner. The office Christmas party or company's annual dinner dance or picnic are other settings in which to indicate their intentions.

They tend to talk a lot about the date of their upcoming marriage and to take wedding plans very seriously, particularly if a transitional living-together arrangement was not instituted. They romanticize their plans for remarriage and arrange large receptions in parish halls, at civic clubs, or at the woman partner's home. They try to contact old friends so that as many as possible will be on hand for the wedding and agonize over which ones to ask to stand up with them. If they are not church going, they tend to ask a minister friend (or someone recommended) to perform the ceremony at home.

They also prefer to have his, her, or all of their children take roles in the wedding. A typical crisis is the problem of whether or not a former spouse will allow a child (if the former spouse has custody and has not remarried) to so participate. These going-steady singles thus tend to direct their activities and thoughts toward finalizing their plans to have a step family, and the custom of having children take part in the wedding emphasizes this. They are usually very eager to resume marital roles and tend to romanticize the new partner while also feeling relaxed and comfortable with that person. Taking quite a bit of time to finalize this relationship is designed to allow children gradually to learn to trust and depend on the new stepparent. Also, ideally, it enables the couple to straighten out some problem areas before the new tie is formalized, although child-stepparent relationships are notorious for causing the remarried pair unforeseen difficulties.

FRESH STARTS

As I have stated, a major problem for Steadies may be the necessity of dealing with a former spouse, because of his or her access to and continuing interest in the children. This situation may persist for a long period after remarriage. Thus, problems of jealousy and divided obligations—a former wife who "cannot seem to get on her feet" or "can't seem to stay remarried", or a former husband who "can't keep a job" or tires to undermine the children's loyalty—may unsettle the courtship and continue after the wedding. One function a new partner may fill is to give advice and assistance in dealing with a troublesome former spouse. Sometimes the former spouse seems to be a "common enemy" who bonds the courting couple early; this is especially likely to happen if the parent member of a new pairing is constantly upset by the former spouse's refusal to be civil or cooperative. Therefore, some subjects reported feeling that a former spouse was almost part of the passage. One subject commented,

> We get everything going happily and it seems as if Josie can tell. We thought it would help that she remarried again and moved out of town, but now we just have to import Bob's daughters further for their visiting weekends, and I know that eventually she's going to start throwing the girls out, one by one, and I'll just be raising teen-agers again!

Another subject said,

> We know she'll be with us always, one way or another. We may end up leaving the state, or maybe the country—actually I have this picture of *her following us any place!*

The subject whom I studied the longest, and encountered just before her remarriage, reported of her ex-spouse:

The Steadies and the Enforced Remarriers

He still tries to throw us into a panic. The only tactic that has ever worked is to try to ignore him, and even that doesn't always do it.

One reason a former spouse may be introduced to a new partner or become almost a permanent feature of the pair's life together is the need for the former couple to plan children's weekend and holiday visits and make financial arrangements. Battles may rage over who gets the children for Christmas or whether or not a grandparent, valued by the child and the new couple, will accept an invitation when she or he is an in-law from the former marriage. If children make a transfer of allegiance to the new pairing fairly easily, in-laws may do so too because of their approval of the impending marriage, or from a desire to continue to see a former son-in-law, daughter-in-law, or grandchild. It is not unusual for a valued and affectionate ex-in-law to be one of the people who gets acquainted with the new partner fairly early. The permutations of these going-steady alliances, then, can affect many lives.

The passages of Steadies are characteristically sedate. Nevertheless, in late passage, Steadies are likely to encounter some typical crises. Among these might be the need for the new pair to fight to get custody of a child being withheld by an ex-spouse, or more likely, the sudden news that a former spouse can "no longer manage" a child and is immediately shipping her or him to the other parent. These developments often precipitate a further crisis, the need to enlarge a house. Another common emergency is when the pair of Steadies is advised by a former spouse that the newly paired spouse must now assume total financial support of children.

Because the going-steady pair does not regard itself as two singles, but as a *provisional couple*, they are not treated as single people and do not go out alone or date other people. Steadies do not contemplate or undertake personality or life-style changes, because they identify their problem as replacing an unsatisfactory spouse with a "proper mate." Thus, they lack interest in other major changes. Some of my subjects, however, remarked with pleasure that they had made certain minor changes in relatively trivial areas such as recreation, observing, "It's nice being able at least to canoe together, as I always wanted"; or, conversely, "Now I don't have to go to basketball games anymore!" That is, Steadies take a lot of satisfaction in such minor changes, since they serve to bring habitual routines more into accord with personal preferences.

Because it is characteristic of Steadies to use the passage not simply for partnership testing, but also for rehearsing a *familial* venture, most of their energies go into this. Professional occupations are continued, but are muted themes, subordinated to this family effort, and children are rarely excluded from the pairing. It is also typical for friends in the neighborhood or from earlier years to include the pair in customary rounds of sociability in which all relevant children are often present. Their motives include being concerned about group solidarity and wanting to be of service to a friend.

It is salient, further, to realize that many living-together arrangements are accepted by the very married, *as if* they already represented a commitment to conventional marriage. This fact is a source of latitude for people in regard to their behavior during the singlehood period. The "as if" semblance of marriage, if not the fact of it, serves the function of preserving group solidarity, because norms are partially honored, or they look *as if* they are, until the union is legalized.

The following example shows how this arrangement can work. One subject entered into a steady relationship involving spending a great deal of time with an enthusiastic suitor. He had a luxurious apartment and was financially secure. She had a luxurious home. For the best part of a year, they stayed together at one location or the other, broken by frequent travel, returning to care for her two college-age children. On the latter occasions, the suitor functioned as the mother's boyfriend, not as surrogate father.

Although the neighbors did not like him or the situation, they knew he was very much interested in marriage. Therefore, neighbors who were her old friends tolerated a normative situation which they personally, but privately, deplored. Some had relatively young children to whom all of this had to be explained. Despite their feelings, the "courting couple" was routinely included in every social event. The intimate nature of the relationship, which neighbors saw as unfortunate and, certainly much too blatantly presented, was tolerated *because the outcome of this romance was uncertain.* They were well aware that this man could become the head of household at any point. They thus "reserved judgment" or tried to, and through a heroic sequence of temporizing and apparently approving measures, they held doubts in check until the woman, herself, reached a decision. Marriage was the decision they wanted to urge on her but not to this particular man, whom they saw as not interested in the children, inappropriate as her mate and their neighbor, and possibly out to exploit the woman. Nevertheless their cordiality never flagged. When she finally decided, rather unexpectedly, to break off the romance, the relief in the neighborhood was extensive. Everyone came forth to applaud her decision, and to express previous reservations. When she did marry, after a second experience of "going steady," someone she had known a short time, all rejoiced. His courtship had been more conventional; he called on her with another couple in tow, and took them all out to dinner. He also met standards for neighborhood participation, as the other man had not been able to do. Neighbors sent rather elaborate presents through a telephone alert system, organized by the wife whose sense of propriety had been most offended the year before. These gifts were, of course, rewards for a restored normative equilibrium.

Thus, the strains of forced cordiality and an awkward "holding pattern" in the neighborhood were resolved to everyone's satisfaction. Then the routines of neighborhood life resumed quietly without much attention being paid to the newly constituted pair. After a round of parties in honor of the wedding at her home and the couple's open houses in which the wife ritually introduced her new husband, the couple took up a rather private existence with little neighborhood interaction. This illustration typifies the anxiety about the outcome of a going-steady period which both Steadies and their neighbors may undergo, despite other social credentials held by Steadies.

The Steadies' characteristic emphasis on the family may involve them in rather complicated situations when their children are old enough to get married themselves. These latter marriages may bring about a comingling of the entire families of the old spouses and new partners. Sometimes the wedding of a child living on his or her own recently may mark the first occasion that former spouses have been in each other's company since their divorce or have seen the ex-spouse's new partner. One woman described encountering her ex-husband during their child's wedding festivities, in a moment following the ceremony when no one else was close at hand; the man refused to speak to her. It is common for the bride's family to seat these divorced parents and new mates so that they are not within earshot during the reception or to assign good friends to see to it that they are kept apart. Otherwise a present husband may attempt to "break the ice" with a former husband or use the opportunity provided to mention that the child support check for a younger child would be appreciated. These weddings also are occasions for friends and relatives from "both sides" to occupy themselves with all kinds of parrying from what are essentially two unfriendly camps.

Participation at these ceremonies can also be even more problematic and result in unpredictable episodes which revive the earlier marital hostilities. Preparations can signal the resumption of the old family quarrel as in the case of several women subjects who spoke of their disappointment when a daughter decided at the last moment before planning her wedding to ask for her stepmother's assistance with plans, rather than that of her mother and the stepfather with whom she had been living. One woman also reported her amusement when meeting her former mother-in-law when her oldest child married. The second woman used the occasion to describe in great detail the former husband's recent wedding.

Steadies are proper and a bit shy, hoping never to divorce again and to fit into the customary neighborhood and familial routines after remarrying. In this sense, they, too, are "normalizing" their situations as quickly as they can. Initially, and throughout courtship, they tend to spend a great deal of time alone together or in family activities and to be tentative about entering social circles as a pair. This pattern stands in contrast to that of Courters who use a network of friends as an opportunity to display themselves as part of a couple and manipulate partner selection so as to enhance their own bargaining position.

Steadies appear genuinely interested in and enthusiastic about the partner and, unlike Courters, to undertake at least several years of earnest and serious courtship before a wedding. Although their sexual roles as a new pair may be extremely gratifying to them, this theme is covert and always muted, because they regard sexuality as a highly private matter.

In public self-presentation, they focus on the benefits to the children of their remarriage plans and the contributions a potential stepparent is already making to the parent's life in this and other respects. This fact alone is often sufficient to win over relatives, friends, and neighbors—as well as the children, as long as the new partner's intentions are viewed as "honorable" and his or her motives as genuine. In a surprisingly high percentage of cases, the first going-steady experience leads to the planned remarriage, evidently to everyone's satisfaction.

Enforced Remarriers

The passages of Enforced Remarriers, the second mid-length passage subgroup, are characterized by an extremely unstable transition and an emotional tone of uneasiness and confusion, rather than happiness and relief. In these cases, subjects were considerably reluctant to remarry at the time or had many reservations about the specific prospect before entering what only looked like a going-steady mode. The prospect was finally accepted only after complications in the passage necessitated a change in plans. One person had this to say, looking back: "I was not very happy about the planned wedding, but I was very touched by my suitor's steadfastness towards all of us as a family."

While people in the going-steady passage have many optimistic hopes for the remarriages they contract after long acquaintance, Enforced Remarriers usually hope to *avoid* the situation they end up in. Generally, the change in direction takes place when divorce is followed by one or more unexpected major setbacks. Among these are: loss of job or a promotion (usually for a male); lack of sufficient income (especially for women struggling to rear children along with stressful occupational problems); loss of parent or sibling; the early, extremely happy remarriage of a former spouse; or a combination of several of these factors. Other unforeseen developments which can crop up to ruin one's plans may be miscalculations about expenses (for example, a lengthy illness or suddenly having to finance a child's education without the scholarship aid anticipated).

Subjects who ended a passage because of circumstances similar to these (which they privately defined as negative and tried to conceal from general knowledge) expressed little direct disappointment to anyone about a remarriage not matching the hopes they originally held for themselves (following divorce) when remarrying. They revealed these thoughts to me much later. A significant clue, however, was their reluctance to discuss the remarriage at all, preferring to focus elsewhere looking back on passage as an improvement over the first marriage. Most importantly, when discussing the remarriage in their roles as my research subjects, positive references to the joys of remarriage, or happy asides, were missing. In contrast, Courters, Steadies, and Passionate Searchers alike continually interrupted a train of thought in our interviews to bring my attention back again to their remarital gains.

Enforced Remarrier subjects emphasized the difficulties of the first marriage in interviews during and after terminating passage. These difficulties were the material they concentrated on and contrasted with a positive appraisal *of the divorced state*, not the remarried one. When these subjects were followed for a number of years, Enforced Remarriers consistently evaded or slighted discussing the remarriage. The other clue to identifying these people was their subsequent "confessions," which came very slowly, that the remarriage had been an expedient.

Sometimes this admission was dropped so casually that it was put in an aside such as, "but it turned out much better than I had hoped."

However, a disappointing enforced remarriage yielding only a modicum of normalcy (or much less than a subject expected) might prove to be a fairly brief one, ultimately used as a staging area to prepare oneself for another transition into another eventual pairing. This pattern was found in a few cases where a subject's partner also married without much enthusiasm and functioned poorly because of an undetected but serious condition, such as emotional instability or alcoholism. One subject said, "For all that my second marriage was a nightmare, when I divorced again, I had my M.B.A. and my own credit cards."

A point to be considered is that many remarriages do not consist of, for instance, two Courters. Although many involve two people in the same sort of passage, remarriages also reveal dissimilar types. A Courter might find someone looking for a Steady and agree to a longer courtship and more stepparenting than he or she wishes. More often, a Courter accomplishes a swift remarriage to an eligible who takes the Courter seriously *only* because the eligible's passage was fraught with such disruption that hopes for the preferred kind of partner or match were destroyed for the time. Thereby, a few Courters "catch" unusually attractive "hardship" prospects in individuals realizing that consequences more catastrophic than a marriage of convenience would ensue from a hesitation to remarry. Here, the person who feels obliged to marry might later lay plans to reenter transition under better conditions, thus divorcing again.

Retaining remarried individuals as subjects in the project meant that a subject's earlier, private calculations about his or her marketability as things then stood (that is, bargaining position) might be disclosed to me later when a second transition ended more happily for the subject. Nevertheless, people were very reluctant to admit to necessity as a motive.

Summary

Two ways in which Enforced Remarriers characteristically control their passages are through exercising the right to reversals during passage and manipulating disclosure (especially to a prospect). Unlike Steadies, who work their way slowly toward building a relationship solid enough to sustain them, Enforced Remarriers are often coerced by circumstances (such as inept management of passage or the development of crises requiring a partner's aid) to rush toward passage resolution. The shapes of the passages of these two subgroups vary enormously. Steadies tend to progress together well, calmly ironing out problems as they surface, using effective interpersonal skills, whereas charting the passages of Enforced Remarriers would yield a wildly fluctuating line.

The hopes of Enforced Remarriers are repeatedly extinguished as more and more problems arise to swamp passage. They usually suffer a series of potential, and then, actual mini-reversals, before accepting a marital candidate as a means of cutting their losses. Therefore, the question of desirability of passage is sometimes at issue. A passage that may look highly desirable at the time of the final divorce decree can rapidly turn into a morass. Wishes to reenter passage (if it becomes possible as a future consideration) may exist at the time of remarriage. As one subject commented, "It's not the long run that worries me, but the short run."

One mechanism for managing passage to which people may not be sufficiently attentive is keeping alert about how a passage is going (scanning for signs predicting the course). Not thinking ahead can mean not being able to forestall an exit not to one's liking. The inability to take accurate readings of one's situation (along with the absence of agents or sponsers to guide and advise one) inhibits some passages. Characterizing many of these passages is the implicit *centrality of passage* itself to a person's life. If the tasks of multiple-role management become overwhelmingly hard, a person finds that every aspect of his or her life starts to be dominated by some form of "fall out" from the divorce. Typical crises in coping occur when occupational goals and/or the welfare of one's children start to be sacrificed to a stalled passage. To remedy such a problem, passage goals may have to be sacrificed for one's children's needs or the demands of an occupational phase. Unexpected disruptions of passage may also arise in the form of an elder's extended illness or a prospective mate's misfortune, for example.

It was extremely difficult for me to collect convincing data to depict Enforced Remarriers unequivocally. This subform remains the most difficult to identify and understand. I found it necessary in my research to follow a number of remarried subjects over a very long period. Sometimes the subsequent success or failure of the remarriage led subjects to comment much more fully and openly than ever before about their attitudes and expectations at the time of the marriage. During this prolonged period, some participants went on to end a remarriage that had not served them as well as they had calculated. Others found that, although their remarriages failed to be happy ones, they functioned surprisingly well for consolidating their affairs, providing a stable base for such important pursuits as launching children or completing an occupational shift, thus greatly raising self-esteem and income or greatly reducing the problems which had prompted the remarriage. Some of these people found that now, by possessing added resources, they were better equipped to control their lives and file again for divorce.

It was *only after* they had "bailed out" of passage into a second marriage that remained less than they had hoped for but that yielded sufficient secondary gains to allow them a *choice* about staying or leaving that subjects were willing to talk with enough candor to confirm retrospectively that the marriage had been enforced. The few cases of this type I encountered led me to recognize that they formed a separate subgroup.

The other characteristic of Enforced Remarriers that makes them difficult to identify is the way they handle disclosure, generally. They are often not even frank with the partner about feeling forced into a solution for such considerations as financial expediency, the education and launching of children, or the need for a mate to help marry off a child or restore a semblance of social stability to bring more order to life. The fact that a partner might conceal from the prospective mate or the interviewer "true motives" (or in some hardship cases, deceive themselves by undue optimism) was not easy to document. People do not like to discuss the necessity of a marriage; it is clear that some simply go ahead and put the best possible interpretation on a "rescue" marriage.

When I looked more closely at every instance of remarriage in the study, a few marriages seemed to be likely candidates for reclassification into other passage types, especially Enforced Remarriage. But on the basis of added data collection, nothing suggested that the original categorizing was incorrect. For example, one male subject followed for five years after his second marriage, that I suspected might have been enforced and eventually unstable, answered my inquiries about his family with, "Oh, we're just fine, thank you! We're waiting for Barbara's son's first child to be born and we are just back from the Orient. Her son lives near us."

In evaluating my data, I became preoccupied with two questions: "Will enforced remarriages prove to be stable, that is, permanent?" and, "To what extent is the permanence of a marriage evidence of its being a successful outcome?" My attempts to answer these questions to my own satisfaction were eventually resolved in favor of accepting subjects' definitions of "success." Except for Graduates who thought that only problems would accrue from remarriage, and Runners in Place who used a long passage to be happily single, most subjects defined a subsequent pairing as the indication of "successful" termination of a passage.

A surprising amount of agreement existed among subjects on this meaning of repartnering. It showed up everywhere—in conversations during fieldwork, in statements directed to me as an interviewer, in listening to people speculate about single friends, and when subjects pondered their own futures. This criterion for success continually revealed itself in offhand remarks, "She's OK; she remarried." A frequent comment was, "I hope to remarry after . . . ", followed by a laundry list of accomplishments necessary to prepare for partnering. A question often put to one single by another, when seeking news of a third, was, "Has she (he) remarried yet?" To my subjects, the success or failure of a romance is a very important matter. For instance, in explaining his long passage as a single Searcher, one man said, "I've had a very gratifying professional life and several romances have gone sour on me." Reflecting on his stable pairing of six years, one subject ended his follow-up interviews by saying, "I certainly went through a lot of women before I found the right new marriage, didn't I?" (He is now again in passage, in the company of a lovely woman.)

A big clue to the significance subjects attached to finding a person with whom to pair also lay in the fact that no one saw the need to complete the following sentence, "I'm still looking. . . ." Some still spoke of past romances in a "what might have been" reference to an aborted love affair (not carried into repartnering for long) as well as "what might *still* be." Both of these themes animate the accounts long-in-passage individuals give of ongoing and prior love relationships.

Therefore, despite the amount of discussion of what might be called "the ideology of singlehood" (which I examine later), a major unexpected finding was a widely held (sometimes tacit) belief in the positive value of pairing. Finding a partner and joining up forces in some manner was to take the word, "repair" in its most literal sense.

Motivations toward this end vary, however. For example, Steadies tend to be in less of a panic than Courters about the aging process, but then they are also apt to be somewhat younger. They do not view divorce or mid-life singlehood as desirable compared to conventional marriage, because they still have children at home. They seem more confident of their capacities to manage passage and to perceive themselves as more "marketable" than do Courters. This is true because Steadies depend much less on agents. However, the children often function as a pair's sponsors (or detractors). This comment from case material on an Enforced Remarrier illustrates the influence children can have:

After my divorce, I fell in love with a remarkable man whose whole way of life was a tremendous contrast to my rigid ex-husband's. Each of us had children though, and neither set was very happy about our romance. Eventually the relationship began to flounder because of another suitor I had who was very shrewd about courting my children, too. Ultimately I accepted him after waiting to see if the first man would fight to be the one who got me; he didn't. One Saturday lunch during the engagement, one of my kids commented how much more he liked his soon-to-be stepfather than my first admirer. To my great amazement and distress, I started weeping and said, "But I *loved* Mark." The children fell silent and then soon excused themselves from the table. I hope I am never again in a position where they can put so much pressure on me for their own purposes.

In general, Enforced Remarriers have to change their initial hopes about partner type; that is, they have to drop their standards in order to get out of a disastrous passage. Although they may start passage with regrets about divorcing, it is the defeating complexity of passage that nudges them into viewing singlehood more and more negatively, and conventional marriage more and more positively, as their experience of transition deepens. Thus, individuals who can securely anchor other roles (such as, occupational or parental) have more options.

A passage's premature termination often hinges on a man's inability to overcome his anxieties about aging, or a woman's failure to achieve financial stability, topics to which I return in my discussion of long passages. However, male subjects of around fifty years of age were also often confronted with realizations that they were hitting the ceilings on their professional careers just as they got bogged down in worrying about their age. In most cases, women subjects felt similarly disadvantaged regarding aging, but a decade earlier. In addition, in an increasingly informal era, and in competing for new women partners, many men discovered that their behavior and attitudes were viewed by lively women as quite dated, especially because of the influence of feminism. To be bereft of the authority of their previously held roles as heads of households, just as they had to deal with new ideas on gender roles, was quite difficult for some of these men, especially with assets diminished by divorce. Therefore, circumstances forced many men to consider women who were highly successful (serious) professionals and more independent then their former wives, since they needed a financial partnership to remarry. For women, the reverse situation often existed. Women may handle the issue of age well, only to be defeated by money management tasks. In either case, a nonconventional marriage can take on greatly increased worth.

Like brief passages, the goal of mid-length passages is restoration to a stable life, in the context of risk-avoidance. Steadies normalize their situation and generally seem to contract stable remarriages, and Enforced Remarriers are engaged in restabilizing and reorganizing a life dangerously out of control. An interesting line of speculation may be that a destabilized state of affairs, *coupled with unnecessarily negative evaluations of one's future,* forces the hand of Graduates and Enforced Remarriers alike. But "stabilizing" is a purpose important to both short and longer transitions. Individuals in all five subgroups involved in brief and mid-length passages were concerned with achieving regularized, "normal" social existences. For Enforced Remarriers, then, it may be primarily that this stabilization leads to a satisfying life or to accomplishments that help in maintaining a remarriage reluctantly or tentatively contracted, as well as in later permitting one to start a partner hunt once again. In other words, among people who value partnering, to re-pair is to mend a broken social connection.

6

Long Passages:

The Hunters-and-Sorters

and the Runners in Place

DURING TRANSITION, people in long passages work to "open up" life to permit the development of alternatives. Doing this may require quite a bit of time. Thus, these people tend to ignore the aftermaths and motives characteristic of men and women who exit from passage earlier. The patterns that men and women in long passages institute during transition largely depend on their interest in and use of current social trends and their dissatisfaction with some of the commitments they made in their early adulthood. Thus, social change is critical to this mode of passage much as it was shown not to be in the passages examined in chapters 3 to 5.

Long passages are conspicuous for the degree to which diversity and creative experimentation constitute the conceptual bases for the conduct of transition. In all three subgroups of people choosing long passages, I found either a personal openness (in the Hunters-and-Sorters and the Passionate Searchers) or what might be called an openness to life experience (in the Hunters-and-Sorters, Passionate Searchers, and the Runners in Place). The Hunters-and-Sorters wish to pair, but they do so at a leisurely pace, after a number of experimental pairings that are appreciated as much for the chance to know someone "different" as for the importance put on any one person. Thus, an individual in this form of transition hunts for partner possibilities and then sorts through them, looking for the "right" person. On the other hand, the Runners in Place are not willing to partner, except perhaps in the sense of a sexual alliance maintained over a long, nonmonogamous period. However, the Passionate Searchers search avidly for a perfect partner with whom to settle into a deeply satisfying pair bond.

The transitions of men and women in long passages initially require a high level of passage-management skills, but become more predictable during the course of transition, especially after one has been in passage awhile. In general, the complexity of passage depends on the individual's willingness to be open to a number of people and a number of potential life modes; coupled with this many reasons exist for guarding one's private life from view. Thus, the degree of complexity rests on the extent to which these people sample innovative ways to live, view life, and relate to other people. Some of the approaches chosen are quite new to most of the people in long passages, although some of the men and women have, in many respects, been rather nonconformist since their university days. Another aspect of the diversity of long passages is the degree to which people slowly institute a great deal of personal change, particularly in regard to their private lives and their belief systems or values.

I formed a number of general impressions about the people

in the three long-passage categories. For instance, the Hunters-and-Sorters are very much interested in partnering, but, at the same time, they are equally interested in the novelty and challenges of living alone on terms that allow a person to remain relatively uncommitted to any lover for quite extended periods. (Since they were once "very married" individuals, they appear to find having a close love relationship, without having to be a fully committed couple is a rather remarkable experience.) The Runners in Place are extremely busy and active men and women who are "all over the place." These people are urbane, sophisticated, and accomplished men and women with high incomes. In short, they are chic. From the start of passage, the Runners are as determined as Graduates never to pair or marry again. The Passionate Searchers are looking for that perfect person with whom they can institute a vital pairing, and they hunt for one, as they live, passionately. Runners are very active sexually; and the Hunters-and-Sorters and the Searchers also value sexual expression highly. However, among all of my long-passage subjects, I encountered a matter-of-fact assumption that sexuality is one of life's boons, and in the contemporary world and among people who have completed parenting, one's sexual life is a private matter, one's own business. Sexuality is nevertheless quite differentially interpreted among these people, because the Runners' utilization of sex contrasts sharply with what Searchers, and to a fairly significant extent, with what Hunters-and-Sorters view as the purpose or "place" of sexuality in one's life.

Long passages are usually "unscheduled" and idiosyncratic in that people don't begin with clear plans, as do some other men and women. These kinds of transition are chosen by individualists. Passage complexity diminishes after a person has been in transition long enough to start finding his or her bearings. Roles tend to stabilize and become enjoyable, and there is less need to be always attentive to passage-management tasks, because patterns begin to take shape and show some regularity, albeit within the contexts of a lot of spontaneity and exploration. However, long passages demand quite a bit of free time apart from work. They also depend on both a willingness and the capacity to rearticulate one's roles and learn ways to negotiate one's way through life with style, ease, and conviction. Long-passage people struck me as men and women who were fleet of foot and rather self-contained. As a social type in a fairly comfortable form of the postdivorce transition, the long-passage person probably best exemplifies what the "average person" thinks of as the hedonistic, "free" existence of middle-aged singles. Be this as it may, many individuals are, however, quite serious people and some of them are earnest about being "good people" living "good lives."

Before examining the first two subgroups more closely, I want to make a few more general observations about long-passage individuals. Men and women interested in and willing to undergo these passages define them as highly desirable from the beginning of a transition. They define long passages this way because they expect to enjoy them and profit from them. Most of the time, they do. To set oneself up in a long passage, one must first get comfortably situated, in the sense of being fairly comfortable with oneself and with one's current daily existence. This usually comes about as a result of important changes in one's life that served as turning points. After this, people wait to see what possibilities exist for them, or else they develop and wholeheartedly pursue what they see as possibilities.

Therefore initially, as a transition, the long passage has none of the settled quality of, for instance, the onset of a Graduate passage, in which matters are quickly decided and do not involve tackling much of anything radically new. Regardless of the way other people view matters, the men and women involved in this lengthy passage value a long, drawn-out transition because of the chances it provides for self-expression and the exploration of a variety of avenues to self-realization. Thus, the long passage is not something one is forced into, but is rather an opportunity one recognizes and seizes. Besides being a chance to enjoy oneself, the long passage is also an opportunity to test oneself and one's mastery of life. Since long-passage men and women are high achievers who have already seen a bit of the world, their frequent references to "exploration" sometimes include inner exploration as well as experiencing new social forms and new arenas of life of which they have never previously partaken. To its participants, the long passage may have its perplexing or troubling phases, but it is an exciting and deeply satisfying option.

..Although the Runners in Place, who are prosperous, self-indulgent, and often, radiant "beautiful people" may not be affected by it; many long passages are characterized by at least intermittent periods of voluntary downward mobility. Accepting an immediate specific lowering of some aspects of one's standards of consumption (such as no longer entertaining expensively) is an extremely functional step by which many men and women organize their passages quickly so they can afford to consider the adoption of many new interests. It is typical of many long-passage men and women in the Hunter-and-Sorter mode, for example, and certainly in the Searcher mode, promptly to take up less expensive housing arrangements until they know how they want to live or with whom. Thus people eliminate some of their customary expenditures (probably related to an earlier, more conventional kind of life) in order to shift funds into areas with which they have little familiarity. One such enabling mechanism might be to share a house so as to reduce expenses to be able to take a long trip through the

Orient, perhaps, with a "new friend." One subject provided the following illustration:

> We built a modern house on a hill near campus, and it was almost poetic in its classical severity and very gratifying. But I couldn't have the new life I wanted with the house and the marriage, so I moved on and bought a big, clumsy house that I renovated. I made a rental apartment out of the rumpus room and servant's room, and I share the remainder with two business people who are often out of town. Recently I ran into the very proper mother of one of my friends from my first marriage, and she said, "What do you mean 'collective living?' " One of the things this change financed was a winter in Guatemala with a fine man, but I omitted that information.

Thus prepared, long-passage men and women will set out consciously to sample a range of life-styles or a particular set of experiences. One woman subject said,

> In the past seven years, I traveled a lot and lived abroad. I have had four crazy lovers, one of whom I married. I could now be bought with peace and comfort. It has *nothing* to do with age— *nada!* I don't think I have to go out to get security, because I have that now—it's just that I am not going to put up with a lot of hassle.

These people are men and women who have both benefited from the recent emergence of alternative life-styles and contributed to their elaboration. They may sample a range of life-styles, savor them, and then often abandon and replace them. This form of going solo at mid-life and this perspective on alternatives yields many valuable transitory experiences that in a general sense facilitate passage. One subject reported,

> I have decided to take a few weeks in Europe, but it won't be my usual kind of traveling. I have never sailed over, so I decided I wanted to book the QE2 and I have. About a third of my time,

I'll be cruising—going over and then going around to the Riviera. I want to go back to my favorite spot and lie around, like on the boat. I'll fly back from Paris so I can get some lingerie. I'll be glad when I'm not poor anymore—you know, always having to hold the line. Going over by boat once is hardly being rich. I'd like to have a lot more money behind me—working for me.

Many forms of recreation or types of experiences these people desire are expensive, particularly at the rate they consume them. By reorganizing their spending patterns initially, they are able to retain a sufficiently steady supply of disposable income to pursue such experiences.

A lengthy passage allows a person to "free up" his or her routine, money, and social identity. However, the predisposition to explore also generates the complexity that requires a person's management skills to be "dusted off" and made operational. People usually begin the change in identity with externals, such as discarding much of a former wardrobe or throwing away keepsakes that weigh one down. A clue that a friend is about to embark on a long passage might be a report that he or she is consolidating life in smaller quarters or doing an extensive house or apartment cleaning in which clothes or mementos are thrown out as a gesture of "stripping the decks for action." Most formerly marrieds in long passages have little idea about what will ensue, but they get themselves ready for it, anyway.

Because possibilities always exist for one's social roles to be reorganized in ways that either enhance or disrupt their potentially reciprocal (supporting) character, the long-passage person must be prepared to handle these possibilities. For example, the occupational or familial role can interfere with a new role as a "man" or "woman" in a relationship. One way to manage roles is to realize that passage may entail a willingness to do a certain amount of "role juggling." This technique works because a person can temporarily focus on the role that is in need of immediate attention, and then shift focus to whatever role appears to be the most promising route to a current goal. My subjects were intelligent about using their roles in a manner that optimized their positions. Money, energy, time, and attention are resources people possess in varying degrees, and one of the first calculations a long-passage person may undertake is how to deploy one's supply of these.

On the whole, long passages were the choice of the research subjects whose experience of mobility had been the most exten-sive, compared to other subjects. These people thought of themselves as "contemporary" men and women who understand and find congenial many aspects of modernity. To a significant degree, and despite a few regarding themselves as elitists, they had never defined themselves as traditionalists, regardless of the fact that many of them came out of highly conventional first marriages. Their histories contained many examples of "good experiences," which were by-products of the necessity to change and adapt along the mobility trail. One woman told me about having to move out of state and not wanting to:

> When I found we were leaving Connecticut for New Mexico, I was really upset. Clyde bought a ranch. I hated horses, and I liked my friends. Besides, things were easy for me before, because everyone in the neighborhood knew us. I always plant bushes and things, but we never stay! Well, I loved the high desert. The air and mountains are unbelievable. When we left, I felt worse than when we left New England. In the West, everything's so *open*. Later on, I was never the same and it was a good thing.

Long-passage subjects seemed to have learned the lesson that something that doesn't look too promising at first may prove unexpectedly profitable. Hence, these people often moved ahead with a lot of hope and optimism. As a personal characteristic brought to bear on transition, this attitude is a valuable tool, since appraisals are rooted in definitions, as in the oft-mentioned point that a glass can be seen as half-empty or half-full.

Nevertheless, when expectations about the necessary future expenditures of time, money, or energy are underestimated, as easily happens in the conduct of unscheduled, entrepreneurial transitions such as long passages, the result may be heavy demands on a person's resources and the need to be able to muster them in a hurry. Unless a person is prepared to move quickly and with determination, there can be unanticipated consequences for professional status, health, courtship progress, or the motivations that originally led a person into a long passage. However, since long-passage subjects viewed themselves as "competent" and also "realistic," they often tended to forge ahead with a "What's to lose?" attitude. In other words, these subjects tended to romanticize passage as well as to enjoy it greatly much of the time. Thus a prominent feature of this kind of transition is its appeal and its centrality to a person's life.

Since long-passage subjects were interested in and comfortable with many aspects of social change, one of the calculations natural to them was examining their values in relation to recent trends. Thus, some subjects selectively changed their personal values while others found ways to get what they wanted in an evolving social context. One subject, a telecommunications consultant who learned how to mass market the furniture he designed commented,

> I have always resisted change but I am stubborn about finally doing what I want to. Some of the changes I made got me a lot

of money, but that's not what caused it. Making money comes only from doing something that deeply interests you and you really want to do. Then you make money, almost secondarily. *Doing what you love nurtures the spirit!*

He added,

> The rational and the intuitive are not necessarily opposed. That idea is leftover stuff from the sixties. The only time I land on my feet is when I follow my feelings. I went along with the corporation shit because I couldn't see a viable alternative. I never believed the corporation line, and I never felt part of it. I thought I had to play that game, but the society and the economy have changed enough that I became "possible." It is more totalitarian in a way, with the centralized computerization and so on, but there's also more freedom for romantic entrepreneurial people like me.

According to one woman subject,

> I couldn't see *when* I would do what I wanted to do, if it weren't then. How long do you wait after your forties? So I resigned my job and took a year off. It was the hardest decision I ever made, and one that was so sound that I didn't think back to it for about five years. I have been truly happy for long periods for the first time in my life, and one year I made more money than I ever had before.

One of the first pieces of baggage discarded in order to "travel light" was some component of conventional values. One woman started out by disbanding her dining room and entertaining in her kitchen, having people for dinner on the spur of the moment. This is not to claim that long-passage subjects foreswore all conventional niceties; they made use of them. But they selected among conventional aspects of life those they enjoyed and respected. Others they used instrumentally (for a direct purpose) so as not to discredit themselves before business associates, for example, or in public places, or when meeting someone new.

Thus, long-passage subjects critically examined and selected from the entirety of "conventional wisdom." Some conventions seemed to them to address superficialities but others to involve serious issues. Social conventions were not taken as "givens" that had to be followed. One immediate gain was their abandoning traditional appraisals of aging, divorce, midlife singlehood, and conventional marriage. This was a most auspicious development because it cleared the way for my long-passage subjects to reinterpret their social meanings, *to them, now,* in a much more positive light. Taking this step worked well for them; in other words, it was functional.

The problematic character of passage was seen simply as an aspect of it, an intrinsic part of it, to be dealt with exactly as they had once handled professional issues—that is, as career problems demanding their attention and best problem-solving efforts. Long-passage men and women were determined to do well with passage. They tried to anticipate problems and assess their resources for meeting them should they occur. One technique some found for handling a problem was to objectify it at the same time they were experiencing it subjectively, as much as they could. This quality of detachment—distancing themselves to measure their progress—helped people get traction over or a good hold on out-of-phase timing. One man said:

> We're heading for a recession that will probably help relationships. People can't walk off in hard times, so they learn to live together. Marriage isn't so much based on sharing and that "grooving together" idea as it was, because from being pagans, we're becoming Puritans. Now we want to know how to handle our money together, and our gurus now plan tax shelters, not advanced ways of cunnilingus.

Comparing previous expectations with present realities often led subjects to modify goals or look at them differently. Being in a long passage also helped many people, because they had sufficient time to experiment with a variety of ways to accomplish whatever subgoal they were seeking. Separating a larger goal into a series of steps (after first evaluating them in order of priority) gave people a way to "sequence" the components of an overall plan. One person reported, "When my psychiatrist pointed out that I never gave enough thought to putting a solid foundation under my life, I set up a five-year financial plan and it worked."

Individuals posed for themselves such questions as, "Where on the road am I now?" and "Where do I want to get?" In trying to answer these questions, many of the research subjects used friends as informal agents (or passage guides) who, because they knew a subject well because of a long friendship and who also had fresh perspectives that might cast light on a problem, helped a person cut the time between a problem's clear identification and its resolution. One subject, for example, went to see films on contemporary life with a friend of twenty years standing, and the two divorced men discussed each film to see if there was anything they could learn from it.

Deviance Disavowal and the Group Movement

No other subjects were so fascinated with passage, open about their feelings, or quick to communicate what it was like to be in transition as were long-passage men and women. The emergence of what I call the group movement was extremely valuable to many of them. As a social phenomenon we are now accustomed to, the group movement seemed to have been an idea which bubbled up from developments with earlier origins that took root in the culture of the sixties. I shall not discuss these origins nor note the many names attached to this phenomenon. However, one of its basic ideas was the working for change in the context of a group of people with similar experiences, problems, or goals. Therapists in private practice, universities, community-development programs, churches, and many organizations set up groups, both for singles and for the divorced. The result was a plethora of group activities in which people could form new ties as they attempted to support each other during the hunt for options. Organizations such as the Sierra Club and Mensa even set up subgroups for singles, determined by age and interests; one could hike or match wits with singles in one's approximate age group.

At the outset, it is important to note that these groups were structured in terms of, and based on, a treasured, middle-class American value, the *self-improvement ethic*. In varying degrees then, the group movement was a useful mechanism for helping people incorporate into their thinking new ideas about themselves and the world, and the value of this process appeared to me to be self-evident in many cases. The groups also existed in such profusion in many parts of the country that one could readily find a group whose rhetoric and principles, to say nothing of membership, was congenial to his or her own situation. In many specific ways these groups provided a setting for people to get together with other individuals who would understand what they were talking about—to work together on human issues.

The benefits of this phenomenon were extensive. First, the movement offered subjects new images of themselves, not as "victims of Fate," but as what one subject called "pioneers of Time and Inner Space." Another subject called such people "a new breed of Self explorers." At any rate, ideas about personal growth emanating from the group movement legitimated the identities of people in transition. Many of these men and women were in the process of combining remnants of previously earned social recognition with the expression of capacities that were only emerging abilities. As a social phenomenon, the group movement gave people a sense of security about being in passage and bought them precious time and space. In their groups, they were quick to see that they were still well regarded in terms of their past records: as conscientious parents, in their occupational histories, and in their prior status as men and women influential in their communities or fields of endeavor. At group meetings, people also easily gained recognition for the talents they were developing as, for example, ceramists, new business people, or simply, men and women with a new, personal style. Nevertheless, some subjects were still in what was, at least potentially, a mid-life crisis, regardless of their assets. In the main, most saw their budding roles as "new people" at mid-life as the first order of business. In part this occurred for a most logical reason: it was a real life-cycle interest for them, and thereby, a truly engrossing one.

Second, the group movement was important to many long-passage histories because it became a vehicle for handling transition by providing people with leaders, *formal agents* sympathetic to and contributing to their new self-definitions. Among them were humanistic psychotherapists, bodywork experts who, like Feldenkrais practitioners, were seen as "healers," and many other types of gurus who played roles that were critical influences on long-passage people. For instance, a person could replace the family doctor who might counsel reconciliation with a former spouse, as if it were the only valuable alternative to divorce, with an advisor who understood and appreciated what a person was trying to learn how to accomplish, outside of traditional family networks. Not all the members of one's old circle might consider the new advisor an improvement on the old, however. One subject who met her second husband (and became his fourth wife) at a somewhat stiff encounter group, was assumed by her first husband's mother to have been nude when they were introduced because of the meanings she attached to such group activities.

Third, the group movement gave its participants *role models* just at the point when they were trying to invent new life maps for their journeys. Other singles were present, too, and if they were not prospects as lovers, they were as friends whom one might emulate, especially if they had been in passage longer and appeared to be handling transition well. Therefore, a further benefit of group-movement participation was that it supplied members with a ready-made set of friends who knew what it was like to be a formerly married and who were similarly interested in the theme of *"becoming"* in many of its manifestations.

This point merits further examination. For instance, many long-passage men and women had been, as parents, quite concerned with their children's full development, another echo of the American "self-improvement" ethic. They remembered the years when they were parents of youngsters or teen-agers and their convictions at that time, that a child's development can be enhanced if parents support his or her interests and talents as they emerge. Many of these youngsters had been encouraged to try on many roles for "fit"; the parents had been in a position to facilitate this, and they did. One subject connected her desire to nurture her children's abilities with her own mid-life experimentation, saying,

> We let the kids try just about anything, though some of this was pretty expensive—like being an amateur naturalist or becoming a sportsman. The neighbor called the Health Department and re-

ported our rattlesnakes, so John took the kids up to the mesa where they let them go. After we joined the Racquet Club so Edward had a good place to play, he turned out to be a fine competitor and went through high school in a blaze of glory playing tennis. He organized a senior class boycott of graduation ceremonies when the Chicano speaker was canceled—and then he found skiing, too, and the young woman he married.

"But now," she added, someone was doing the same kind of encouraging—for *her.*

Another extremely significant function of the group movement was that it gave long-passage men and women the chance to go through transition as members of an aggregate that perceived itself as a collectivity. After so many years of moving and always being "outsiders," except within a company, and then becoming members of an "out-group" in their neighborhoods and circles of relatives after they divorced, these men and women now could be members of an "in-group." It was not a reference group that one envied and wished to join, but was excluded by, as had often been the case for these people on the mobility route.

This sense of *belonging* was very important to some of my subjects. Being individualists with backgrounds of mobility experiences meant that long-passage men and women were, to some degree, people who were "cut off," and they knew it. Because of the new social bonds that many forged through participation in the group-movement enterprise, an interesting kind of "group consciousness" was born. Viewing themselves as a body of people trying together to create new opportunities for themselves rekindled their excitement about life. Thus, for some people, one consequence of this sense of a collective history was that they not only "belonged," but that they formed part of an elite that was bound neither by the limiting world views of an earlier time in their lives nor by the hold of tradition. They were inventing new social patterns, and trying to break ground, not just for themselves, but for others to come. As was the case with subjects undergoing briefer passages, the problems that long-passage men and women had to deal with were important problems of human existence; and because of this fact, the siren song of group-movement rhetoric was "good news" indeed. Its ideals and its rhetoric were especially attractive in any comparison with corporate or familial ideologies. And throughout the process of participating with peers, one's fellow pilgrims became the new kinfolk.

While these people had not necessarily thought of themselves as "joiners," some of them had invested a great deal of time in the past to secondary group life. They tended, however, to use secondary groups instrumentally, that is, to achieve specific practical ends in a goal-directed way. In so doing, they had not consciously sought (or secured) the emotional sustenance that group life can provide. They had been oversupplied with the influence and material benefits obtained by always scrutinizing organizational and other forms of secondary group life for the purpose of capitalizing on its potential contributions to them with respect to maintaining or advancing their positions. But they were deprived of other, much deeper forms of nourishment often found in the intimacy of primary group life. This was a tradeoff characteristic of their pasts, and it was one of the costs they had endured, even if they had not always consciously or knowingly bargained for it. The group movement proposed to address this deficiency.

Last, and most importantly, group-movement beliefs functioned as an ideology which offered somewhat imprecise, but almost limitless vistas of human development, coming within a person's reach just when conventional wisdom suggested that he or she had arrived at renunciation time, middle age. Accordingly, in addition to providing such practical services as giving a person somewhere to go for the weekend and someone to be with when there, a primary function of group-movement ideas lay in their utility for converting what might seem to be a dilemma into a respectable, enviable pathway. One could even handpick one's group, choosing people most apt to be congenial as well as those who could fulfill one's personal needs. The organizers of some activities, such as Mensa regional coordinators, sometimes approached recruitment and program planning so intelligently that they structured lectures and parties on the basis of zip codes instead of just townships. A person could solve an immediate problem by attending an event with expectations of meeting people from one's locality. This was a boon to singles living in the far reaches of some vast urban sprawl as most came to do.

So, all over the country in metropolitan regions, around seven in the evening, people started looking for their car keys. To the question, "Where are you going tonight?" posed by a person in the next apartment or a housemate or someone at the office, these people could reply, "I'm going to group."

In and of themselves, the activities offered by the group movement in their total range were never instantly profitable nor were they panaceas. The abuses of this movement are well-known. For example, many people deceived themselves or others in the course of participating, either as leaders or group members; there was a potential for damage as well as growth. But even this fact was well used by some of the people who recognized it, and thereby learned more about how to discriminate between the spurious and the authentic human gesture. Although much of what went on was trivial or mere amusement, the influence of the group movement was in many essential ways a profoundly positive turning point for some subjects. It gave them new friends and the means to leave behind some of the artifice and pretense with which they were accustomed to dealing with the world, with significant others, and even, with themselves.

By no means were all of its devotees only dilettantes who wanted to try something "trendy" they could then talk about at parties, though many were. Some people had suffered grave losses on the mobility trail, and for them, taking stock was not a light matter. Many were serious men and women plagued by the realization that they had, up to that point at least, somehow failed to grasp what life might best be understood to be all about. Professional ambition, for instance, had become tainted because the road up was littered with casualties. It was becoming evident to these high achievers that achievement and affluence were not, by themselves, very good answers to the ills of the human condition or to important life questions which they had neglected. Many people had lost significant others and failed to appreciate the nature of the bargains they had made with life, even though these had brought them financial success. They felt they had not accomplished a balanced or very wise way of looking at their existence.

Some among them were not yet ready to concede that they had "lost the way," irretrievably. These people used everything available to them in the group-movement setting, to try to work seriously to set their lives in order, with a degree of integrity they had never formerly been capable of. The movement gave these adults both sustenance and hope. The psychological value of its connections to emotional security and an unfolding and deepening of personality during the maturation process of some of my subjects appeared to me very important. The developmental issues these adults began to address, at the very least, indirectly, and the developmental tasks some of them began to perceive as occasions for working on themselves, did result in more self-mastery. Some Searcher subjects, whom

I had known a long time by the study's conclusion, expressed to me around that time their feelings that, as an outcome of a pilgrimage, they were somehow better human beings. In this regard, as in many other instances, I tend to believe that what men and women declare has worked for them, ought to be listened to with respect.

There is almost no limit to the uses to which an individual can put the group movement. Over several years of fieldwork, I logged thousands of miles driving to the group events at which some of my data were collected.

Subjects' Responses to the Issue of Aging

In a general sense, subjects in long passages reworked the imagery associated with various life stages. Instead of young adulthood being later envied, to these men and women it was an apprenticeship for the vastly more exciting work of the mid-life stage. At that time, one could be free of a novice's restrictions and more fully alive, human, or spiritual. One woman discussed it in the following way:

> The internal struggle is always there, of course. But in one's thirties or early forties, a lot of energy still goes into problems of self-esteem. One is still defensive and engrossed with the self. In middle age, your energy is no longer so often going into emotional conflicts. You are "clearer," you can pay attention to other people, and you can put your energy into relating to them. That's why older men and women are so at peace. The Chinese were right about this possibility for wisdom in old age. I'd just as soon have the younger *body,* because mine doesn't always do what I want it to; but I have a lot more energy I can put into drawing people to me, when I want to.

Another said,

> When I divorced at forty, I relaxed because I thought it was "all over," so I began to be much more comfortable with myself, and more spontaneous and direct.

And still another commented,

> After my divorce, I assumed I was too old to be a suitable companion for younger men. I was stunned when they started coming at me, as if from behind trees, and I told them so. The more honest I was, the more new friends I acquired.

Long-passage subjects who participated in the group movement were well aware of the criticism of many of its ideas and of the negative images sometimes associated with middle age, but neither had much effect on them since they were busily pursuing their new lives. Detractors were seen as likely to be people without the willingness or capacity to "move and grow" themselves, and hence, as men and women who felt they would lose, not gain, from change.

The possibility that some participants were so inspired by movement ideology that they were in danger of flying about like Icarus (and suddenly plummeting to the ground) seemed not to worry these enthusiasts. The point is not to generalize about the validity of specific ideas or try to decide which people may have over subscribed to them, but to recognize that participation apparently yielded a variety of benefits.

The group movement was used to justify all manner of innovative attempts to improve life, some of which had positive consequences for the individuals involved. For instance, a woman subject who married a younger man after they lived together, commented on the yield to the marriage of their commitment to Gestalt therapy as well as its separate benefits for her:

> Those of us who used Gestalt extensively are a serious minority of highly educated people who look at the world in complicated ways. I wish there were more of us! It's hard for me to speak of the gains without being emotional. Now I am less stressed, more direct, and much happier with myself. Certain basic things are needed to be a happy person. For one, understanding and *liking* yourself. Gestalt helped me learn who I was, because, like many people, I was all covered over with other people's notions of who I was. But I got lots of positive feedback in Gestalt groups. I was delighted and, I remember, kept saying "You mean *I'm* like that?" when people commented on what they saw as my good qualities. Birch and I did one or two intensive weekend marathons and the follow-up each year for about ten, and during crises, we could take part in ongoing weekly groups.

She went on,

> It helped me develop parts of myself that weren't developed and control negative parts, and now I am a happy women who has what she wants. It taught me how to relate to others in a balanced, human way about my needs and what others needed, which is very important to a love relationship. I had the most trouble with the male-female thing. We rarely worked on our relationship, I mean, as a couple; we each worked on our own problems, which had a great effect on the marriage.

Thus the long march of a durable passage was often recast by long-passage men and women as a heroic journey with a moral purpose.

At the heart of the attitudes engendered in some of these subjects from their interest in the "new culture," was a new way of looking at one's responsibility to oneself and to what one was contributing to a love affair. The Bloods, in describing the contemporary social climate, speak of "profound changes taking place in American marriage and divorce" that reflect a current value shift toward an "ethic of self-realization" that departs from the older ethic of "obligation and duty." They have researched the social phenomenon of "amicable divorce," by which one presumably can replace the traditional adversary mode, because they regard it as symbolic of the direction of these changes. They note, in discussing new conceptions about the issue of personal responsibility,

> Many persons of both sexes now see their primary commitment to themselves, rather than to the relationship or to the other. *Their only permanent commitment is to themselves as individuals, to their own growth and fulfillment.* No marriage can flourish, they say, unless both partners are authentic persons, true to themselves, pursuing their daimon wherever it may lead them. Each partner is engaged in a life quest, a journey, a pilgrimage, a spiritual calling, a vocation which includes an occupation but much more besides. When a man and a woman find that their paths converge, they may choose to live together and perhaps celebrate that common life with a wedding ceremony. But their commitment to one another remains ultimately conditional. It lasts only as long as their journey takes them in the same direction. As soon as either partner finds that his/her journey leads in a direction which the spouse does not wish to pursue, it is appropriate for the couple to separate. *As soon as the marriage becomes an obstacle to one's own spiritual growth, the new moral responsibility is to divest oneself of the impediment to growth by leaving the partner.* [1] [italics added]

They add,

> Better to go their separate ways than for either person to give up his or her personal vision quest . . . but this does not mean that change automatically brings divorce.

One subject, another veteran of Gestalt therapy principles, explained how change had kept her partnership alive and each person growing:

> As a process, Gestalt therapy has dramatic effects, because it teaches you to watch yourself acting, and to do so without all the usual criticism, editing, and censoring. By learning to observe what I was doing and how I felt at the time—*why*, in other words, I liked myself and became much more self-accepting. The process teaches you to observe at the same time you are acting. Of course, sometimes I didn't like what I saw, but faith in Gestalt gives you the power to feel that you can change the parts of yourself that you don't want to retain, and that adds to a feeling of self-esteem. For instance, I have changed and so has John. That gives me a great feeling of strength and being able to cope. The way the process *works* is that it is enabling, because you get the *tools* you need to become your own "best person." For instance, you can rid yourself of fears which prevent you from partnering "well" because you are afraid to surrender to someone; i.e., make a commitment, because of your fears of abandonment.

According to the Bloods, leaving mid-life careers of all kinds is now seen, not as evidence of any failure but as an "evolutionary leap" that enables individuals to develop new potentialities, life-styles, and/or partner changes. In this model, then, changes are opportunities rather than admissions of failure. To such people, changing occupation or partner is an accepted or expected step in leading "rich and full lives." In other words,

> Each succeeding marriage [or pairing] may be seen as good in itself as long as it lasts [and] meets the other's needs at that particular stage in their lives. . . . Only traditional couples wait so long to divorce that bitterness is inevitable.[2]

The foregoing ideas illustrate many of my long-passage subjects' attitudes toward love and pairing as well as the transitional period and show the consequences of their commitment to an "ethic of self-discovery."

The Hunters-and-Sorters and the Runners in Place

Those who hunt and sort their ways to a paired exit constitute the first long-passage subgroup I will discuss. Unlike the Courters, the Hunters-and-Sorters do not feel the urgency to pair or the threat of aging, and they can be differentiated from Steadies, since they avoid an immediate commitment. Repartnering in a hunting and sorting passage is characterized by much trial and error and the successive experiencing of a number of partners and pairing types, at least as a preparation for the final, successful pairing.

This kind of a transition focuses not so much on hopes that it will conclude in remarriage, which do exist, but more on the idea that one can "grow" through a series of tentative explorations of partnering. The Hunters-and-Sorters show considerable reluctance to pair permanently because of a concern that by not waiting long enough, they might prematurely opt for a partnership that proves to be a poor choice, probably for both of the partners in it.

Although to me the issue of "emotional readiness" to pair seemed to be implicated in many long-passage love affairs, and certainly for Hunters-and-Sorters, it was probably sometimes an unconscious motive for postponing pairing or breaking-up a promising match, the people hunting and sorting were not inclined to examine their actions in this light. They tended not to be interested in reading books about "stages of recovery" or in looking for psychological causes for forestalling closure of the transition. They also did not seem to include considerations of emotional readiness in their calculations. An interesting and related fact is that while these subjects did value becoming paired as a desired end, they were inclined to take its accomplishment for granted. They saw it as something that could be achieved eventually without difficulty, but that it should be selected only when the "right person" is found or when the "time is right." Thus they tended to view Courter and Steady passages as not sufficiently open-ended. They faulted Courters for their willingness to marry anyone halfway appropriate in terms of the old circle, and the Steadies for "closing out their option" on the basis of their first partnerships (that is, having insufficient information about themselves and the world) perceiving both groups as concluding passage prematurely. Thus Hunters-and-Sorters viewed the fortuitously happy, rapid repartnering of early exiters as "too good to be true." They tended to be wary of being "trapped" into rapid pairing, and failed to understand what others hoped to accomplish by acting so quickly. In addition to not being anxious about passage outcome, these subjects also tended not to display much concern about the course of a passage. They kept a weather eye cocked for impending trouble, but they were much more able than earlier exiting subjects to be reasonably relaxed about the irresolution in their lives.

In many instances, the Hunters-and-Sorters seemed to have a gift for managing passage. They seemed to be more able to take the "long view" and not be disturbed by something momentarily out of phase. The hunting and sorting subjects had different *expectations* from many other people's about the course of passage. For one thing, they expected rather horrendous developments from time to time, and met them with humor. They tended not to swap horror stories about either marriage or divorce but, rather, funny stories about passage, describing, for instance, an incongruous thing that happened to them lately. Posing to one another such questions as "What would *you* have done?" or "What do you think she *meant* by that?" or "Has this ever happened to *you?*" their debates centered on how interesting it was to be engaged in so unpredictable an enterprise as passage. They often confided in someone, soliciting advice which they proceeded to ignore.

In addition, subjects hunting and sorting through a series of partners tended to try to use the researcher as a resource person, as did all late exiters. It was often necessary to be very persistent as an interviewer to prevent a session from turning into the advancement of a subject's strategy. Late exiters were curious about my research findings and invited me to discuss and compare long passages, rather than simply telling their stories.

In later interviews, a late exiter might ask, "Does this jibe with what you are seeing?" Sometimes a subject would jump to become my friend and suggest more interviews than were necessary. One invited me to offer him advice. Subjects were quick to suggest other people as subjects to recruit and said, "I hope you publish a book about all of this." They were enthusiastic respondents. In short, an important component of hunting and sorting passages, and of all long passages in general, was the subjects' relishing of many aspects of passage which they thought were becoming "encouraging attributes of contemporary life."

Like other people in long passages, Sorters seemed not to worry about being middle aged. In the main, they ignored it, or discussed and dismissed it. One advantage shared by many long-passage subjects of which most seemed unaware, was that they tended to be less burdened than earlier exiters. For example, because they divorced later, married twice, or undertook passages of such length, they were usually without children at home; in other words, they were a bit older than early exiters.

Hunters-and-Sorters and Runners in Place

In probing for the significance to passage of middle age, I found that these subjects judged age as becoming increasingly irrelevant. The long-in-passage person simply did not view middle age as all that much of a disadvantage. One man said,

> Well, age is important maybe, if the man is twenty and the woman forty; but if everyone is over forty, they're all more or less the same age, aren't they?

He went on to say,

> In the case of a man of twenty with a woman of forty, the age difference could be novel and interesting for both. I had such a relationship early in life. But in a pairing of a man of forty and a woman of fifty, not much of significance is involved in such an age gap.

Another subject, when asked about the potential disadvantage of being in mid-life when divorced, said,

> Some young people belong to the knapsack culture. If a relationship breaks up, they can hitchhike somewhere, crash at someone's place, and start a new life easily. Middle-aged people have to keep up appearances and have made more permanent investments. On the other hand, that is really probably better, because one has so many more resources at mid-life.

The fact that long-passage subjects were less likely to have children at home than say, Steadies, greatly facilitated hunting and sorting, making it easier for subjects to remain in passage. Not having much responsibility for children was implicit in a great deal of the freedom all long-passage subjects enjoyed. It was a necessary component of their conduct of passage, especially regarding their definition of it as an opportunity.

Whatever the reasons subjects were no longer directly caring for children (because they married early and thus completed parenting early, or a former spouse had custody out of state, or children left home early (perhaps at onset of divorce) and were rarely heard from, or they lived independently at young ages and were engrossed in their own lives), their absence permitted extraordinarily independent life-styles. As one woman put it, "Since I live by myself and do not intend to remarry, it really isn't anyone's business that I go out a lot with twenty-five year old men, is it?" Another woman said, "My second husband was a European, a gentleman, and a family man. It was a marriage for family reasons. Afterwards the situation was different. I could look for someone to suit only me." One finding in studying long passages was that subjects consistently chose options that would have been virtually impossible with children living at home, but they tended to overlook this fact. One man said, however, "I wouldn't think of seeing a woman with children. I wouldn't ever even *consider* that."

Many of the Hunters-and-Sorters had married high school or college sweethearts and went into and out of marriage with little other experience of heterosexual relationships. One exception to this was the romantic affair of the type that often takes place in the last stages of a marriage once it becomes apparent the marriage is deteriorating. In fact, the pleasure with which some subjects briefly experienced such affairs seemed to assist them with the divorce transition. Also, the supportive response many people received from other unhappily married (or single) friends sometimes provided subjects with the first clear encouragement of their hopes for passage. One woman said, "When I began to be treated as I had always hoped to be, I began to feel as I had always hoped to feel, and I also became very much more comfortable, and all of this stiffened my resolve to leave the marriage."

Therefore, as a rule, long-passage people had undertaken

marriage and family life very early and honored these commitments for what came to feel like an interminable length of time. On becoming single at mid-life, some began and maintained a round of multiple relationships which looked to me suspiciously like living out the fantasies of young adulthood, perhaps particularly compelling to them, because "freedom" was an ideal in sharp contrast to the marital and parental burdens they assumed when quite young. Although this advantage of being past the time of day-to-day responsibilities for children seemed to be appreciated by only two of these subjects, it seemed to be a factor at the heart of long passages. It was most significant in terms of subjects' experiences of sexuality and the whole issue of their sexual roles, which I will discuss in more detail below.

On the whole, I found that divorced people appear to "recruit" others to the single state much less often than one might expect, and less than the "very married" are apt to imagine. People in long passages gradually pull away from married friends. There is little commonality of interests among them, and it is considered "poor taste" or "bad faith" to toy with a married friend to amuse oneself or to become a threat to a married couple. It is also perceived as a waste of time, since a married friend is seen as "not available" and as a distraction from the very people one "ought to be seeing." Nevertheless, with such high divorce rates, it is clear that the factor of availability can change quickly.

Often, the person encountered inadvertently, who becomes a romantic intimate, is also in the process of divorcing, though this may not be immediately evident to anyone. The point is that sometimes before the extent of a deteriorating marriage is fully understood by one of its participants, his or her brief intimacy with an already single person may be symptomatic of the impending marital collapse. These "new friendships along the way" often do not eventuate in new pairings, but they bring a great deal of support to the person already single, reciprocal support for each, or courage to a person about to have to face a marital estrangement process already well underway. If both divorce, these relationships may later be converted to solid friendships. These early supporters (or informal agents) may be later described to a new lover as "a person who was a big help in my divorce."

In many cases, the absence of children at home (or a separation that leads one spouse to live alone in an apartment), permits these friendships to develop at critical junctures. The practical consequences of the absence of children in the home and their lack of impact on the single's choices are extremely important. It facilitates all kinds of experimenting and allows privacy. For example, one man who did not want the woman he was currently seeing to know how important she was to him (that she was his only interest), convinced both her and his visiting children that he was interested in someone else, too. The absence of children, added to the absence of parental influence (since, in many cases their *own* parents tend to be back home in another state) often makes the passage the first opportunity for people to sample dating and partnering *without an audience.*

Otherwise, when children are present, singles tend to use them as agents, turning to them for advice and ratification. This can, of course, greatly complicate and inhibit a parent-child relationship. This fact was referred to by one subject who said of her son,

> It's odd but after his father and I divorced, I leaned on him too much. It seemed to prevent either of us from finding someone. At least, as soon as I found a very nice man, my relationship with my son improved.

Another subject spoke of the breakdown of a formerly close relationship with his daughter:

> She was always my favorite, and her mother was always jealous of her. But when she got old enough to date in high school, she became very critical of me and rarely came to visit at my apartment. When I finally found Marie again—the first woman among several I fell in love with after my divorce, and we married, I thought I'd see more of my daughter. Barbara likes Marie a lot and stays overnight sometimes, but it's never been the same.

A problem for people involved in sorting out partners, however, is that there are no children to prevent living-together relationships, and a promising person may nevertheless refuse to enter into or maintain a nonmonagamous relationship. Individuals who, in an earlier stage, might have had children at home and used them as an excuse for not consolidating a relationship "yet," have no such justification. Therefore, arguments over the issue of fidelity are prominent in the hunting and sorting passage. In general, however, Sorters may choose other Sorters to be involved with, and people may stay overnight together when each knows who the other will be spending some time with next.

Since Sorters tend to value casual sexual encounters as such, another likely problem in this type of passage is that one person will become attracted to someone new, who is not similarly responsive.

This possibility is written off as one of the potential costs of what is viewed as "recreational sex." One woman subject replied to a friend's query about so-and-so with, "Oh no, that's not serious at all. He's just a good fuck." Other people who are sorting may retain a friendly, casual sexual relationship simply because it kills time or enhances a period of waiting around for "someone important" to arrive in one's life. One subject said,

"For quite some years I've gone to bed every week or two with a pleasant man I find rather boring. It sort of takes the pressure off my finding the right man for keeps and he knows where he stands with me."

People unfamiliar with mid-life singlehood in long passages often appear to view sexual interaction as its primary purpose, and as the sole aim of organized singles activities or such casual pursuits as going dancing or out for a drink alone. They also sometimes assume that sexual activity takes place as soon as a couple meets, probably in a motel. But actually participants in long transitions seek friends and potential mates as well as sexual partners. Furthermore, divorce may diminish incomes. Among single people sometimes both time and money are dear commodities. My long-passage subjects gave little evidence of the popularity of the motel so ubiquitous in American imagery. When meeting new people in their own towns, these subjects would almost always invite a new person to their home rather than go directly to a motel. Furthermore, except for out-of-town encounters, or in the case of Runners engaged in "one nighters" or couples taking a vacation together, using a motel was rejected by these subjects.

Use of a motel at which two people are registered during a conference both are attending when they meet is not regarded as "using a motel," because both are already there for other reasons. Use of hotels or inns for sexual encounters is more frequent in a transcontinental rendezvous between lovers with a well-established relationship. They come in by plane from opposite directions and enjoy the comforts of a good hotel during what is probably a briefer meeting than either wishes. If pressed for time, they may choose to stay at an airport motel when both have to make early flights out. If meeting amid friends at a resort, a motel may be used simply for privacy of negotiations. Or two singles who each have business out of town may pick an intermediate city, meeting briefly en route to separate destinations. More often a pair picks a peaceful, beautiful, or romantic resort for a weekend tryst. They may have a "favorite" glamorous locale. But when a romance is "heating up," they forgo luxury in favor of frequency.

Like other long-passage subjects, the Sorters have homes they enjoy and like to share or show off; and they may also be happiest with "homey" routines. Hence they usually meet at the residence of one, although travel time (distance) from their meeting place can be a problem because of having to get to the office in the morning. But the time, energy, and money once required for raising children can now go into housing that offers privacy. It is typical for long-passage people to move around and look for a variety of places defined as exciting to live, such as a houseboat in Sausalito, an apartment on Manhattan's East Side, or a woodsy retreat.

Sexual interaction also takes place at the single's home, since place of residence, like clothing, is used to rehearse or announce one's current identity. (People also sometimes use sexual encounters for this same reason as well as for sexual gratification.) One subject into the stalking of hunting and sorting, reported practicing a new personal style:

> I am trying to get used to wearing Ivy League suits. I think I am handsome in a large, rather roughhewn way. But I think I am too ugly to try to look conventionally Eastern. So I have combined my new clothes with this pair of dark-tinted glasses I wear all the time. I think they help me have a slightly ominous appearance, which, taken with the correctness of my clothes, makes me look "interesting." I really have enjoyed losing a lot of weight and not being a big fat slob for the first time in my life. I am still not used to women turning around and staring at me when I pass them on the street, and I love it!

Later in his identity explorations, this man affected jeans, long curly hair, moccasins, and a slightly disdainful expression, reporting, "This works well, too, but it's interesting; it's with a different, classier type of woman."

In long passages, a person's "staying over" at the other's place is handled casually—ceremony is an aspect of life with which these men and women dispense in exploring experimental life-styles—although they may provide all kinds of romantic accompaniments to sexual interludes, such as a fire in the fireplace, candles, and special goodies to eat. A new male friend, for example, may sleep on the sofa so that a budding relationship can be resumed on awakening, but it is much more usual for the couple to sleep together, especially if meeting on a Friday or Saturday night when the next day is not a workday. The acquaintanceship is then resumed over the Sunday paper or over coffee before a dash to work. One subject described the "best things that happened to me lately":

> I went home with a woman I liked, stopping to get us a Sunday paper enroute to her apartment. We discovered we had both recently left large houses in the same exurbia and felt we might have met there at a dinner party. In the morning, she served brunch in bed and we spent half the day there—making love, lounging, and reading the paper. It reminded me of the hopes I had had for how marriage might feel. We saw each other a couple of times but then both got interested in someone else.

Additionally, this "staying over" may have a function which reflects both interest and a somewhat guarded comraderie, as this subject reported:

> A man I have seen on and off for awhile took me for an all-day drive in the country one day, and the next Saturday, I invited him to stay overnight when we got in from a party. He did, going home the next evening. This saved him a long drive back to his apart-

ment that night and gave us a chance to enjoy a long leisurely Sunday. I didn't invite him to stay because of wanting a sexual interlude and I doubt it was his reason for accepting. What happened was that we slept until noon, as each of us probably would have done anyway. There seems to be quite a bit of attraction between us but neither of us is ready to rush it. People used to the sexual revolution don't have to prove it, and, since sex can be a powerful addition to a relationship, sometimes you'd rather take your time about dealing with it.

However, when a Sorter encounters someone "important" enough to pursue seriously or to want to live with, monogamous sex is usually instituted, if in a serial way. But living together is not taken as a final decision unless the pair so agrees privately, between themselves; and this situation tends to be characterized by at least temporary fidelity. The Sorters are inclined to be tolerant of each other's point of view on this, however. Some living-together arrangements break up because one partner insists on monogamy or on a marital commitment and the other will not agree. A man who eventually entered a stable "arrangement," which resembled marriage and then was legalized, commented,

I really liked Margaret enormously during the time we were together after we both divorced. Actually, we had an affair as I was divorcing, and it certainly was a love affair afterwards. But Margaret was set on marriage and I was set against it. When I met Janet, after a number of "arrangements," I was attracted to her at once. I was sure she wasn't hung up on marriage. We stayed together all weekend; but, not wanting to jump into anything, promised each other we'd not call the other for a week. But Thursday night she telephoned me to say she just couldn't wait to see me. And I asked her if I could go over to her house that night and start moving her things to mine. We were all settled by Sunday and haven't talked about marriage yet—that was eight years ago.

Since in hunting and sorting the decision to live with some-one is assumed by other singles to "take one out of play," at least for the time being, people not ready for this restriction keep their own place of residence. A couple will spend time at his place or hers, although each is only *one* of the men or women invited. One man commented,

> At the moment, I'm seeing three women, all of whom have some of the qualities I want in a woman. They're quite different and no one of them is "right," but it keeps me too busy to look elsewhere.

As a variant situation, a residence may contain housemates or roommates. People sharing a house or apartment with some-one else often describe this person (not a lover) as a "room-mate" in leftover-from-college-days vernacular. Sometimes a single person, living with a housemate is interested in a number of people whom he or she invites to the residence, and only a housemate gets much idea how each guest is evaluated. Since housemates are potentially intrusive, most Hunters-and-Sorters prefer not to have them.

But if they are temporarily necessary for financial or other practical reasons (such as meeting one at airports upon one's return, or caring for a house when one travels), intimacy with a housemate may be circumscribed and held to an instrumen-tal function. Trusted housemates are confidants, however, and may become "friends of the pairing." Nevertheless, housemates are a potential source of problems, since they must be introduced to people one is interested in, may com-ment on a pairing without being invited to do so, may regard a lover as intrusive, or may attempt to seduce a lover. Some housemates may be drawn into a "game" between dynamic lovers.

Because the housemate is becoming a common phenomenon, it is an issue to be managed. Some housemates are supportive of Sorters who are interested in each other, but others (such as a man's male housemates) may become a continual source of friction between lovers. Also, as with Courters and their circles, a person newly-interested in a man or woman may include housemates as indicators of the person's desirability. An unattractive housemate, or the interaction between a housemate and one's lover, may reflect badly on a person. Additionally, interaction between one's lover and his or her housemate may reveal aspects of a lover's character which lead to the lover's devaluation. Housemates can serve other functions, too, as in this case:

> Sam and I have been seeing each other for two years, and I would like us to live together. He seems to feel that he would be demeaned by moving in with me, and his office and apartment are too far from my office for me to be there. So far, it has seemed silly for me to stop sleeping with the young man who is my housemate, but I don't believe that Sam has ever suspected this of us.

Sorters are characterized by frequent switching of partners and general enthusiasm about the sorting phenomenon. Like all the long in passage, they value passage as an end in itself, not just as a means to an end. Sorters enjoy sorting through a series of partners, when each offers something never before encountered. One man explained to one of his lovers his interest in another by saying, "she teaches sculpture." Thus, passage may be either a chance to sample different life-styles that are seen as inviting, while keeping one's "options open," or one is temporarily in a life-style that is dictated by professional commitments, and thereby relatively fixed. One subject reported,

FRESH STARTS

For two years I was with a man who held a high government office and also taught at the university part time. He was a member of a minority group and had an interesting philosophy about upward mobility. We planned to live together ultimately, but things kept getting in the way, like the play he was writing and wanted to finish. We worked in similar settings, and he was a great resource person for me in my career. Often he escorted me to company parties or we went to conferences together. When he continued to put me off, I broke up and met someone else at a party. No one had ever taken me to such deluxe places or bought me nice clothes. One day he announced his decision to pursue someone else, "more his age." He was a dynamic, powerful man —new experience to me! But soon I met a lawyer working in the poverty sector. He lived in my suburb and was interested in holistic health. We often spend some time at the golf club walking around the course on nice mornings. I am learning a lot from him and don't miss the other two men.

Thus there is an element of casualness to sorting not present in briefer transitions. As one man put it,

> The relationship I'm in now has gone on for two years and is relatively satisfying, probably because each of us has an apartment. There's a lot to work out yet, but I don't get uptight about it, because I know there's more than one woman who could be right for me. If it fails, I'll know it was just an affair.

And, a woman subject evaluated her relationship this way,

> We're a lot happier than we were in the beginning and don't "blow it" nearly so often. I'm not sure he's the one for me, but with the expansion in my career, it's not the time to go looking. I don't know what will come of it, but either way, I have learned a lot, so I'm not worried about wasting my time.

Another woman spoke to the issue of permanence, which some people in long passages jettison as an unattainable goal:

Hunters-and-Sorters and Runners in Place

Have I found anyone special? Yes, two or three men. It looks to me as though I will end up giving up on permanence, because the intensity I've got to have just isn't possible in a long-term thing. Any *one* of these has been more important to me than my long marriage.

Running in Place: Activities as Ends in Themselves

Another form of long passage is that of the Runners in Place who opt for an unpaired exit from middle age. Although Sorters eventually tend to settle down with someone (and doing so is always a goal), Runners in Place, like Graduates, early in passage arrive at an equilibrium that includes a great deal of sociability. Runners, however, are the most socially active of all the subjects I studied. Early in the passage, Runners in Place take stock of their situations and arrange their lives to ensure a continued high income, a high standard of consumption, and lots of leisure time. Like Graduates, they feel same-sex friendships are an important source of gratification. These friends are usually other singles, known for a long time, perhaps since their early marriages. If there is any rule of thumb for the Runners, it is "keep on the go." One subject, an eligible, attractive lawyer summed it up:

> Soon after my divorce, I reinstituted some friendships with men I'd known in law school but seen rarely during marriage. There are three or four of them. I go out to dinner with one of them about four times a week. We may eat at 11:00 and if we do some wenching, that's OK, too. New York is full of great places to eat and good-looking girls. I have had the same steady girlfriend for a year or two. I see her once or twice a week—and that takes care of sex.

In response to my questions designed to find out if this was a temporary adaptation, he added,

> What do I want to be doing in my late sixties? Exactly the same thing! It's great! I like it! All you have to be careful about is having too many free evenings where you can sit around feeling sorry for yourself. I weight train and take fencing lessons—that takes up a lot of time in the evening, and I'm taking painting lessons. These are all things I was interested in much earlier but couldn't follow up. I'm awfully busy getting it all in. All you have to watch is that you don't end up sitting around in your apartment. I have a weekend place in the country, so all the vacation I need is two weeks skiing at Vail where I go every winter.

Thus Runners do not worry about the prospects of aging, but they do dread "accidentally" ending up married. One woman said,

> I greatly doubt that I could put up with a man as a live-in partner, nice as it might be to have that much of a companion. I have a great job, very high income, and travel at every opportunity, often alone. Every time I work abroad for a few months, I have an exciting live-in romance; but it's all based on being temporary. I've learned that if you entertain often and well, you're never without something to do on the weekends—which is one thing I always keep going.

Although no data actually substantiate the hunch, Runners appear disinclined to risk the vulnerability and self-disclosure essential to developing an intimate bond. As a subject said,

> As you know, sometimes I'd give my right arm for a man around. I'm always asking a couple to Sunday brunch so I can coax him to fix a faucet or something. But I know that I give off an air of invincibility, no matter how desperate I feel. And every time a really nice man has waxed romantic, I end up being the one to point out to him how self-sufficient I am. I guess I am just in the habit of "talking my way

out" of everything that comes along; but then, I haven't "accounted to" anyone for anything I spent, or any place I went, for years. I can't see myself starting at this stage in life.

Another subject reported,

> As you know, Charlie and I used to live with one another, and there is a terrific erotic bond between us. However, he cannot handle fidelity; I think because it makes him feel powerless. I have learned not to try to force my views on other people—or my wishes. Giving him the right to other partners without withholding from him lets him demonstrate his love for me. He still "takes care of me" in many ways, despite all his protestations that he cannot do this. I think we're preserving an important relationship by accepting its limitations. Things may change, but at the present, I cannot take him more seriously, since he is not capable of more than an episodic commitment. Isn't this kind of tradeoff at the heart of many marriages?

Because the Runners do not live with someone for the purpose of testing out a relationship, or enjoying one, they rely mainly on friends for a supply of confidants. These other people may be the only people who know and understand a Runner's problems. One woman spoke of how much she depended on her colleagues for getting assistance with personal difficulties and that this also involved the husband of one helping her with house repairs.

Thus Runners treat both friends and sexual partners as ways to meet basic life needs. But while eroticism is an important aspect of running, commitment to "falling in love" to the point of contracting partnerships for the rest of life is assiduously avoided. Runners do not intend to re-pair, in any significant sense, so they are not looking for friends' approval, as are Courters. They often compartmentalize aspects of their social life. As one said,

FRESH STARTS

There are a couple of marvelous little inns on the Cape which are perfect hide-a-ways for romantic weekends. I suppose it is a little odd, but I've been going to one of them with this or that new man or an out-of-state lover in town for a few days, for years and years. Everything is so luxurious and pretty—and I never run into anyone I know from home or from the firm.

Another Runner phenomenon is the readiness with which an older woman professional may engage in a friendship with a gay male who is interested in "passing." Gay men may show a woman more courtesies than the man she sleeps with. Gay men are also into a variant life-style; they "understand" how it is to get along outside of the mainstream. They are among the few males whose advice on clothes may include going shopping with a woman every season to help her select clothes. Additionally, gay men are apt to propose outings where their knowledge of the theater and what is "in" is far ahead of that of most of the men she sees. One woman reported the following observation: "Whatever Justin is interested in in the art world this year, will be all the rage in New York the next. He's a sweet friend and through him, I'm always well posted."

These friendships could make a woman more critical of her lovers or direct her attention away from the worlds they inhabit if she is interested in pairing. But since eroticism is linked not just to pairing but also to life, these men can fill valued functions. Many women discuss their straight lovers with their gay men friends. It is possible that fairly stable pairings with gay men (with or without sex) may become more common. Often these relationships represent a bisexual state for the men, as male erotic friendships are generally not abandoned when they are also in a relationship with a woman. But since no one is expecting either a full commitment or a conventional marriage, these non-exclusive relationships serve some people well, especially if the woman needs the facade of a partnered (straight) existence in connection with entertaining at home for business purposes.

The Runners and Sorters are relatively open with others about their lives and frank in discussing pairing with sexual partners. Additionally, the Runner and Sorter passages are quite visible. Neither type of individual depends on neighborhood interaction as do Steadies and Graduates. Usually Sorters and Runners discourage familiarity with their neighbors. However, in settled neighborhoods and among subjects who often remarked, "I hardly see my neighbors," the neighbors themselves may be quite interested in these singles. One busy, long-passage woman was startled to notice that her neighbors had stopped greeting her as they went in and out, and she wondered when their disapproval had started.

Runners achieve a high degree of stability without partnering as do Graduates, and generally, with considerably different results. Along with their mutual dislike of the idea of pairing, the Runners' tendency to avoid people who want to get "serious" is as strong as that of Graduates, but they tend to have even more trouble getting anyone to believe them. Both aspiring partners, and I, as a researcher, questioned the protestations of Runners. In some cases, I clung to the possibility of a Runner changing his or her mind for even longer than did an aspiring partner. But at this writing, no Runner has yet surrendered to a paired commitment.

The Hunters and Sorters customarily share a lot of information about their lives and plans as they sort through tentative pairings. Discussing mid-life singlehood is a favorite pastime of the long in passage. Their recreation patterns exhibit informality and long talks as part of ordinary interaction, which reflects their sense of a *collective* situation. In these ways long-in-passage individuals distinguish themselves from other middle-aged formerly marrieds. However, Runner passages differ from other long passages in the ease with which Runners dismiss the idea of seriously undertaking pairing. Re-partnering is a definite objective and an issue not taken lightly by Hunters-and-Sorters and Passionate Searchers (who are discussed in chapter 7).

Sorters define tentative partnerships much differently from the way a Runner views even a long-term sexual "engage-ment." The latter kind of relationship is episodic and relatively unimportant, since sexual partners are seen as replaceable. But Sorters value each of their relationships as important *ends in themselves*, whether or not they are stable. Sorters define even a brief pairing as the source of happiness or an extremely useful contribution to one's experience. One man explained, "The whole thing with Sallie was a mistake—it was all about a fantasy I uncovered years ago; but I had to go through it again before I could return to Allison." Another said, "It was only a three-months affair, because that was all it took to remind me I didn't want an 'Establishment' marriage."

Both the Sorter and Runner pathways lead to *restoration* of stable life-rounds, but the continuity established by Runners involves familiar routines which combine compartmentalized segments of one's life: professional associations and activities, small friendship networks, and extensive sexual interaction by means of a large network of partners to which additional ones are continually added.

Runners define sexual alliances as instrumental. They are valued for the function they serve as sources of sexual gratifica-tion, rather than being viewed intrinsically as sources of inti-mate human connection. Runners' sexual allegiances are not generated by an interest in and appreciation of a person's qualities as a human being so much as by that person's reliabil-ity as a lover who "delivers" in the physical realm. One woman who understood her Runner partners, remarked, "When Dalton is making love to me and raving about 'how good it is,' I know he's talking about 'it' and not about me."

In this regard, what appeared to me to be a liberated mode of adaptation, (and is so seen by male Runners who compare it with marriage), sometimes resembled a conservative value choice dressed up in contemporary finery. Male Runners are "macho men." However, several of the Runner males I studied had originally come from extremely conservative backgrounds; hence, their opinions had some basis in their traditions. However, what *is* news about the Runners, as an emerging phenomenon of increased incidence, is the present number of women Runners who take a drastically new position on sexual behavior and marriage. Many of these women also approach sex objectively—or somewhat exploitatively, perhaps as evidence of their power or attractiveness. In other words, sex is viewed dispassionately by women Runners too, who may speak of it as a "nice way to spend some time, although I don't like him very much."

Advertising oneself as a person who will meet other people's sexual needs can backfire on Runners, however, just as possession of wealth can lead to doubts that one would be valued without it. Women Runners tend to think "Men are just useful for *sex;* who needs them for anything else?" This can depersonalize men to an extent to which men are not accustomed. Men, formerly proud of their sexual prowess, suddenly begin to feel, as several put it, like nothing more than "a big cock." One man declined a subject's dinner invitation by explaining, "I haven't time for a new woman; I am already booked having dinner and sex with as many women as I can handle."

Runners separate sex from love, if not from the possibilities of making commodities of themselves. Demonstrated adequacy in sexual performance is a resource always open to one's manipulation as an attribute by which to obtain social recognition and an increased share of social rewards, in the same way that female beauty and male wealth are classic formulas for this, both in and out of marriage. Within an intimate relationship, furthermore, centered primarily on sexual gratification, performance proficiency can become a trump card in a power game that can destroy a relationship. Nonintimate Runners ardently advocate soloing through life, and they view this form of singlehood as a tremendous advance over marriage.

When the Sorters discuss passage, not only do they focus on their partnerships and on finding "that special person," they are equally ready to emphasize "learning about life" in the partner-hunting process. Here, Sorters are expressing ideas about self-development via personal encounters. However, they do not pursue partnering as a goal with the same intensity displayed by the Passionate Searchers. Thus, Sorters' ideas about the meanings one attaches to pairing stop short of the lengths to which pairing is significant to the Searchers.

Individuals in anyone of the three long-passage subgroups may reject, out of hand, the choices of those in the other two subgroups. This is nowhere more true than in the reactions of Sorters and Searchers to what they perceive as the Runners' impoverished sex life. To Sorters and Searchers, not being intimate and caring with a sexual partner could defeat the purpose of sex, rendering it almost meaningless. Engaging in sex without affection is defined by Sorters and Searchers as being "into occasional kid stuff." In an ongoing love affair, they consider secretive "sport-fucking" to be inauthentic, unethical behavior. One male subject commented, however, that sport-fucking was an old male technique for retaining control of himself and of the women he had sex with. Despite disagreement over the place of sex in one's life, all subgroups engaged in long passage exhibit to some degree a preference for nontraditional values, especially in regard to sexuality. The further meanings connected to sex by long-passage subjects will be enumerated in chapter 7, showing how response to sex distinguishes among the long-passage subgroups in certain additional respects.

But to make the point about sexuality being an aspect of long passages that unites all of them to some degree, I suggest that my claims about the importance of sex can be checked by asking a long-passage woman how she stands on this issue. If you know one, ask her "What is the greatest single gain from a mid-life divorce, in your opinion?" The first time *I* did, the woman replied, "I now know why the Mona Lisa's *smiling.*"

7

The Passionate Searchers

and the Transformation Theme

Parameters of Passionate Searching

The last passage form I studied was that of the Passionate Searchers who engage in a highly transitional long passage. Searching is somewhat like hunting and sorting except that it is qualitatively different for a number of reasons. First, searching is unique from sorting and all other subforms of passage because of the depth of the Searcher's wish for a pair bond with a perfect partner. This makes partner change not merely a matter of novelty, erotic transport, or having "fun" trying out another kind of person, as it often is to those engaged in hunting and sorting; but a possibly very painful route to a paired outcome after many relationships have been attempted, or many relationship crises have been surmounted. Searchers are therefore very serious about their sorting and earnest when describing their past love affairs or a tentative long-term relationship.

Second, searching is also in a class by itself with regard to the idealization of all of the following ingredients: *(a)* the process of searching for a perfect partner, *(b)* the growth and transformation of the Self (sometimes referred to as "finding myself"), *(c)* the romantic partner, and *(d)* the vital (perfect) pairing. In the opinion of Searchers, then, the road to mating implies much more than patiently sifting through a series of people whom one enjoys knowing.

The difference comes primarily from the function ascribed to the purpose of pairing, as is best seen in contrasting the nature of Courter with Searcher partnerships, using Cuber and Haroff's model of two different types.[1] The Utilitarian Marriage, for instance, is established or maintained "for purposes other than to express an intimate, highly important *personal* relationship between a man and a woman." This well describes the Courter marriage. But the Intrinsic Marriage is seen when "spouses have an intensity of feelings about each other and the centrality of the spouse's welfare in each mate's scale of values." This point captures the essential quality of pairing among Searchers. However, once partnered, many Searcher pairings take on the appearance of long-term marriages, whether or not they are ever formalized.

Third, in addition to looking for "someone right for me," as the Bloods, and Cuber and Haroff point out, Searchers want pairings that are right for the other person, too. A partner's welfare is part of the equation by which both people are supposed to judge a partnership. In other words, one is supposed to examine one's motives within the partnership. Despite the fact that in presenting their accounts of what they are doing and what it means, people can be conveniently self-serving, the Searchers seemed to try to take literally many tenets of the "new culture" in regard to what the Bloods termed the "New Age Ethic."

Searching is most easily contrasted with the Runner passage. Although subjects in both of these forms of long transitions rejected conventional marriage, disparaging such a goal and defining it as an unacceptable alternative for them, the Searchers' determination to pair (and expectation of this outcome) is as passionate as is the Runners' avoidance of it. But Searchers differ from Runners in many other major respects.

While the bonding of Searcher couples may ultimately prove to be impermanent, it is always of great moment. Besides intending and expecting to leave passage with a cherished and engrossing partner, Searchers put a heavy burden of conditions on themselves and on the partnership. (Obviously, since Runners do not bond, they do not go through breakups.) As for the Searchers and the Hunters-and-Sorters, the way that they talk about the lover after a breakup reveals the different emphasis each group puts on the former partner. One Hunter-and-Sorter said this, "We broke up against my wishes, because she didn't really know what she wanted, but she thought she did." But a Searcher would make a more generous interpretation, as this one did, "We were right for each other, and I still think a lot of her, but it wasn't the right time for her."

Passionate Searching as an Expression of New Age Ideals

The Searchers abide by New Age ethics as much as they can. The Bloods' description of the philosophic principles of such couples approximates what I observed when I studied Searchers. As a subgroup, Searchers display not only an unusually positive evaluation of pairing and an unusual ability to take responsibility for their feelings and desires, which are seen in their capacity to alter criteria for a partner as these operate in mate choice, but also in their efforts to make a total commitment, which includes a spiritual obligation to the loved one's growth as a unique individual. This involves respecting the degree of maturity a person has already arrived at or appears able to attempt. As two human beings who are part of a larger unity, partners may be seen as not only separate from oneself and distinct individuals with their own "stories" and with hearts that have "their own reasons," but they are also viewed as part of a cosmic or universal connectedness.

Therefore, Searchers were and are reluctant to attribute blame or shortcoming to a former partner. They also work hard not to be too defensive or self-righteous. It is also seen as futile to reproach someone who was not able to "be there" for one or who had to forgo, with one, a promising partnership that turns out to be only a learning experience for each person, albeit one about which both have very mixed feelings later on. Thus Searchers feel there is too much at stake in a pairing to be casual or mean-spirited about its conduct or its termination. In contrast, Sorters are a bit offhand. They view the future as "something that is still down the road," and they live together somewhat casually. A partnership is satisfactory as long as it pleases the couple. But Searchers see partnerships as part of a larger design by which life brings one important lessons or important new "teachers" in the form of each successive partner.

Sorters tend to discard successive lovers with ease, since lovers are not invested with so many important *meanings* as they are for Searchers, who are apt to retain former lovers as intimates, if not sexually. One Searcher reported taking part in a long, mystical ceremony by which a prior partner celebrated her marriage to his successor. He described this man as "pretty conventional, but good for Melanie and the security she needs right now." A woman subject described her new romance and her delight in this man's having the same first name as a treasured (former) husband, saying, "I hope the two of them get along. I wouldn't want to be with anyone who couldn't accept Charles as an important friend of mine—and therefore, ours." Another Searcher continued his support of a former lover in her efforts to help her young daughters become more independent, and another continued to assist his former lover with the repairs and maintenance of the house in which they had once lived together very happily. In comparison, Sorter accounts reflect complete ruptures, as this account shows:

> I know it was hard on her when I insisted on an abortion, but the next thing I knew, Marcy went to Vermont and married a dentist. Can you imagine—a *dentist*, after she lived with me in Soho? The woman I live with now doesn't mean as much to me, but you know how it is, she's here in New York, and Marcy's in Vermont!

The following, by contrast, is a Searcher's reference to an important ex-partner:

> You remember Marge, whom I lived with when I was finishing that research? She completed her project and took a job in Northern California. That way she gets to see her kids who are there in college. Did I tell you I'm a grandfather now? And I live in a great house in Santa Monica. When I went up to San Francisco to see the new baby, I saw Marge, too. She's just doing fine.

Another characteristic of searching is the extent to which the lives of Searchers exhibit New Age perspectives on life in an across-the-board fashion, not simply just in pairing. These people are in the process, then, not merely of trying to partner well, but also of following what is essentially a strict moral code (embodied in "new culture" ideas), applicable to all facets of human existence. Whether they have been encounter group afficionados or Jungian analysands, they try hard to attempt some form of personal transformation, perhaps to gain more emotional strength or learn to relate to others with more openness and courage (in other words, basic trust). They try to be true to New Age ideals such as "being in touch with my feelings in order to be more authentic," rather than being stilted and lacking in spontaneity. Therefore, being less defensive and self-protective is goal of Searchers, and this means that some of them are quite vulnerable from time to time, particularly with people who are afraid of disclosure and thus inclined to be either skeptical or cynical about the openness of others. Searchers sometimes undertake Wagnerian struggles involving what one called "self-work," and this is especially true in their conduct of love affairs, which they take to be occasions for their emotional honesty to be tested. One friend who had many reservations about the relationship a Searcher was involved in, said, "I realize that it's a pretty enthralling romance she's trying to pull off, but who needs *that* untidy a life? She must *like* it!"

This motive for understanding oneself better and being a more "centered" and open person is an ongoing goal, related to how one reacts to and generally behaves with a cared-for other person. Thus, despite the ups and downs of private life, people attempt to institute more direct ways of dealing with others, and these attempts often pay off very handsomely in private life, although Searchers do not see this as the only reason for doing so. Commenting on her psychological evolution which ended in marriage to a perfect partner, a woman Searcher said,

> Timothy and I have been together for twelve years. For two, we pretty much lived at my house, but he kept his apartment. Then

we married. I know we couldn't have made it without Transactional analysis. There's always been a lot of stuff going on to handle. Now I'm dealing with my brother's death and Tim, with all the fallout from his promotion. If our story has any message for anyone else, it's that you have to be patient if you find a marvelous person, but each of you has a hell of a lot of problems. I *always* knew it would be great if we could get through all the bad tapes from as far back as childhood. God, it's taken a lot of patience! Like the time he thought he wanted a sexually open relationship, and I nearly collapsed.

Among Searchers, conventional marriage is seen as mainly related to *family life,* much more than it is to pairing. The *paired* aspects of the first marriage, furthermore, had a great deal to do with the obligations a husband and wife had to meet together as a couple who were "company people." Because of the importance to children of the role performance of their parents (as parents), and the salience to the couple's mobility aspirations of their roles as a "company couple," and for many other reasons, the emotional quality of their marital relationship was neglected or simply ignored, or else played out through a dependence on a stereotypical enactment of social roles. In other words, the social side of marriage dominated the psychological. This fact partially accounts for Searchers' delight in, concern about, and obsession with the emotional state of a partnership or the possibilities in a person one has started seeing quite a bit of. This woman subject described the point at which a partnership began to look really promising to her, from the vantage point of emotionally successful (truly intimate) bonding:

After all his doubts, one day he said to me, "We are beginning to really learn how to stand in for each other when the other person gets upset." It excited us to realize that this is true now. There are enormous satisfactions in working on a relationship until it starts to work, and knowing you have picked a good person to do this with. It also means that you *do* get to know each other on a deep level and it builds the partnership and makes it very alive. Seems like I was getting ready for that, for the first half of my life—like training for the Olympics.

A Searcher male said,

I had two long marriages to two special women. Now it's like there were two separate lives and this is the third. Allison and I have not been together nearly as long, and each of us has our own house. I can see that the closeness we have has a lot to do with my finally being able to be open about my feelings. Before, I left the emotional work to the woman.

Searchers know that their occupational commitment did pay off well for them in many other ways, if not for the furthering of the emotional richness of their lives. During passage, Searchers try to organize their work so that this career line serves many functions related to emotional life, and the emotional security derived from one's professional status, greatly strengthens the hand a single Searcher holds during the transition.

Therefore, while all the Searchers I studied agonized, from time to time, over the issue of partnerships, they also focused on their work. This part of life is, for this subgroup, a factor in which gender is a passage dimension by which women often are advantaged. One woman spoke of some upcoming plans,

This summer I am going to take part in a special program at _____ on a grant to look at the biological work on that question. There's a good stipend, so I won't have to rent the house. It will be good to get out of here, and some of the people there are bound to be interesting. It amuses me that I'll be put up at the delightful inn where I spent my honeymoon as a green twenty-eight year old the second time around. I'll be there as a reputable scientist. It won't be too much déjà vu, and I might meet someone fine.

Implicit in these benefits is the continuity an occupational status gives to life and to one's social identity. Another woman told me about refusing a promotion:

> One thing I can say about my career is that I'm never bored! At forty-seven, I have a lot of options. My work has led me to live on both coasts. The best opportunities lie between New York and Washington, but I like getting a stint in California, too. It's also let me keep my options open for a while longer. Did I tell you I turned down a teaching job at _____ because my middle son starts there next fall? I didn't want either of us inhibited by the presence of the other. It's good to straddle both coasts and both life-styles. I think the best position you can be in is to be a "sharp" Easterner who's spent enough time in California to be laid back. Also, in my work, I belong to two networks, and it was easy to translate that into a national reputation.

One's professional work also facilitates experimentation, because it helps compensate for the defeats that may follow some of it, such as in the sexual area. An occupational career can be an ongoing source of stability, because a new equilibrium can always be reached at least partially on the basis of professional competence. A woman talked about the part her professional work played in her life:

> Chauncey and I have been important to each other for quite some time now. For a long time, I thought my work was interrupting my romance. Lately, I have started to think of it as the most stable element in my life. Whenever anything is wrong in any other part of my life, I have to keep my work going, and it just takes over.

A remarried male subject who had "cut back" professionally reported,

> I no longer invest 100 percent in my field, but I still turn up some good contracts. Last summer we went to Japan for a large American corporation. I took Jessie, and we saw my sister. My interest in the trip was behind my taking the contract.

Explaining the opportunities his profession provides, an academic said,

> As you know, I am a Mann scholar. I have an arrangement with my university that, anywhere I travel, I will try to add to our Mann collection; so, no matter where I go in Europe, if I take in several cities and major universities, some of my expenses are likely to be underwritten.

Men also find that contributions from the occupational sphere add to their resources during courtship, as this businessman described:

> Having been in the same business for twenty-five years is useful to a single man. I'm involved with a new woman now, and it's easy to show her a good time. She wants to go sailing? I have a friend with a boat. It took me some time to realize that all my accounts are with old friends to whom I give my business, and their favors are part of the system of "perks." If Natalie wants to go to the mountains, I just pick up the phone and get the offer of someone's house.

Multiple Role Management in Deviant Women

Women undertaking long passages at the same time they continue ambitious careers are in "double jeopardy," because to be both unmarried at mid-life and pursuing a career seriously are both considered deviant by traditional standards of womanhood. One male commented of this kind of woman,

> They're too much "overhead." The good kind of a woman to have is the one where you take her to the opera, she's happy! You have to *give* in a relationship, but some giving hurts less than other kinds and fits better into the rest of your life.

And a woman subject observed,

> It takes a pretty secure man to live with a high achieving woman without having to constantly make comparisons between his accomplishments and hers, as if life is all a contest. Some men automatically label any high achiever woman "competitive." You can laugh and say "Of course!" but that doesn't change the fact you get tagged with a dirty word.

Another subject tied feminism to female achievement:

> What do I think is going on with women? Well, for one thing, a lot of men are snickering. Why? Because feminism is turning into a disaster. Of course there are many women in established careers who refused to marry a decade ago, and are now thinking it over. Who do I think would be right for them? The same men they wouldn't marry before. The divorced older professional woman? She shouldn't get herself a passive young househusband —that was the sixties' model. She needs a man her age—or an unusual one she can regard as her peer.

The status of "formerly married" is capitalized on by both Graduate and Searcher women, but it is less useful to the latter group who tend to minimize family ties. My point is that the Searcher woman must dispose of the stigma attached to being serious about work as opposed to treating it merely as a "job."

Many long-passage women find ways to turn things around

with respect to their professional ambitions. One subject said,

> The first thing you have to remember is "Never apologize!" The minute you agree with him that your work may be a disadvantage to both of you, you're lost. Because it *isn't* a disadvantage. It's really a neutral area, that's been overworked. A man doesn't have to be "proud" of you, and he doesn't have to "feel threatened." Couples that are staying wrought up over "her work" are beating a dead horse. Some of us struggled for three decades over "Am I feminine?" Were we? Yes.

She continued,

> As a college girl, I wasn't "feminine" if I didn't want to "put out." That's all the debate is about, even now. Heart-to-heart talks about your work just mean a man is sneaky enough to slip in the idea you're maybe not frigid, but you're still "flawed." I bet many a man is kind of disappointed when the woman he has an eye for takes the bait.

Effecting a redefinition of herself that includes the work she does can be advanced with more success if the woman is able to decide what her work *means* with respect to her gender. Examining the strategies with which some long-passage women tackled both work and the exigencies of partner search shows both the negative and positive sides of the equation. Both elements must be combined in a way that optimizes maximum leverage.

Early- and mid-length-passage women tend to be relatively conventional; hence, for them, status inconsistency at mid-life (being divorced and working) is mitigated and less of a problem. Their occupational achievements are less outstanding than those of long-passage women and their approaches to pairing more conservative. Women with higher professional aspirations and longer, more individualized passages are "bucking the tide" if they approach pairing as do their more tradition oriented sisters. Since earlier exiting women usually have less access to a large income and a high degree of professional recognition, they also may seem "eligible" to a larger number of potential mates.

Our culture encourages pairings in which men "marry down" into a pool of younger women of somewhat lower socioeconomic rank. Thus women with lower (rather than higher) social rank, such as some early existing women, face fewer dilemmas regarding status. In addition, lower ranking women may perceive with accuracy that they stand to gain more from remarriage than from work, as it will provide them with levels of economic security and a status otherwise unattainable. Marriage rates are lowest for the most highly educated women. These women have a *choice* between marriage or singlehood. While some of them see life in terms of a continual dualism between work and love, for example, other higher status long-passage women find that possession of such professional rewards as high incomes and more choice lead to a contradictory mix of perogatives and handicaps that they must reconcile as innovatively as they can.

High-status women in long passages customarily begin their transitions by emphasizing their occupational roles. In so structuring their priorities, they assure themselves a source of economic power and the intrinsic satisfactions that lead to emotional security. Thus, they may elect a long passage without anxiety about the outcome, since having sufficient means provides the necessary confidence to remain in passage. These resources put women in a stronger bargaining position vis-à-vis many other formerly married women. While Searcher women want to pair, they are less dependent on it than many women. One Searcher said,

Searchers and the Transformation Theme

My career has always supported my role as a woman. At any hang-up in my private life, I turned to the social aspect of my work. After any romantic setback, I can always walk into a meeting and begin again. I used to hop planes like some people take taxis. If I needed to, I'd go to a meeting in my field wherever it was and never failed to run into something or someone important to that phase of my work. Half the time, I got so interested in these meetings, I didn't remember feeling low when I left.

Professional success is an alternate, additional route to ego strength and the self-acceptance that can enhance a woman's personal life. One woman reported,

When I started doing research on sex, I was puzzled by the audiences that the topic draws. All sorts of people started to buy me a drink or ask me out to lunch. Many of them were men who wanted to "come on" to a sexologist, just for kicks. And everyone had a "problem—of some friend." I was pleased when I learned how to handle the traffic.

For Searcher women in long passages, the present is a satisfying time. But a partnerless old age is another matter. The question posed to oneself in mid-life, "How will I feel later on, if I don't take a partner?" is comparable in import to that of a younger woman wondering, "How will I feel later, if I don't do mothering?" In each case, as for Scarlett O'Hara, postponement is often the answer. Nonetheless, being too engrossed in satisfying work to concentrate on a partner hunt *now* tends to worry long-passage women. Temporal dimensions of long passages can be urgent and poignant. Therefore, these women must make rational calculations about how much time to allot to what roles and purposes, they must begin to clarify their goals early in passage, and they must consider any and all means by which to use income to "buy time." One subject addressed this point:

> As someone who fought for minority rights, it galls me to know that my best chance to secure enough time for my own goals is to buy the BTUs of less advantaged women.

Another said,

> I do "health checks" with my therapist. I don't see them merely as people you consult after something goes wrong.

And, describing her concessions to the exigencies of time, another said,

> When we were in Asia, I refused to have domestic help. As a political activist and feminist, I don't feel comfortable with it. But I am also a corporate executive, and I need a housekeeper and a gardener. I don't feel as right about it as I do having help at the office.

Integrating one's worlds of work and private life as a single career woman can be difficult for some women. Higher status women are usually well aware of the contradictions between personal and professional status. One woman said "I live in the contradiction"; but others decide to compartmentalize. Nonetheless, many handle the conflict more or less continually. For instance, the achievements that bring these women "strokes" in work settings may be a disadvantage in relating to men, or there may be particular problems when one is interested in a man who is sensitive about his having a lower standard of living than the woman.

Because these women have a solid occupational basis for receiving recognition, they are sometimes especially disinclined to sally forth into unfamiliar singles settings. A woman may flinch from the uncertainties inherent in amorous encounters, feeling she lacks knowledge of what the "rules" are or fearing she lacks the personal attributes needed to secure equivalent recognition. Not knowing what will be expected of them, or what they should expect will happen, some women hesitate to launch a partner search with the same determination they bring to career advancement. One woman said,

> I know finding another partner is a "numbers game," meeting many men until one is right, but I seem to be dragging my feet.

Another said,

> I never find anyone if I'm looking. It just happens in the course of one's life. It happens a lot more often when I feel good about myself and I'm heavily booked and quite busy.

My impression is that, in most passage categories, women lag behind men in finding another prospect after a breakup. Men tend to line up a new person and make progress in consolidating a new romance before permitting a breakup to occur. Many professional women are much less realistic and rational about getting what they want in private life than in their work. Despite the fact that the very tactics by which long-passage women secure recognition in public life (namely, insisting on it when merited) may have to be suspended or subtly revised in searching, both life arenas demand the same active pursuit and clearheaded planning.

The business and professional worlds are organized around formal and informal procedures which long-passage women have learned to read well, but some have more difficulty understanding other social worlds. Dealing with heterosexual transactions is, furthermore, a complicated business for men and women alike. Locating and interpreting many muffled, oblique cues, like hints about a partner's responses to one, requires both persistence and some finesse. An acutely important attribute is a woman's attitude. One commented, "I never know what I'm doing in romance as much as I do at work, until I settle in with a man. But I have one maxim: 'Keep all your banners flying!' "

These women may find it difficult to locate role models or mentors. One recalled,

> When I was coming up in my field and throwing myself into my work, there were lots of women to emulate, but I don't know anyone who has—or seems to want, the combination of professional and personal life I want. All of a sudden, there aren't any role models.

Women are slow to share "inside information" about partner hunting to the degree that they share tips about finances or careers. Men, too, have a stock of privately held strategems they have an equal investment in concealing. However, after a divorce, long-passage women become sensitive to the social contexts in which they must circulate to meet additional men. They try to sharpen their self-appraisals as a precondition to a partner hunt. In addition, manipulating the amount of, timing of, and type of disclosure about occupational life, as well as raising one's comfort level with men outside of work settings, help maximize all the positive aspects of a woman's public and private life.

The issue of the carry-over between elements of a woman's private and public selves is a matter of gender much more than it is of age. Younger women are alert to these problems, too, as Broadhead noted in his 1979 study of medical students and how they handled role conflicts.[2] His female medical student subjects recognized that occupational success might backfire on them and inhibit the receptivity to them of the men they dated. Therefore, they tended to be wary about disclosing that they were in medical school, leaving men to infer a less prestigious level of training, such as nursing. This ruse is less available to women in well-established, highly visible careers. Therefore, rather than choosing to down play work, some long-passage women look for ways to turn its handicaps into the advantages which "give them the edge" over women of lesser achievements. One of the best ways is to highlight career gains.

The Conversion of Higher Status Resources into Supports for One's Role as a "Woman"

The first resource at the disposal of long-passage "career women" is, of course, their money, a factor that can put them at once in either a strong or weak position. This is a truism, but it is nonetheless of huge importance to a woman needing to equalize her position in one sense and flaunt it in another, all at the same time. For instance, having sufficient income makes it unlikely that a woman will have to ask a prospect for a loan for dental work or have to decline an invitation on the grounds of being unable to buy the proper attire (such as tennis clothes), or disappoint a friend who would like a loan. One woman made the point by saying, "Being poor just wasn't sexy." Some women tend to forget their lean years of training when in their comfortable present existences and do not see all the ways in which this latter state can function as a springboard to the pairing goal.

Second, another positive function of her professional life is the long-passage woman's mobility. Not only do these women usually have to travel on business, they are free to attend the very conferences at which they will meet congenial prospects. Access to these men is greatly enhanced by being present in one's occupational role, rather than having to wait to be invited to accompany a man as his guest. Once there, they have ready-made roles to play. Unlike the dancers at the singles clubs, they actually *are* there for the business of business—as well as for pleasure. Meeting in this manner facilitates courtship, because it can take a pair out of the familiar round of work (back home) and provide the partners with a common preoccupation that justifies their presence together. If theirs is a colleague court-ship, or they are in related fields, they can test how well their professional interests mesh or how much they can accomplish as a professional team as well as audition each other as "newly mets."

Conferences are notorious as locales in which participants "suspend the rules" for a time. At the very least, a woman's attendance may provoke a transitory interest on the part of a new man otherwise occupied and this "time out" can sustain her spirit and expand her horizens. For long periods, many higher status women maintain relationships with professional men who live and work at sites too far apart for regular daily contact. But work interests may provide the continuity neces-sary to develop a relationship that neither party is yet prepared to act on in so drastic a manner as relocation. There are other considerations, as the following comments show. One woman recalled,

> Eventually we decided against marriage. I would have had to make a move that could have damaged my career. He had just received a promotion he worked towards for years, and I was several years from knowing what direction I would take. We met in the Midwest or the Rocky Mountain area—midway between our jobs. It was a romance which changed my life and we are now very good friends.

Searchers and the Transformation Theme

Another woman said,

> My stage of work is critical right now. A cross-country romance is absolutely all I can handle.

While women Searchers enjoy the freedom they have for self-indulgence in decisions about travel, housing, and spending money, other problems plague them. Foremost is the fact that professional success is only partial legitimation in the case of women. The life that leads one to a secure occupational status is much different from the route to establishing oneself socially in a community. One Searcher commented on this:

> I find it easy to entertain colleagues and friends at buffet suppers, but it is harder to cultivate the new friends I'd like to know, without a husband.

Searcher women have little time or interest for the community activities often used by other people seeking to widen their social circles. Searchers are characterized as "different" and often discover that they must explain their work at otherwise pleasant social functions. One subject noted,

> Saturday coffees at my tennis club are well attended, and I've met nice people. But when I try to "connect" with a couple, I find they already have stable friendships. At mid-life, couples settle into regular routines. They go on cruises or are tied up with their children. Everyone's cordial and the men are easy to talk to. They include me in shoptalk. The women are terribly nice, but we live in different worlds. They listen to me as they do to the men. *But they don't treat me like a woman.* It's just the opposite of our set from married life, where I feel like an ex-wife; but it isn't any more comfortable. The main roles for a woman at the club are to be somebody's wife or somebody's date.

Women face more social pressure to remarry than do men. There is also an assumption in the case of a woman that professional work is *compensatory*, characterized by the comment, "nice, since she doesn't seem to be going to remarry." In addition, while married friends are receptive to the man a woman Searcher brings along, they tend to be too receptive and to scrutinize every pairing for its potential for remarriage, as the following illustrates:

> I was well aware of their hopes I would remarry, so I did not take the man I was most interested in. My date and I sat on the floor by the fireplace with our plates, and we were soon engrossed in conversation that was more interesting than I expected. When people began to leave, we didn't pay much attention, but soon we noticed no one seemed to be around. We found our host and hostess waiting alone in another room, as if waiting up for a daughter.

Since the man a woman Searcher includes when accepting an invitation is apt to receive more attention than she likes, women sometimes "strategize" parties by going alone. But the main result of pressure to remarry is that it further reinforces the privatization of personal life that already characterizes searching. Searchers often do not introduce a potential mate to old friends. Once a tentative living-together arrangement is instituted, there is a tendency to view old friends as "outside of" or threatening to the pairing.

This state of affairs can become a vicious circle; to avoid exposure of their pairing explorations, Searcher women accept and get fewer and fewer invitations, which results in their entertaining less. Thus the normative ambiguity of the Searcher woman's social position is reinforced. She may resolve this contradiction in status by seeing friends from former days primarily by herself. Once in a relatively stable "arrangement," she is too happily immersed in her work and the relationship to have many unmet needs for sociability. Either way, the outcome is generally that she gradually drops some old friends.

Feminism was an important component of the lives of all Searcher women in my study. Most take the ideals of women's liberation for granted; it is habitual to their thinking. But it is not as exciting now as it once was, when they were incorporating its ideas into their lives. One subject had this to say:

> Feminism was crucial to me but I seem to have new concerns about all our lives—as human beings.

Another said,

> After divorce, I avoided any man who attracted me, joking about it to friends. I put my career first until I was so starved in my personal life, I had to rectify the imbalance.

Still another woman said,

> My career was so rewarding and in such an important phase that I avoided entanglements. As a feminist, I saw remarriage as a series of obligations which would destroy what I had worked so hard to get. Some of my friends felt the same way. Now most of us have become committed to some man. The conflict between career and love seems to have been overshadowed by a relationship.

As ambitious professionals interested in self-determination, women Searchers cannot dismiss conventionally oriented men, but they avoid them whenever possible, as a rule. As they become more occupationally successful, feminist principles are so firmly established in them that the views of traditional men surprise and irritate them.

However, for many Searchers, feminism has taken on new dimensions. Most of these women continue their commitments to the advancement of women, but the longer a woman Searcher is in passage, the more she focuses on private life, sometimes tending to be less "modern" in her love relationships. One spoke about the matter:

> When you get out of a marriage that inhibited your work, it's hard to trust men. I stuck to seeing men who were as little interested in being serious about love as I. I was very anxious about being able to combine work and love. I thought only men could do it. I was terrified of falling in love, because I equated it with failure on two fronts. Then it simply happened to me, and being a feminist hadn't misled me at all. I can stand on my own two feet as a professional, and really loving a man showed me I can stand my ground as a woman, too.

Searcher women among my subjects were not concerned that they had "hidden" in their work, but rather that they had invested themselves too much in women's issues to the detriment of their chances in partner searching. Many women realized they were conflicted about the competing tugs of public and private life. They did not wish to make "unconscious choices," as one put it, between work and love —or to be forced to choose between them at all. One said,

> Professional women have not been talking about the dread they feel that careers and marriage can't be combined. We are not afraid of failing at work, but of succeeding! Feminism taught us to deemphasize private life and identify with our careers. Some of us had fathers who imbued us with the idea that only professional

work was true achievement. My therapist did. My father was ecstatic about my Ph.D., saying, "I'm glad you didn't take another M.R.S., instead."

The Expansion of Private Satisfactions in Searcher Lives

Despite the advantages of their professional careers, some Searcher subjects began to temper this commitment. They did so by giving some other role, usually the interpersonal, top priority. The success after struggle that characterized their professional careers seemed to encourage my subjects to tackle other areas of life to secure a similar degree of gratification. Success at work may thus pave the way for success in other areas after a mid-life divorce. A male subject said,

> At the point where I could have moved again to a better post, I didn't. I had a sabbatical coming up, and I didn't want to miss it. In the meantime, I learned to play the Conga drums, and I found a woman to merge with. I still rent the house in the desert, and the kids are grown up. We live a pretty quiet life. I have a laboratory of recording and filming equipment, and I do stuff just for fun. I never anticipated this sort of a life at fifty. It could be titled, "Another Freak Goes Free!"

After savoring professional achievement, some of my subjects were ready to tackle the awesome task of transforming their private lives.

The goal of a deeply happy private life was a prominent theme and a dominant image in Searcher reports of passage. It was as if professional success were sufficiently gratifying to embolden people to try to fulfill personal aspirations in an

area of life they perceived as more risky, less easily understood, and much more important. People "understand" professional work, but not romance and the opposite sex. Becoming a modestly successful scientist is, for example, a matter of
following a rather clearly laid out path, compared to the mys-
terious business of furthering one's "career" as a man or
woman.

One way to concentrate on private life is to start by resting
on one's professional laurels. Upper-middle-class professionals
who have "made it" and divorced at mid-life frequently become quite interested in decreasing the amount of effort they
put into work. Many times married professionals do also, but
the issue is quite central to Searcher passages. This fact is
especially true for men, or for professionals who made financial
investments that later paid off in the form of increased leisure.
But all kinds of Searcher men and women, well protected by
investments or not, respond to divorce as if it were a signal to
take some time off. Women tend to back away from the 200
percent commitment to work, common in many histories. One
subject said,

> At first, I couldn't get anything right *but* my work. It was a lot
> of consolation for messing up marriage and about everything else.
> But I've been steaming along enjoying myself there for fifteen
> years, and I want something on my tombstone besides my creden-
> tials.

One man was surprised when he found himself questioning
professional success:

> For a long time, I got a lot of satisfaction out of being an
> important man in my field. I was always in the newspapers. For
> years, I took it for granted, but that kind of stuff begins to pall.
> When you're alone, you see it just isn't enough. I never noticed

that when I was married. I took a year off; it really helps to have some time to yourself! I'll never work so hard again.

A woman related,

> When I was pushing my career, I was always leaving in the middle of something in the marriage. Since I'm divorced and take quite a bit of time for myself, anytime anything important is going on in my relationship or we want to go off—*I'm there*. We have a level of intimacy that is impossible in a whole lifetime if one or both are totally into careers. When we "took time" together, then the "we" happened. And if middle age is prime time, then I'm not going to spend it hustling on my career.

This man expressed similar relief:

> It's good to schlepp around in boots and jeans and not worry about status. I'm especially pleased to have gotten out of politics while I've still got pretty hair and my own teeth. My ex-wife is still in the big house, and Valerie and I have an apartment in the Village that we never straighten up.

In general, deemphasizing the occupational role to gain more leisure time helps Searchers achieve such goals as pairing. However, as this shift to the interpersonal is taking place, an intermediate step may first occur: the decision to make the sexual role, temporarily at least, the most important. An unequivocable, unanticipated finding in this study was the importance of the sexual role to Searcher transitions.

This shift in emphasis almost amounted to a condition necessary, if not sufficient, for identifying a newly recruited subject as a Searcher. It is inextricably linked to people's wishes for transforming themselves and their lives during passage, and ultimately it is also closely connected to partnering intentions. If marriage is the winning sweepstake ticket to a Courter, a gratifying sexual bond in a living-together arrangement rings the bell for Searchers. A uniform perception among these men and women is that one of the greatest gains from a divorce is a chance to find this kind of a relationship.

However, with respect to the importance of sex to their lives, Searchers hold disclosure of this fact to a minimum, except among other Searchers. Here, there is no hesitation about the topic, no lack of consensus about sexuality's place—in other words, its worth—in the scheme of things.

However, responses to sex as an issue are usually enormously personal. For instance, in Cuber and Haroff's research on the role of sex in upper-middle-class life as it relates to overall life satisfaction, half of the men and women in their sample were both currently unhappy and regretted their original evaluations of sex.[3] Fifty percent of the unhappy men felt they had put too high a value on sex (perhaps jeopardizing a marriage to pursue extramarital sex) or that they had been foolish to forgo sex to the extent they had. The same split was true of the unhappy women. They were dissatisfied about the role they had assigned to sex; but half of them believed they had erred by emphasizing sex too much and the other half, too little. Most interesting of all, among the happy men and women, half attributed their present contentedness of having given sex a central place in their lives, and the other half, to not having done so.

Sexuality is indeed differentially apprised; however, among my subjects, the Searchers' stories did not show any such disagreement. All the Searchers felt that a major part of their previous marital unhappiness derived from not having given sex an important role. Searchers were glad to have gotten out of the first marriage and still voiced numerous complaints about the marriage; but when I interviewed them, they were mainly complaining about the sex. Men complained that their ex-wives avoided sex as much as possible or were willing for it to be perfunctory; women insisted that their ex-husbands had refused to acknowledge the presence of sexual problems in the marriage or claimed the ex-husband directed all of his energies into work. Everyone complained about the clumsy, inexperienced, "sexless" first marriage. The following is a typical account:

I am resentful about growing up when brides were supposed to be virgins and people knew little about sex. How would *you* have liked to go through fifteen years of marriage without a sexual climax? I was crazy about my ex-husband when we married, but after ten years, I began to suspect the source of our incredible emotional distance and my unbelievable tension. I had constant asthma, probably because I was repressing anger, and I also needed to cry. Everybody kept telling me how lucky I was with a fine husband, fine kids, and a fine house. I kept wondering, "Why am I so unhappy, if I'm so lucky?"

Before feminism, I even thought I *was* lucky. I never saw how much I contributed to Paul's success. Finally, I asked him if he thought "everything was alright with us sexually," because I thought we should see someone. He was really angry and said, "If it weren't, I'd tell you, but if you think something's wrong with *you*, I'll pay for a doctor." I knew nothing about male sexual problems, and I thought I was frigid. Two years, one divorce, and one affair later, a delightful man turned me on and wrote me a sonnet to celebrate the fact. It was like turning on the lights! It was worth the costs of a divorce.

A man commented,

I think as far as sexual gratification goes, there's a lot going around. Nonetheless, I also think that people get "burned out" in other areas of their lives, and it affects sex. The last satisfaction I would relinquish is sexual gratification.

Speaking of the choice of a sexual partner, one woman said,

> Part and parcel of conventional marriage, it seems to me, is that the husband is supposed to be the sexy partner. Under the double standard, he was also the more sexually active partner. I think going to bed with someone is the height of a political act, and I wouldn't want to with any man who wanted an inexperienced woman "follower."

And one of my male subjects found that,

> the sexual revolution's changed a lot more than attitudes. I know from my own experience with divorce at this age that *everything's* changing! A lot of the women I go to bed with are lawyers or physicians. They can go to bed with whomever they please. Frankly, I find it a turn-on to be seen by such women as attractive.

For another woman,

> My chief reward for getting divorced has been learning to be multi-orgasmic. You probably won't be surprised to hear that I kept on looking until I found a man I liked, who put the same value on sex that I did.

A common theme in Searcher discussions of sexuality was their regrets at having married early and on the basis of very limited sexual experience. A Searcher woman whose story differed greatly from the others in terms of the point at which she appreciated sex reported,

> The one thing that was a plus in my first marriage through the whole dragged-out thing—the motherhood part, moving West, the divorce, and going back into training—was that I always enjoyed sex! I kept having affairs, or thinking about having them, the entire time we were married. When we divorced and I got a job, sex was a positive part of my life. I already knew how to get a good

thing going sexually and how to go on being a mother. What I had to tend to was my career. I'll say one thing though—if Mark died tomorrow, and I had to start all over again to find a partner, I'd be terrified, but I'd *find* one.

An equally emphatic male made this point:

> Any time there was a really big attraction between a woman and me, I considered living with her. As I told one of them, "If the sex isn't there, nothing else will be; but if it is, anything else can be worked out." This was my first rule.

Therefore, when a Searcher reaches the point in passage at which the importance of sexuality is evident, the question that remains is *how* to integrate the sexual role into the whole of life. It is not at all uncommon for a major goal of a Searcher to be to become comfortable with being fulfilled as a sexual being, and this can require one having a somewhat awkward phase of trying to learn how to acquire new abilities and changed attitudes. Fitting one's occupational and sexual roles together can be a problem area; for instance, one may be very much more adept in the professional than the sexual realm, a contrast which can be painful to contemplate.

One interesting way that many subjects integrated these roles was by using the professional role as a cover for the extent to which sexual considerations began to take precedence in their lives. For instance, one may excuse oneself from attending the public functions connected with a profession by claiming one is overloaded with work, explaining, for example, "I took a briefcase full of papers home to work on that night." This enables a person selectively to decrease the amount of time devoted to work-related activities without anyone's suspecting the reason.

Thus, one's professional role is amenable to all sorts of manipulation. It can be used to allow lovers to remain in bed together all day, or to travel together in a holiday spirit as long as they attend to essential business. If one is seen out at night, others may assume one has worked late at the office. Men wishing to diminish their level of commitment to work may be assumed by friends to be cutting back simply because they are sufficiently well off. These friends rarely ask for an explanation. Many Searchers start taking time off, however, for their new interest in sex, particularly for its exploration in the first tentative postdivorce "arrangement."

However, Searchers do not much value the "recreational sex" so highly prized by Runners. The following reasons for this explain more clearly how Searchers view sex. First, Searchers link sex to a relationship. No relationship without a substantial degree of sexual pleasure is seen as significant enough to be a relationship. Thus, no truly intimate pair bond will exist unless it is customarily and regularly celebrated and sealed, erotically. Second, Searchers tend to connect sex with "acting with authenticity." They do not stick around in a romance without good sex, but, when it is present, they consolidate a pairing and do not have much interest in additional sexual partners. Third, there is a great deal of cloaking of sexual experimentation or its salience to life, particularly early in passage, because these people think that their absorption in sex might discredit them in other's eyes and that it might offend their very-married friends who appear to have organized their lives around other interests. Though Searchers view their present lives as a triumph over the earlier limitations of leading sexually impoverished existences, this change takes place in private, and it is handled as "inside information." One woman described the situation as similar to that of a Catholic priest getting a "hole in one" on the golf course but not being able to tell anyone because it happened just before Good Friday mass.

Fourth, an important fact to note is that sexuality in general, and sexual expression in one's pairing, in particular, is part of a basic but larger issue that reveals the centrality of "new culture" ideas to the Searchers' passages. Sex is a component of a fundamental commitment to health and sensual body pleasures, which is a major theme both in pairing as well as in one's life as a single person. Just as Courters view married life as necessary to well-being, Searchers believe that sexuality and living a life full of robust physical activity is a basis for well-being. This is not to claim that Searchers are sensualists. A common belief among Searchers is that well-educated people tend to stay "up in their heads" too much, intellectualizing their ways through unsatisfactory lives. Searchers are well educated and trained to deal in abstractions; but most of them can look back to a period of therapy after divorcing when they tried to "listen to my feelings" and "be more in touch with my body." They tend to think that talking about living often becomes a substitute for being really alive—*acting*. And they assume that a person cannot make much progress in making personality changes or transforming a life if the "life of the mind" leads one to ignore what one called "the truths of the body." For instance, when dealing with what was a lack of sexual responsiveness for some of my subjects (exhibited in premature ejaculation or nonorgasmia), they discovered in therapy that their bodies were delivering a message they had not been aware of, or were too frightened to convey: "I don't like you enough to be doing this with *you.*" One woman said,

> I always used to be too polite to acknowledge even to myself that I didn't want sex with my first husband. He didn't want it with

me, furthermore. However, each of us knew a lot of changes would follow any clear statement of this. So our bodies would just "shut down." First of all, my body was telling me, "You don't *like* him; *listen* to me."

From this standpoint, Searchers believe that learning to "stay in the body with what one is feeling" rather than merely thinking a situation through, is an avenue to living a more authentic, *grounded* life.

Therefore, slogans for the long passage are "be good to yourself" and "take care of yourself." All the long passages I studied were enormously pleasurable to their participants. The Searchers were often glowing with health, radiant from all the laughter, hiking, picnicing in the fragrant sunshine, and making love with someone they enjoyed. Being sufficiently good to oneself to "live the life of the body" is viewed as living the healthy life. Certain aspects of this pattern are taken as "natural" to a healthy existence: massage; plenty of exercise and fresh air; moderate amounts of nourishing, unprocessed, delicious food; and engaging in strenuous play to the point of feeling a "good tiredness." The latter is a physical tiredness that relieves the nervous tension and the fatigue that once were such prominent features in these people's lives. Searchers view sports as "play" and encourage each other to be playful. This may lead a Searcher pair to spend Sunday flying kites, swimming, napping on the grass in the park, and talking there to children and oldsters. The point is to get into the stream of life —and *love life!* Most long-passage subjects were environmentalists who wanted to "save the trees" or "save the whales," and they sought out wilderness areas as a source of joy, peace, and truth. Searchers are often found at the beach taking long, invigorating walks which they follow with long naps. One woman commented,

Searchers and the Transformation Theme

I have had more fun with my partner than I ever had as a child. Much of it involves a childlike playfulness. There is also a sense of wonder, high spirits, and a great feeling of security—of being *safely at home in the world.* It's like it ought to be for children but sometimes isn't. It certainly wasn't anything like that in *my* childhood!

Among the joys of the "good life," then, appreciated as a source of feeling "alive" but also for its bonding effects, is sexual expression in the partnership.

Thus, pairing is greatly facilitated by putting one's occupational role on the back burner to give first priority to sex. After the sexual role is incorporated into the interpersonal role and leads to a tentative pairing, sex may become the focus of a person's efforts to restructure life so sexuality is a common, vital part of it.

It is interesting that while the sexual bond both expresses and cements the partnership in most cases, this situation can be maintained only if a couple has dealt with, or does deal with, a variety of psychological problems of the type common to many kinds of couples. For instance, only if a couple can avert or work through the potential power struggle that may arise between them, will the coupleship remain stable. It is my impression that many promising Sorter and Searcher pairings (seen by both parties as "egalitarian"), flounder on the rocky issue of power; that is, who will control the relationship. Commonly, in the midst of a happy Sorter pairing, or an intensely felt Searcher pairing, presumably "open" and democratic, a power struggle develops and unsettles what seemed to be a successful match. According to one woman,

We'd lived at my house by means of a contract for four years, when he suggested we buy a house together as an investment. I refused, reminding him one provision of the contract was no commingling of surplus funds. We contributed almost equally to fixed expenses of living together. He kept at me, saying we'd had four good years, each had money that needed to be invested, and so on. Do I think he was calling for a renegotiation of the contract? I don't know, and I didn't care. It was already covered in the contract. So, he said the contract stipulated monogamy unless one party notified the other to the contrary, so he was now notifying me. That went on for a month with him gone a lot. So I told him that the contract permitted either of us to call for the partnership to be dissolved, and I did it.

Normally, decisions about whose turn it is to cook, at whose residence the couple will live, how money is to be spent, and who pays for what, are minor issues easily settled. Maintaining separate residences is also a common mechanism for helping sustain monogamous Searcher relationships. A Searcher woman explained,

> It helps that each of us has a house and some privacy, and both of us have good incomes and a lot of free time. We live fifteen minutes apart. Often we are together twenty-four hours a day but we have other periods where we do not see each other for several days, and I like to be by myself. This weekend, we have tickets for three plays and dinner reservations every night. Last week we were at his cabin in Vermont, not doing much of anything. We have taken the worst parts of marriage out, and what's left is the good part.

Typically, this kind of a harmonious pairing occurs only when a couple has spent months together. Many tentative Sorter and Searcher pairings are consolidated through having a very good time together over a long period.

The courting rituals of Searcher couples profit from the resources these men and women command at mid-life and the fact that they value the simplicity of informal activities at that stage of life. These people are not under a strain, and they see each other in the best light, compared to couples who have little money or time at their disposal. A woman described a courtship built around her future husband's hobby:

> We met at group, and all that next summer, he courted me in his sailboat with the gorgeously colored spinnaker, and we'd come in with the wind as the sun set and do some dinner over charcoal on the deck and watch the stars come out. Eventually we married on that deck amidst all the flowers I could pot, and then we built a house in a woods at Inverness.

The fact that, during passage, Searchers and Sorters adopt many ideas from the "new culture" does serve to protect them from discouragement and self-doubts, but if a pairing proves to be unstable, passage can become more difficult. Searchers are less interested than ever in indiscriminate sexuality after an intensely satisfying pairing fails, but the cohort of divorced men and women with whom one has been in passage, starts to thin out as people pair off. Without a pairing prospect for a significant amount of time, a Searcher has to take stock and continue to believe in the possibility of a vital pairing. This can prove to be a large order to fill.

During this time, a person may adopt one of two strategies: accept a temporary period of celibacy, or engage in multiple sexual relationships. Despite their emphasis on sexuality, occasional periods of celibacy among my subjects were not at all unusual. Searcher subjects were also capable of indiscriminate sexual activities, and most had partaken of them at least at one period; in other words, they had been ratified as sexually desirable. But casual interaction does not please this kind of person for long, and Searchers are soon engrossed in testing out new tentative partnerships.

Searchers do not object on moral grounds to one-nighters, but see them rather as illusory and unlikely to lead to what they are looking for. Nevertheless, some pairings begin this way. Searchers believe a continual round of casual sex is best for people "into sport-fucking," such as Runners. However, they are not judgmental; they merely seek for themselves more of a prize than recreational sex. Therefore, many prefer "time-outs" between relationships, turning to celibacy or restricting sex to one or more friends also in a holding pattern. Searchers seek intimacy through sex, and tend to view superficial relationships, that might be Runners' mainstays, as "trivial."

However, another mechanism that Runners enjoy, singles activities, are sometimes used by Searchers after breakups. On the whole, a new partner can be found fairly quickly. Searchers recall people to whom they were attracted in a previous year or while they were partnered and not available. They also are comfortable with going to groups and use them well. A woman subject told me about going to a singles dance, after a breakup:

> I was watching the dancers, and the place was mobbed. Only one man interested me. Just as I noticed him, he started towards me. I pulled myself together, stuck out my foot; and when he started to walk past, said as clearly as I could—because those places are always so dark and he was so surprised—"If you're not in the mood, it's OK; but if you'd like to, I would love to dance." He was terribly pleased and acted like a cowboy reining in his horse. It turned out he was a physicist and former neighbor of my former lover and just back from several years living abroad. Our mode of meeting seemed to recommend me to him. Well, he wanted to move in with me, but I didn't even want to go to bed with him, and after several weeks, I was seeing John again.

Searchers are adept at initiating conversations with people they find attractive and practiced at reading people's clothes and demeanor for clues about their interests and inclinations. Both men and women welcome the new freedom women have to do some scouting around. Most men are flattered to be asked to dance, and women are not offended if a man declines. One woman said that one of the funniest things that had happened to her was asking a man to dance and then realizing he was stoically bearing up throughout the dance, as she had herself often done in the past before there was this role reversal.

At singles parties, friendship is often extended by someone as an opener. Then a man and woman can subsequently eye each other from a distance and proceed in the other's direction if they desire. A problem herein is determining the extent of the other's interest, particularly if he or she knows other people, who stand and chat with the individual as if the two of them were intimates. A number of Searcher women talked about this, and about returning within range of a man they had taken as interested in them, because he had generated *their* interest, only to find him looking "taken." One said,

> When I got back to that part of the house, he was sitting talking to a woman who had her arm on his, and I thought, "Oh, shit!" But I sat down to one side, just to wait and see, and shortly he noticed me and joined me. I immediately suggested we take a walk outside. We walked and talked for an hour and pretty well got all the preliminary information each of us needed, as we were frank in our questions and in the answers. We've been together now for a year.

One subject reported meeting a delightful man when both took refuge on a patio at a party they regretted attending. They confided their mutual discontent and shortly thereafter left the party together:

> He is really a nice fellow with a big house and pool and three horse-crazy daughters. They keep two horses down the road at the Hunt Club. He was at my university, but we never met. He was just the sort of man I was looking for then, but now, we have very different life-styles. I helped him chaperone a party to which one

of his girls had invited couples; he said it helped because all the mothers call up to check if there's not going to be a woman there. Sometimes I went over for Sunday morning, and we presided at the brunch table together. I stopped seeing him after that, because what he needs is a wife-and-mother person.

The fact that men their age often seem overly traditional is sometimes not recognized by the men Searcher women meet. Men whose behavior is quite conventional sometimes are not comfortable with making room for a professional woman's work life, or they feel odd if she is more assertive than a former wife. This leads many women to look to younger men as partnering possibilities. Men who are traditional in outlook are at a disadvantage with "new women" regardless of their other assets. This leaves a narrowed field for Searcher women who then tend to define nonconventional pairing as possibly their best route. One such woman reported the following conversation with a traditional man,

> He said it was "nice to have a woman ask me to dance," but then, the next thing he knew, she also invited him to go home with her. "What did I say to that? Well, I thought it was pretty damn forward of her, so I told her, *'I'm* used to doing the asking, thank you.' "

This man was typical of the kind not seen as self-possessed or interesting, but as unacceptably old-fashioned. The subject said that an answer of "No, thank you," would have been quite sufficient.

Male adherence to traditional attitudes and behavior appears to inhibit men from dealing well with the mid-life transition, especially when it is accompanied by divorce. Some men complain to Searcher women that "today's woman is too independent and is just out for a good time." These men are written off as not able to be comfortable with the weakening of male perogatives and, therefore, completely "out of it" (meaning, the modern world). No male attribute "turns off" Searcher women faster than the oft met patronizing attitudes with which some men approach them.

Nonetheless, while Searcher women are relieved to lead less circumscribed and constrained lives, role strain and role conflict are often present for both men and women during partner hunting. Women not willing to deal with traditional men have to keep looking. One complaint of the most accomplished and confident women subjects was that almost the only way to keep a somewhat traditional man happy was sometimes to be unable to run one's life. The conflict in expectations between Searcher women and traditional men paves the way for younger men, whose views are "contemporary," to rate well with these women; they, too, are receptive to nontraditional pairing.

A complication here is the confusion that exists about ascertaining age. A common approach is to ask how old children from a prior marriage are. But younger men tend to be less interested in age and less uptight about an age gap. One Searcher said that, when a man she knew was continually interested in the fact that she was older than he, she was alerted to the fact that he was himself troubled about getting older—and that the nearer in age they were, the more it upset a man that he was not the older of the two. One said that "some younger men tell me that they like older women, since they are not so set on a house in the suburbs and not so helpless."

In the case of mid-life males, many subjects could not adapt to changing sex roles. They did not realize however, that this meant they must forgo being able to attract a professional woman enjoying a fairly autonomous life. Many women

Searchers passed up men, who might have looked like "good catches" to their mothers, simply because these men were unhappy about the new definitions by which women stood to gain. Having no foreknowledge of the other person's expectations often resulted in awkward disjunctures. Like the young women in Broadhead's research (who felt that women could make good physicians, but physicians might not "make very good women"), many women who were enthusiastic Searcher professionals worried that they therefore might not be very acceptable as "women." Thus, locating a man with a fairly strong self-image can become urgent business.

Although they have these fears that work could lower their opportunities to pair, most Searchers tend simply to plunge ahead, dealing with whatever comes along. Nevertheless, many promising-looking pairings immediately fail in the face of negotiating sex role issues. These issues are closely related to a Searcher's perceptions of his or her options and some people are too clumsy to discuss the matter with much skill.

Sex roles have been undergoing so many modifications and are still in such flux that people must be willing to improvise as they go along. In fact, many male Searchers have come to enjoy cooking and buying washers and dryers. One woman said she had never been allowed to prepare a meal for, or offer a cup of coffee upon arrival, to the man she partnered for a year, because he still felt smothered by memories of the solicitude of his motherly former wife. During the rest of the time she was seeing him, they sometimes cooked dinner together in the kitchen he had remodeled. Searcher women have grown accustomed to receiving all kinds of household tips from men friends (including advice on how to clean burned pots). Because of the ages of Searchers, the single father as an example of role reversal is not common. Some Searcher subjects found that in their hunt for a highly rewarding form of couplehood, it was sometimes necessary to live with someone to determine actual attitudes on sex roles.

Searcher men and women use psychotherapy extensively, and it often functions as a tool for becoming rapidly "resocialized" after divorce. In addition, therapists can assist people in relinquishing marital roles. If emotional conflicts from an earlier time are present as unfinished business that threatens a pairing, these can be worked through during therapy, and new possibilities may be elaborated. Therapy offers Searchers a source of support for their experimentation. This fact is important since the trial and error period sometimes requires a rather random casting about for social identities that will work with the kinds of people a Searcher wants to attract and enjoys being with. One Searcher recalled the process:

> I went to considerable financial hardship and lost some time to do three years of Jungian analysis. It meant sticking to a dull clerical job and holding my course work to night classes. My marriage had offered me a high standard of living, but nothing to look forward to, so it was easier to skimp and wait than to go on with being transferred indefinitely. I was fascinated with the law and wished for a lawyer for myself. Finally I ended up telling my analyst I'd like to be one. I think he expected to hear that for a long time before it occurred to me.

Many Searcher women enter professional careers rather late and do not gain the income levels they originally hoped for. Nevertheless, with a salary and some investments made with the proceeds from the divorce settlement or from astute financial management, their financial situations are much better than they ever envisioned when first married. Searcher women romanticize their entry into business and the professions, although they might be behind compared to sisters who trained early, or men who receive higher salaries for the same training.

Subjects reported much satisfaction at being valued professionally, particularly if they were bored in or not appreciated in their marriage, as was so often the case. The approval and acceptance these women command at work is a very positive factor at middle age.

Nonetheless, both men and women discover that career success tends to "get stale," or it becomes "cold comfort" if one's personal life is not yet in order (for example, pairing has not been accomplished). Women Searchers also recognize that, while men also take refuge in work, most men are much more matter-of-fact about work.

A major problem for all Searchers, but an acute one for some women, is that the structural realities of life leave much to be dealt with, apart from work life. Searchers who want "new culture" people for partners may have to look hard and long or compromise on some issue. Men tend to watch a "new woman," who claims to be an independent one, for signs that she will prove to be as possessive as an ex-wife seemed to have been. And most Searcher women will remain on guard, not completely satisfied with a new friend's insistence that he is not upset with career women's ambitions, watching for indications that he will nevertheless pull away from her the first time he watches her savor a professional or personal triumph. Thus, despite protestations, people wait to see if behavior and stated attitudes are congruent. In addition a woman who retains a circle of married friends from a former marriage, whom she sees occasionally, may eventually abandon her tie with them if they have little understanding of the implications of the fact that she has since become a well-established professional.

When Searchers entertain at home, it is usually with impromptu invitations to a couple or to several friends. Because their single friends work hard and travel a lot, it is hard to collect them, since they tend toward spur-of-the-moment plans rather than committing themselves ahead of time. This is especially true among singles when a new relationship is beginning or an old one ending. Furthermore, devoted very-married old friends tend to dodge Searcher invitations or, more often, book things so far ahead that they are never available at the last moment. Although such friends are interested in the single's welfare, the two types lead such disparate lives that the relentless Noah's ark quality of what Searchers view as "mainstream life" may seem to a Searcher to offer too many problems to be worthwhile.

In other words, while Searchers tend to be wistful for extensive couple friendships, they tend to discard these hopes. By middle age, social circles have narrowed and Searcher couples live fairly solitary lives except when they get together with their parents, children, or other relatives. Nevertheless, this is not a serious problem for Searchers, since they tend to emphasize the pairing over other relationships. Because their aims are so opposed to those of say, Courters, they end up forgoing rather than cultivating the invitations that were once part of married life, leaning toward considering this more active social life "what goes on when you're younger."

Searchers learn how to handle feeling a bit isolated, especially if not paired, or around the holidays, by joining a group of people who go out together regularly for gourmet dinners or a group like Mensa, which has a yearlong calendar of social events both in and out of town. In this fashion, acquaintances become friends and a joint history can be constructed which compensates for the loss of marital ties. A number of male subjects mentioned this kind of group membership as an "alternative family." However, long-passage subjects may admit to each other that "without children, Christmas loses a lot," or "the holidays seem strange without a lot of invitations." One Searcher woman in a living-together arrangement reported her shock at being rebuffed by neighbors who found excuses for not getting to their New Year's Eve party, saying,

> Because the house was so pretty and it was our best Christmas since we started being together, we got some cocktail stuff and called a few singles and the neighborhood for New Year's Eve champagne. But the neighbors seemed a bit floored by this cordiality. All of them said they were "too tired" or "had plans." This was the first indication I had that our relationship might have disturbed the neighborhood.

One male subject mentioned he had joined a men's group, because he "wanted to make friends," adding that, after six months, he hadn't noticed that he felt any male bonding.

Searcher women tend to be in good physical health and have high energy levels, another reason they interest and are attracted to younger men. In general, they were somewhat nonconforming as young women despite marrying early. They were women who were bored with coffee klatches and community roles, once they grew accustomed to them. One such woman explained,

> I adored having children early, and I had no idea then that I might ever leave Mike. I might have guessed it, I suppose, because I always *was* a rebel, like going back to college when they were in grade school, and it just wasn't done. You know, I really didn't want to pick up a baby again until I had my fifth grandchild. I'm really enjoying this one.

These women make friends readily and use women who are old friends as confidants, more often than do male Searchers. Many women rehearse transition by looking for role models among the single career-women they know, to prepare for adjustments to come.

Generally, women remain enthusiastic about being accepted

in professional and social circles. Their job titles generally out-run their salaries, but work is a major resource for organizing passage as well as a source of immediate gratification, and all of this stands in sharp contrast to their first marriages when the husbands' work and children's needs always came first. The women tend also to have been somewhat uncomfortable in their early conventional marriages because they felt it was necessary to stifle their aspirations so as not to "rock the boat." One remembered, "My rather stiff young husband did not want it known that I smoked, and he asked me not to mention having *graduated* from the university, although having attended was 'alright.'"

Thus, while some Searcher women perceive their career accomplishments as somewhat more limited than what a younger woman might achieve, nonetheless their achievements are the basis for more satisfactions than they'd originally expected to garner. They also view their existences as tremendously privileged in comparison to their stably-married sisters who command neither salaries nor independent status. One subject referred to her conventional life as a wife and mother being followed by a modicum of career success, as

having the best of two worlds. Of course a younger woman would not have settled today for not being a full partner in the firm, as I was glad to do. But for women of my generation, I've done well. Doing family life and then a career in succession, rather than simultaneously, worked out quite nicely. For one thing, I didn't have to worry about how you deal with a dual-career marriage and raising children. I never would have wanted to take that on actually, so not having had a chance doesn't bother me. The women I like best now, who have done well professionally and are also mothers, had their children later than I did. On the whole, they did better in their careers because their training was behind them so early.

Another commented,

> In my opinion, if you're dead set on children as well as a career, you have to do one of them very early and the other very late. Since I don't think American women get around to understanding being women very early, you might as well have children first. Then the best part of your life is left to middle age, when you feel you have earned the right to some goodies for yourself.

Searcher women tended to have their children very early. It is typical of them to have enjoyed their children but to have chafed under the restrictions of motherhood, or more significantly, *never to have identified themselves primarily as mothers.* One woman reported,

> I had beautiful children, a great house, and a lot of money, and nothing like the problems of working-class women. But do you have any idea how lonely it is to be responsible for so much when you are married to a man who is always off somewhere doing well? Housewife? To me that means being married to a house! I did a lot of mandatory stuff, like entertaining boss after boss. We were promoted a lot! The winter that I had to be a Cub Scout den mother for the fourth year, I had a headache and went to bed every Tuesday afternoon after the den meeting. I am happy now, and I don't care who thinks what about it, because there is one thing I am *very* clear on: *I have paid my dues!*

As for Searcher men, in order to search widely, they must willingly relinquish at least a few of the privileges masculinity carries, or used to convey. But for many men, as for Searcher women, the Searcher passage offers an opportunity to live out some of one's wishes formed earlier. One said,

> I've always been a little bit disappointed in men. I never got off on that macho stuff, and the friendships I hoped for didn't seem

to be what my men friends defined in the way I did. I really don't care for the stag fishing trips, where everyone drinks too much and walks around with their balls hanging out all the time. I used to think something was wrong with me, but now I tend to think that I may have been a little ahead of my time.

Another said,

Careerist? I guess you could say I was into it pretty heavily for years. I was not only a "big man" in town, I was all over town. They couldn't hold a meeting or form a committee without me. Frankly, though, I think a lot of it was "running." I hated my marriage, and it never occurred to me there would ever be a way out of it. I was on the go all the time, because it kept me from thinking about how miserable I was, and everyone expected it of me. Since I found Margaret, I'm happy and I can afford to sit down and feel how I feel. I think a lot of men are running around in the rat race, because somebody told them it was their role.

Thus, to some men, passage brings a welcome relief from their accustomed roles of being all-around heavily committed performers. I also found that some Searcher men who do not make it to "the top" but who do moderately well in their professions, are greatly advantaged today because of their interest in social trends. The following comment reflects such an attitude:

All that male competitive stuff really tees me off. I never did enjoy it, for all that I could play that game. I hate guns, and I think men who collect them are dumb. I never let the boys have them around the house, and I think that settling things by fighting is pretty boring compared to using reason. I guess you could say I've always been pretty tolerant, and I got tired of being faulted for it.

The flexibility and relative lack of male chauvinism of many of these men, along with their interest in New Age living, stands them in good stead with "new women." Thus, they are in a strong position vis à vis the career woman whom society increasingly defines positively. For these "new" men and women, the increasing legitimation of careers for women and less competitive attitudes for men means that "time is on their side" and they are "in tune with the times." Middle-management men with fair salaries, or higher status men with assets depleted by divorce can, if they are not rigid, undertake a mid-life partner search with a new sense of self-worth and heightened social currency. These men are particularly well received by late career women, who divorced prosperous "workaholic" husbands whose work left them too heavily scheduled to have much time for personal life.

Many of these men, additionally, still hold positions providing them with an adequate financial base and a measure of status, which is all they perceive they need. They sometimes emulate or look like much younger men, and they are easily distinguishable from Establishment men in singles settings. They are visibly popular, and often monopolize attractive younger women and sought-after older career women. Potentially, they are role models for males in their age group. A stage of life that can be more traumatic for their "more successful" brothers, who soon face competition from "young comers," may be rich with unanticipated gains for these more adaptable men. Their styles of self-presentation (reflected in their clothing, vocabulary, and manners) are more similar to those of younger men; but, most importantly, so are their *values*. All of this helps them mitigate the potential disadvantage of being older and without substantial assets. By so exploiting shifting norms, both men and women Searchers maneuver to their own benefit.

The Ideology of Singlehood

While the "going solo" model certainly appeals to Runners and Graduates, Searchers and some other subjects use it only as a stage in passage, albeit a very useful one. Stein has made a good case for singlehood as an end in itself, which is currently being supported by an increased incidence in this social phenomenon.[4] Thus, the debate that has been underway, as to whether this emerging social form is permanent or will be proven to be merely a temporary adaptation to a number of conditions, seems to be leaning in favor of proponents of the first position. Today, the single status carries with it an enhanced aura of prestige. In a general sense, it is beginning to be viewed as one of the privileges of middle age.

However, Passionate Searchers simply do not perceive singlehood in this way. They put little energy into denying the importance *to them* of pairing, even when they have not yet achieved it and when being less frank might also be less painful. On the other hand, Searchers make extremely good use of periods of "time alone" if these are dictated by the course of a relationship or the need to collect themselves afterward. One shift they make is to enjoy playing "catch up" in their professional work. But like Runners, Searchers think that singlehood is greatly to be desired over traditional forms of marriage. One said,

It is almost unbelievable to me that I live such a self-contained life with or without a partner. After our breakup, I saw a distinguished but very rigid man for four months. This promptly put me in mind of my marriages. At the end of each of these, I had nothing like the pleasant life I can get for and by myself now.

Breaking up the "arrangement" was really rather positive because for the first time, I came out of something to an absolutely beautifully appointed life, which now includes another interesting man.

But even its utility "between engagements," or the fact that "time alone" is important to some Searcher courtships and marriages, does not diminish Searchers' enthusiasm and determination to find a gratifying partnership as an ultimate good. Despite being retrospectively most discontented with memories of an early marriage, Searchers will not only "go back to the mat" over and over again, they can hardly wait to do so. These men and women hang onto the ideal of finding a perfect partner, regardless of how well singlehood works, seeing singlehood as a "fallback position" one can adopt with integrity if one is self-sufficient and simply has not yet found and won the partner with whom one can honestly love, honor, and play.

In probing for the significance of being middle-aged and alone while attempting to pair, I found that Searchers do not seem to suffer the pangs of mid-life singlehood since they find it so much more desirable a state than their unsatisfactory marriages, and always define it as a "stopgap" state of affairs. One woman subject said,

I think any woman would have to be hardy to follow the path I chose. Maybe I should say "foolhardy." It always struck me that I was "going for broke," holding out for the kind of a man I'd always wanted, especially when I was an older woman, but I went on the assumption that not all men were looking for a youngster with hair down to her waist.

In all categories of passage, subjects tended to assume they would get out of passage what they wanted, except for the

Enforced Remarriers, who at least defined their remarriages as right for them, at the time. In this regard, Searchers were no different from the other groups. They did tend to leave passage by pairing, if only by their considerable efforts to do so. In the process, they created and attached a world of meanings to both pairing and mid-life. When they evaluated their passages, they tended to justify their choices as "responding to the times," especially as expressed in the "new culture" and the group movement. For instance, they described periods of celibacy or a temporary sexual alliance with a "friend" (not a "new friend") until a prospective partner appeared on the scene as "taking responsibility for oneself." In hoping for and working toward a partnership, they were "confronting the facts of my existence" and "giving myself permission to believe in getting what I want." By experiencing singlehood and finding it unexpectedly pleasant and possible as a life mode, Searchers had a chance to reconsider pairing if they wished. They didn't. The point I am making is that they clearly had a *choice*, after trying singlehood, since it tended to increase their self-confidence. But it actually led them to believe even more strongly that some kind of pairing would work out, if they would entertain tradeoffs. One subject reflected,

Singlehood? It was what I thought I wanted when I got divorced. What I *thought* I wanted was to be free and single and date the men I liked. But it was just a stage. Within a year, I found this didn't suit me at all well. I wanted the security of *knowing* the person I cared about, and his caring for me.

I found that superficial, casual things weren't enough. In fact they turned me off. I could have friendships, but whenever the romantic sexual ingredient was involved, I had to feel good about him and "know" him. For me, sexual relationships are a big vulnerable area. I can't go to bed and be that vulnerable, physically and emotionally, with a stranger. I did have several sexual relationships with friends, but while I was secure with my work and with friendship, I wasn't about romance.

I'm not sure what other reasons were involved; I've been in therapy —after divorce. There I learned that what I wanted was *a very close one-to-one* relationship. I identified this as a prime value. Now that I've got that relationship, it's still a prime value.

Another subject said,

> I am still perfectly capable of meeting a pleasant man, talking together over a drink, spending a night in bed with him, and then saying, "So long, it was nice to meet you." While I had to work for the confidence to be *able* to enjoy it, I have had it for a long time now.
>
> But more than that, I want to partner—and not with a man who'd encourage or overlook infidelity. If he did, I'd no longer think highly of him nor want to stay with him. I am also capable of not telling him; but that's not the point. I prefer to be partnered, but I can take care of myself, if it's necessary; and I would choose it over being with the wrong man.

Discussing the practical realities of her life, and her evaluations of singlehood for the long run, one woman commented,

> Sure, I know how to drop in at a bar and find myself an attractive man. But I also know that it takes a long time to develop a relationship. I live a time-limited life. Why waste time getting to know a man a bit and then begin all over with a second one? I think that the ideal of singlehood is very simplistic, because there are many considerations nobody seems to be talking about.
>
> Another point is that I have a lovely teen-aged daughter who is often with me. I'm not going to drag home a series of men to present to her; I'm not going to have different men staying overnight; and I'm not going to hang out in bars. It wouldn't work for me, any more than it would for her. . . . Besides, I like things warm and comfy with lots of continuity—like they are now.

A male subject said,

> I've always thought multiple relationships would be fun, but I
> never could manage them. Furthermore, I want lots of intimacy
> and to be absolutely sure of my woman.

Another subject reflected on her evolving attitudes:

> I felt like a free soul after my divorce, and I had a lovely affair.
> But I wanted to be honest with Michael and faithful, as soon as
> I saw how I felt about him. I wasn't sure it was consistent with
> my claim to be an independent woman, however. I thought he
> might accuse me of misrepresentation. Instead, he was shocked,
> accused me of wanting to *get married,* and said I "wasn't very
> liberated." I was furious. I've seen lots of marriages without
> fidelity. It turned out I was fighting for a monogamous relationship
> and calling *him* conventional.

Searchers give themselves plenty of time for long passages.
Just as Steadies spend considerable time testing out an emerging
new family unit, Searchers put both themselves and their pairings to the test. Nevertheless, most of the time, the pairings of
Searchers depend on one last contingency, a willingness to
change one's expectations for the kind of partner one would be
willing to settle down with. One woman subject, talking about
the surprises that this latter fact can impose on passage, laughed
and said, "But you know, according to John Lennon, 'Life is
what happens to you, when you're busy making other plans.' "[5]

Redefining the Perfect Partner's Characteristics

Searcher passages sometimes stretch the patience of well-wish-
ers who wonder how they will turn out, but Searchers stand

ready to stretch themselves in the course of self-improvement and throughout the mate selection process. This shows in their willingness to amend or bend their requirement for the type of partner they would consider appropriate. Often they meet someone who does not fit the list of characteristics they think they are looking for, whom they initially do not take seriously, but whom they quickly realize they should take seriously, be- cause of the person's growing importance to them. Since Searchers give high priority to a person's intrinsic qualities such as intelligence, or personality rather than to objective criteria such as income level or having gone to the "right" schools, many unconventional pairings result because conventional cri- teria are discarded. One woman commented on this, saying,

> It's funny but many of the men now attracted to me, are almost caricatures of what my mother originally wanted for me. They're Establishment men with inherited incomes who bore me silly because they're so conservative. I would never be able to settle for one of them now.

Another woman said,

> One of the strongest points in my present relationship is his intelligence and the fact that he is so enormously well-read. Only recently did I realize that is important to me as I *have* to have good conversation. I was once married to the most boring man in Con- necticut.

A male subject said of his remarriage,

> I fell madly in love with a girl from an ethnic background when I was in law school, but my parents raised so much hell that I married what they called a "patrician." My second wife is Italian- American and yells a lot; I love it!

Searchers and the Transformation Theme

The laundry list of desired characteristics, then, soon comes to match the qualities that actually please an individual rather than matching a list of social assets, conventionally derived. This may involve personality characteristics or, less often, physical attributes such as an individual's appearance. For instance, I was surprised to see how often my Searcher women subjects were clearly interested in or influenced by a man's mere size. Two rather small women had different reactions to this issue, one commenting,

> I know it's crazy, and I cannot figure out where it came from since my father (whom I liked very much) was about 5 feet 7 inches, but I am never comfortable with a man who is under 5 feet 10 inches or 5 feet 11 inches. This cuts out a lot of great men. Also, as I am small, if he's over 6 feet, we really can't dance, and I am embarrassed because he leans down to hear me sometimes. A second problem is that they have to be blue-eyed blondes. I wonder—does that mean that I am imprinted like a baby duck by my first husband's appearance? At any rate, when I went off to school, small men made a beeline for me for the first time in my life, and they *scared* me.

And, the other,

> I really love small men, about 5 feet 5 inches or so. My father is 5 feet 4 inches, and he's a lady's man. I always go for men that size, and most of them have been high achievers.

A larger woman said,

> I just love the way Ronnie comes up to my eyes. I think one of the reasons that I just couldn't go anywhere with my doctor friend was that he was so tall, and I felt he was looming over me and was going to control me.

Unions that derive from highly individualistic choices often cross class and age lines, especially when a woman Searcher is involved. While marriages of two people of nonequivalent social rank are hardly news in a democratic society, the forms these pairings take are interesting, and so are the larger societal influences behind them.

Bernice Neugarten theorizes that our society is increasingly an "age-irrelevant" one and explains, "Because of pervasive changes in economic, political and other aspects of social organization, the age distributions of industrialized societies are changing [so rapidly that] arbitrary constraints based on chronological age are removed, and individuals have opportunities [that mesh well with] their needs, desires, and abilities."[6] These remarks apply to the cases of Searchers who see age-grading (using age as the primary basis for regulating social interaction) merely as a vestige from tradition not binding on them. This is often particularly true of the innovative ways in which Searcher women sometimes handle pairing and its potential dilemmas, which are both intensified and remedied by their being nonconformists who entered the professions. In other times, women like them might have given up a wish to pair, as the price a nonconforming woman must pay to have a professional career. But Searcher women not only insist on having a partner, they want to find a man who attracts them and to whom the idea of having a high-status wife is very appealing. As one such woman said,

> Why am I supposed to apologize for my credentials and my standard of living? If my father had left them to me in his will, that would be OK to everyone. Well, as far as I am concerned, he did, in that he encouraged me to achieve, at the same time that he thought I was his "darling daughter." I mean, there was never any suggestion that I *had* to have a career as marriage wouldn't be an option. I had boyfriends from the time I was ten.

244

Another said,

> Look, I've worked very hard, and I had a rotten first marriage.
> I am forty-five, and I am worth several million, by my own efforts.
> I expect to have a man who wants to put something into *me*, not
> the other way around.

The following type of marriage is common in the stories of
Searcher women:

> Natalie is a woman lawyer "married" to a fisherman twelve years
> her junior. They have been together for seven years. Last summer
> Peter accompanied her on her annual summer visit to her family
> outside of Boston. Because of his interests in conservation, Peter
> spent some time at a nearby marine biology station while Natalie
> and her mother lunched with a number of her mother's friends in
> the town where her family has summered for three generations.
> Like her father, Natalie graduated near the top of her class at
> _____ law school.
>
> Although she often goes abroad on business for the firm, she
> has recently set a limit of two weeks as she misses Peter so much
> when they are apart. Peter and Natalie live in a modest apartment
> overlooking the harbor in a major coastal city. They have not met
> their neighbors since she moved in with him, but most of the men
> are merchant seamen, fishermen, or men who work at the harbor.
> Peter has not met Natalie's associates and does not care to.

As potentially stigmatized, middle-aged divorcées, women
like Natalie seem to succeed at maximizing what Neugarten
calls "opportunities for both self-enhancement and extensive
new modes of social participation."[7] At any rate, they take this
to be the case. In a general sense, although Searcher life-styles
at home center on emotional expressiveness, egalitarian routines, and exuberant sexuality, they are nevertheless middle
class or upper middle class by virtue of the professional involvements of one or both partners. In other words, they are *private*

(or "closet") nonconformists. The following description shows how one Searcher and her partner handled this matter:

> Diana is a surgeon on the staff of a famous teaching hospital. She and Brian live primarily on his salary as a park ranger on a small wooded homestead in what once was a colony of summer homes. Her mail from the hospital goes to a post office box in the country village she drives through en route to work. Her colleagues do not know about her "marriage," and her neighbors do not know she is a surgeon. Since her divorce many years ago, Diana has been an amateur naturalist. She met Brian while visiting a national park in _____, and he immediately took a new job in order to move near her. Originally, Diana termed the relationship an affair, but now both of them describe themselves as a stable couple. Diana obviously takes great pleasure in Brian's presence and teases him by telling people that the last time they were separated, he fell ill.

A common theme in Searcher accounts was a newfound capacity for expressiveness. Men talked about their former emotional rigidity and women of their satisfaction about being able to live less constrained lives and the energy they derived from this liberation. Three Searcher women spoke of having "kept younger men" as a good stopgap measure. One of them said, "It's cheaper than paying for therapy to try to 'adjust.'" A typical male observation when making comparisons was, "I was only the person who paid the bills in my first marriage." Thus, men spoke of leaving obligations, but women of going forward to opportunities. The reason that Searchers spent so much time talking about how much their lives had changed and how much better they have become, is that they now live lives that seem to them unexpectedly rich.

For many Searchers, the partnership "arrangement" they finally arrive at and which terminates passage amounts to cohabitation, although it may later result in a legal marriage. What seems more important to Searchers than legality is that the pairing offer a great deal of intimacy without threatening a professional or business commitment. Several Searcher men studied chose women partially on the basis of their acceptance of a limited mode of cohabitation (going back and forth between two residences). Both partners in such situations indicated to me that a demand for more closeness might prompt them to reconsider the partnership. Therefore, these men and women either accept or creatively solve a collection of situational difficulties in order to pair in some fashion with a person they enjoy. This case material illustrates how ingeniously some Searcher pairings work out:

> Abigail is a nationally known professor of _____ whose books are avidly read by a wide audience. Her husband is a radio operator. He has a fairly good income, but he is at sea for six months of the year. She writes during this time. On his return, they party and frequent their favorite waterfront bars with his friends who do not know of her work. They have been together for a number of years, but only a few of her intimates know about him.

Many pairing problems are seen as worth enduring if a couplehood is regarded as unusually gratifying in comparison to previous experiences, as is usually the point in Searcher pairings. One woman compared a brief period of cohabitation to two fairly long marriages she experienced:

> The time we lived together was not only the only time I really enjoyed living with a man, it was also the only time I felt married. He has a wonderful English sense of humor and a very good mind. I think I could talk to him for years and never get bored. I appreciate him most of all, however, for his unreserved capacity to be "emotionally available."

Because the alliances Searchers contract are relatively unconventional and the intimate bond so gratifying, most Searchers "live two lives," as a means to guard privacy. Despite the degree to which work structures life, they find the private world more important. While a major contribution of professional life is the confidence it gives them to take an idiosyncratic path, the benefits of keeping work and private life separate seem to Searchers to be obvious.

One woman Searcher reported that she shielded her private life from view by leading her colleagues to infer that she was unhappily unpaired. Another said she made it a practice never to go escorted to any function attended by business associates or friends from earlier years. Another woman said, "My new friend attended a conference with me for several hours on the spur of the moment and we ran into several of my colleagues. I was proud to show him off, to my surprise, as I tend to avoid such disclosures." While men go to fewer lengths to conceal a partner's existence, they may conceal the details of a pairing. One man told his visiting father that his lover was his secretary. Since many Searchers had been high achievers since childhood and remembered being carefully groomed by a series of coaches —including watchful parents, teachers, and mentors—they relish a chance to sidestep agents, limiting the role of advisor to therapists and special (confidant) buddies they see by themselves.

Thus, agency is not important in Searcher passages. Once a romance becomes stable, Searchers make their own decisions about the pairing. One woman said,

> I rarely talk about a romance which is underway. Once I went to see my old therapist about a man, and he said, "Break it off." But I didn't want to, and I didn't. Later, he said, "Follow your feelings." I had done this in the first place, or there wouldn't have been a relationship. When my feelings had gone to someone else, I broke it off.

Searchers and the Transformation Theme

Searchers are a bit wary about discussing their pairings for several reasons. They know some of their unions will be fragile because of their unofficial nature and because they are not bound by some of the built-in factors, such as children, that sustain other relationships. Thus, they have many motives for not inviting comments on the details of their private lives, to which many persons once were privy, welcome or not, and they value privacy. Secrecy about a growing romantic involvement is a protective device that adds to a Searcher's already considerable delight in an intensely felt romance.

While earlier exiting subjects wanted to be restored to life in groups, Searchers were interested in transformation, whether this took the form of a transformed partnership, life, or self. For Searchers, pairing with the desired type of partner becomes only one of several aspects of a changed existence. Sorters' lives are not so different during passage from those of Searchers except for the importance Searchers place on the transformation theme. In both of these groups people had moved a long way from the original small towns they left as young marrieds—and sometimes they talk about this fact. For some Searchers, their goal becomes a special quest: to go down the road of life as a more "fully human" person with a greatly enlarged view of life and a newly found perspective about one's role in it. A number of Searcher subjects spoke of the fact that the pairings they finally made were the result of the many changes they made in their lives, not the cause of the changes, and this seemed to be the case. Other Searchers found that their lives came to involve going between several houses and several parts of the country fairly consistently; they had become cosmopolitan to a degree they never could have foreseen, when younger. Because of the extent to which they did seem to have different *kinds* of lives in mid-life, compared to their expectations in early adulthood, it appeared to be true (in whatever vocabulary they used to express it) that there had been a degree of change in their lives that amounted to transformation. They had changed, among other things, many of the rules by which they lived.

No long-passage subject thought any longer of mere restoration to life in traditional groups. Runners did not seem to want to be tied to any particular person. All long-passage subjects continued to think of traditional groups as the coercive, not nourishing groups of earlier life, and a fate to avoid. The dyadic couple is certainly a group, though Searchers seemed not to think of it in this way—and it was here that Searchers made a large investment. Nevertheless, Searcher pilgrimages looked rather solitary during and between partnerships, although they wanted life to be organized exactly as it had been during the course of searching.

It was somewhat surprising to me to find that long-passage men and women fit in and enjoy many kinds of group life in Establishment settings such as their professional and business circles; but the impact on them of this life is mediated by the care with which they maintain and protect their private lives. Searchers do not by any means relinquish all forms of traditional interaction. Their conscious, selective use of traditional social patterns is what is significant. Throughout their lives, Searchers never relied solely on traditional values; this was evident in their departures from small-town life, which they found confining and not sufficiently stimulating. One defined a small town as a place where "you can't get the *London Times* and everybody gossips and knows your business." They stay fairly close to cities, because they value access to such cultural advantages as museums and concerts, and they think of small towns as places where "nothing ever happens."

Therefore, after divorce, Searchers look to all manner of problem-solving ideas, all avenues they can locate for meeting their needs, not simply to traditional answers. This is because they believe they can find better alternatives or invent answers by being innovative. To many, the demands of public and private life are so contrastive that they must be handled in separate ways. By using ideas from the "new culture," rather than traditional notions about how, why, and with whom they should mate, they gradually build the new self-images that lead them to be surer of themselves than they might otherwise be.

Searchers eventually become the kinds of people that, since the divorce, they had begun to want to be. The new definitions that accompany and facilitate this development lead them to take an increasingly broader view of love and marriage. They make new interpretations of divorce, middle age, singlehood, and pairing that widen their opportunities and cast them in a much more positive light. While I do not fully understand all of the details of how this evaluative process works in reestablishing a new identity, it seems to me that the general process of redefinition enables people to construct useful and enhancing definitions of their postdivorce situations and appraisals of future options. They gradually come to a sense that they have more freedom of choice than they originally saw any reason to expect when the first marriage was ending. By this, I mean to make the point that they *perceive* their alternatives at mid-life as quite numerous because they weigh them from a perspective colored by the "new culture" that is at once radically different from and yet clearly consistent with much of their earlier lives, an aspect considered further in chapter 8. Searchers believe they deserve and can obtain, even to the point of personal transformation, the aftermaths they seek. One very direct means to this end that some utilize is to compartmentalize life. Their new hopes and plans are rooted in their new self-images and their pictures of themselves as "winners," but in another time and place, and on a new set of terms, their own.

For some of the Passionate Searchers I studied, trans- and intercontinental air travel became both a practical vehicle and a way of life. One woman said, "It really makes me nervous not to be catching a plane every so often." Thus, while flying literally furthered Searchers' experiences in mobility, it was also seen as a metaphor for the psychological and emotional exploration in their lives. Technology was making a global village out of the world. One subject observed, "I seem to have a Rolodex on my desk which lists international area codes and I am not positive when all of this happened."

Another subject had spent so much time abroad since her first marriage that she had friendship networks in many countries including Poland, and her home became a stopping-over place for these new male and female friends as well as *their* relatives and friends. Because the United States is for Europeans, a midpoint on the way to Mexico, South America, and Asia, her life became a series of ever-expanding concentric circles of more and more people, until she was familiar with the theater and politics of several other nations. She made innumerable visits to London on the way to Russia, until it became a second home to her. Other "bicoastals" shuttled back and forth from the East to West coasts so often that they read the *Los Angeles Times* and the *New York Times* along with their hometown papers. Others lived in the woods with their Mercedes, had the *Wall Street Journal* come with their mail, and kept up with property in many locations.

In other Searcher cases, people had broadened their views of life through other means. Although they did not travel so widely in a literal sense, they had greatly changed their patterns of thinking, extending, and enriching their inner lives. Some were extremely well-read and very well acquainted with other cultures, especially those of the Far East, and with their religious and philosophical traditions. On the west coast, the term,

Searchers and the Transformation Theme

"Eastern," probably now connotes Asia, not the eastern seaboard. One subject said, "This summer my friend will be in Istanbul with the Sufis, but I've decided not to go out, too." Another said, "I got a good tip from my friend who is abroad for part of every year: always travel with your dog, it's a basis for conversation." Another said, "My work has been very confining and I've not gotten back to Europe as soon as I expected recently. Now I realize I shall probably be going to Asia instead."

Among other subjects, I sometimes heard discussions or a reference to the "transformation of human consciousness." For some, becoming transformed meant learning how to live without having continually to make so many plans. These people were eager to be "open to experience" and they thought that one's attitudinal change might be as important and exciting a life development as any one specific event.

For some Searcher subjects, the once powerful "achievement" theme seemed to have become muted and to have reemerged in new evolutionary dress, as part of the transformation theme. This theme involves inner as well as outer life. Thus, among my subjects, I saw a change of focus from externals to the interior life, but also, many external manifestations of this shift. Searchers are people who tend to talk a lot about what they have *learned* since their twenties and thirties. By way of explanation, one woman said, "I have *learned* so much. About pain, for one thing. I learned that you can hang onto it, or you can *let go* of it."

There was a lot of self-acceptance in Searcher accounts. People who had once thought so much about "getting on," and "fitting in" seemed quietly assured and not trying so hard any longer.

A subject who was a male college professor said,

FRESH STARTS

The other day it struck me how very profound that children's ditty is. You know—about rowing your boat gently down the stream. Not "against the current," resisting what life brings, but down the current, going along with life. You know, whenever you find yourself resisting, *what* you are resisting is where your work is, where your lesson lies. And the line about "going merrily" realizing that "life is but a dream." I mean, of course I'm not saying that there isn't a reality—you have to keep going out for groceries; but on top of the reality are all the illusions, expectations, and judgments we put on it.

All the business about the evolution of consciousness is interesting. I don't like the metaphor about "growth," because it implies some people are ahead of others. I think in terms of awareness and taking away the veils with which life is covered. I was familiar with different states of consciousness because of experiences with drugs and Eastern philosophy, but, for years, I resisted spiritual ideas since I objected to anything that hinted of religion. But remember what Jung said, "Somewhere around your forties, if you haven't returned to your childhood religion, you must find another, or go crazy."

Recently I took a year off and spent five months sitting in a Zen temple, meditating, just looking at all the things going through my mind—all the absurdities and judgments about people, including myself. As soon as you see through the ego games you're playing and become aware of the ones that are causing you misery and suffering, the awareness lets you see the connections between the mental games you run on yourself and your bad experiences. These games are the defense mechanism parts of the ego by which you declare you are independent or autonomous—separate from God and other people, and can "do it your way" or "have my way."

It has changed the way I read the Bible. Phenomenology is another way to look at life and see how we have many roads to God. Satan is just the ego. Sin is our ideas of separateness from others and from God. Once you gain awareness, you learn to let go of negative judgments about yourself and about others. This is different from making choices. I don't mean that making judg-ments and making choices is the same. You have to make choices. But you can see that you must also give up some of your positive judgments; these also can be used to manipulate people and try to get your own way. Of course, we choose to close some doors and open others. But you can let go of trying to control everything and start to be less attached to the outcome, so you can *let life be.* You can't do anything about a lot of it anyway! Why not go along with it? Look at the mess we have made trying to control nature and conquer everyone. Why not go along with life being gentle to ourselves and each other?

In some instances such as the forgoing, New Age concepts provide people with a philosophy of life and other people with whom to share it, much as professional work can provide a life structure. Searchers tend to think they are a fortunate group in being able to move into new life arenas, enacting alternatives which once would have seemed too alien to them and which were never before so widely evident in "regular people" at mid-life. (People who made similar choices in earlier historical periods, such as George Sand, are still often dismissed as mys-tics or rebels.) Thus, for Searchers, as for most long-passage people, life is an exciting, great adventure.

Social trends are of tremendous significance to the conduct of Searcher transitions, much as they are of little moment to shorter passages. To the Sorters, Runners, and Searchers, a fundamental gain from divorce is the right to seek the freedom to radically change their life-styles and themselves. Quite apart from the possibility that some of their reports may have been unduly self-congratulatory, subjects' claims to having achieved some of their goals of self-actualization (or some measure of an evolved consciousness) were taken seriously in my research, because they spoke of something very real to them. As for

FRESH STARTS

Searcher pairings, while nonconventional experimental pair bonding is hardly a new social phenomenon, these men and women were neither young nor Bohemian and they knew it was a new adventure *for them.*

8

Looking Ahead

THIS BOOK'S portrayal of the eight variations in adaptation to mid-life divorce shows that the primary organizing principle of each kind of passage lies in an individual's perceptions of his or her needs and life chances, in the light of that person's values. Values mirror our beliefs about how life works and what counts. For the Sorters and the Searchers, who weighed and pondered the worth of their entire value system over a long period of time, doing this during a loosely structured, long transition resulted in substantial changes in their perspectives on life and love. However, for all of the men and women in my study, gaining some measure of the "good life" was a benefit in many ways. For one thing, once some of an individual's goals are accomplished, that person can better apprise the meaning of such accomplishment, in the last analysis. One of my subjects spoke about that fact in this manner,

When I was young, and "hungry," and hopeful, I had a lot of false values. There were so many things and experiences that I wanted, or else, I thought the possession of them would solve everything. Now I'm older, wiser, sweeter, not so greedy. Isn't that

257

process part of growing up? We keep changing, refining our experience and zeroing in on what works for us, as we go along. Until I got half of what I'd first wanted, I really couldn't freely choose anything. You can't very well renounce something you can't have, for instance. What I mean is, when more things become possible, fewer things are necessary, or you know what *is* truly essential.

Some people found that gaining affluence through occupational achievement meant less to them than they had expected it would, or that, in themselves, achievement and affluence were not enough. The meanings of affluence, then, to look at a decisive factor in their lives, had been put to the test over time. Some people simply took affluence for granted as a valued "given" which greatly adds to life's pleasures and is a major foundation for a strong self-concept. But to other people, status considerations later proved a bit spurious, inflated, or simply inadequate.

Among the experiences that mobility and a high degree of affluence (compared to that of one's family of origin) gave to my Sorter and Searcher subjects was watching their children throughout both the 1960s and the 1970s responding to questions about values in the context of their having had relatively affluent childhoods. By the early 1980s, many a former student protester had become an adult whose occupational security was rooted in the Establishment. Other young adult children had partially dropped out for good, in that they had built lives that involved settling down somewhat out of the mainstream. Either way, watching this generation react to and rework the meanings of affluence was a crucial experience for some parents. In many other ways, too, the 1960s proved to have been a watershed decade. One woman said,

> At the end of the sixties, my generation was irrevocably divided among itself. Some of us were on one side of the great cultural

divide, and some of us were on the other. There was a finality to it, like being on different sides of a great glass door. We can see and hear each other, but we don't touch each other's lives much anymore, because we have such contradictory views about the meanings of everything that matters: money, sex, love, and time.

It is now clear that after mid-life divorce, or during middle adulthood itself, there exists a whole range of possibilities that one can explore, which people are increasingly *prepared* to explore. Some people greet this fact eagerly, just as some people are not very interested in it. But, much as anyone in the postdivorce passage might feel in need of a guidebook, all formerly marrieds must invent their own passages out of their own (possibly evolving) values. I hope this book will serve to guide some men and women to making their own choices with a great deal of conviction, understanding that no one else can know as well as each person does what values are the most important.

Part of my motive for writing this book was my original puzzlement over the fact that while it seemed to me that people do surmount the trauma of a mid-life divorce, little had been published showing by what means anyone manages to do so. There was no clear picture of the "how" or "why" anywhere, and I wanted to discover the patterns of behavior and the attitudes that led people to a successful outcome, in order to report them. If you are yourself in passage, I hope my picture of what I learned provides you with an appreciation of the richness of the options that abound as well as a sense of how satisfying a passage outcome can be, if it is grounded in your identity, both in terms of who you once "were" and who you "became." The eight approaches to passage reveal not only the great diversity in people's responses to and interpretation of the mid-life divorce event, but also show how differently people look at various important life questions and how valuable each personal perspective is to the person holding it. And with respect to the middle adult years, and apart from considerations of the occupational career, the satisfactions of personal life can be greatly expanded whether or not one's subsequent decisions confirm or alter one's early, previous life pattern. Increasingly, among our well-educated, and sometimes divorced population, certain newly available life patterns which are part of the adult development story are emerging. But before I look at some of these hints of things to come, I would like to comment further on points that I have not yet fully elaborated.

The Issue of Control

One issue I have not yet closely examined in this book casts more light on the highly personal ways people view passage and attain their goals. This issue is the perspective with which a person views "control." Examining it directly also helps me to summarize and compare the passage subgroups. For example, some people, such as the Courters, realize at a passage's onset that *being in control* is important to them. Tightly controlling what happens next seems to work for them, and they learn to rely on this mechanism.

But long-passage people feel that having had a tightly run life in their first marriages seemed to work out to having overcontrolled, stifled existences. For the Sorters and the Searchers, furthermore, having a tight rein over themselves during passage could extinguish rather than enlarge the spirit. These people are therefore willing to set out into the transition without timing, direction, or even a very clearly enunciated goal well determined in advance. In the case of Searchers, the wish to avoid tying down anything but the essential passage-management tasks (for instance, regarding one's work) leads them to devote a great deal of time to letting a passage unfold.

All mid-life passages are replete with opportunities for disjuncture, delays, reversals, and reassessments. But attitudes toward "the unexpected" vary greatly and seem to depend on the extent to which a person is disposed to define "the unexpected" as *potentially,* the start of a good new direction. The Immediate (Planned) Remarriers take a very dim view of the unexpected, for good reasons; whereas the Searchers try to open up passage in order to "ride the wave" of an increasingly rich, multidimensional passage crammed with strange and often, lovely experiences. The "lovely experiences" are paid for, however, by the Searchers' ability to tolerate irresolution, to handle disappointment, and to enjoy a taste of risk-taking, seeing the latter as an intriguing, "long shot" adventure. The men and women in brief and mid-length passages, in contrast, tend to be cautious people who shepherd their resources, have clear aims, and play their cards "close to their chests." Many long-passage people are, by comparison, somewhat extravagant spenders who are ready to expend themselves.

In brief passages, being in control involves thoughtful attention to timing and disclosure, because these factors are decisive for outcome. For instance, the Immediate (Planned) Remarriers admit few others to their confidence because they seek the highest degree of control. The conspiracy to rewed is hidden until the last possible moment in order to leave intact the uninformed spouse's customary web of expectations. No Immediate (Planned) Remarrier wants to have to deal with a spouse who stumbles onto the news, especially in states with rigid divorce laws. Theirs is an adversary approach to divorce, but one that succeeds. Pandemonium can follow on such a crisis as the two (formerly unaware) spouses of each being put in touch with each other or getting in touch with each other, to compare notes on the pair of lovers. No brief-passage subject wanted to play the game of life in a form that included "wild cards," that is, unpredictability. The following observation is by an Immediate (Planned) Remarrier's son:

> Mother wasn't interested in being single. She knew that right from the start. I knew she was not very happy with Dad, but I am sure she would never have left him without being sure of Leo.

This instrumental view of passage would go contrary to the perspectives from which a Searcher would define the purpose of transition. If definitions are to "work" for people, they must be anchored in each person's definitions, personal history, and present sense of what it all means. For instance, the Searchers often see a moral dimension to passage. For them, leaving a mate *only* after the next mate is located (and found to be receptive to one) would be considered unsatisfactorily expeditious and not sufficiently "open," whereas doing so is an acceptable and sensible approach for the Immediate (Planned) Remarriers. One Searcher subject discussed the gains she felt had accrued to her from getting her divorce without locating and advising a former lover of the fact that she was changing her life, partially in response to meeting him and falling in love with him:

> For eighteen months, I didn't see the man to whom I am now partnered. It was a lonely time. My lover wanted to try a trial reconciliation with his wife who had withdrawn her divorce suit against him on hearing of our interest in each other. I felt I needed more experience of being entirely responsible for myself. Often it was a happy time for me. I dated, but I was faithful to him, even though I wasn't positive we would resume. I knew that he knew

that I would like to. I thought that if I contacted him about my divorce, he would not have so free a chance to make up his own mind. My therapist said, "If he wants to find you, he will."

I went on with my work and got my divorce quietly. I found many things to enjoy. I very much enjoyed the feeling of self-respect I had. A friend said, "Just let it happen. If it's supposed to, it will." The idea of just letting *anything* happen was alien to me at first, but they seemed to be saying "Trust life!" Anyway, when he did decide to find me, I had made many good changes in my life. I was a stronger person. It was quite a celebration when we got together.

Searchers think that it is not only impossible to control all aspects of a passage, it is also undesirable. If a passage is highly controlled, it is not the "right kind" for them. For one thing, it would not fit into their "new culture" ideas about "becoming a new person." Thus, the Searchers seek to create a passage that evolves naturally, in keeping with the changes in their own attitudes and behavior.

While earlier exiting people find that careful control of the transition enables them to secure desired outcomes, the Searchers view passage metaphorically as an open-ended treasure hunt. They fight to increase the chance of unexpected developments leading to enhanced options until they have found a partner to whom they can make a full and permanent commitment. They approach life at one moment like a kid looking for the prize in a box of Cracker Jacks, and the next, like a child who ponders a slice of orange a long time before eating it.

Earlier exiters work to close off interruptions, some of which might have turned into options, because they know what they want. They are like hardheaded shoppers. The brief- and mid-length-passage subjects I studied bargained well. The degree of security they obtained in the transition by managing their passages fairly conservatively, they paid for by accepting goals that were narrower in scope than those of Searchers. In the final analysis, differences in approach are grounded in a person's perceptions of what life is all about. They are very much a part of one's personal style and philosophy. One woman subject said,

> I suppose my life has looked disrupted and provisional to some of my friends since my marriage to a successful man ended, and my future is still somewhat unknown. But I almost never feel ashamed anymore, and I do not have to pretend about hardly anything, not anything important. I am sometimes flustered, but on the whole, I am very happy.

These differences in perspectives are also reflected in the nature of the questions men and women put to themselves about how well their passages are going. These differ substantially. In order for me to make any sense out of what subjects were doing and *why* they were doing it, it was necessary for me to first seek out and understand the meanings each of them attached to various things going on in their lives. There is no hierarchy of purposes or values from which to choose, but rather, a repertoire of adaptive modes (the "reasons of one's own heart") from among which to select a course appropriate to the rest of one's life.

Certain themes woven into one person's account of passage may be absent from another's. Tracing the handling of the issue of control revealed that, when similarly colored threads are present in two types of passage, they may be woven into quite distinct patterns. A unique pathway can lead a person into a specific course and an aftermath hand-tailored to that individual. The factor of control is an easy way to demonstrate that each formerly married person holds many more cards from the start of passage than are usually seen or than most people suspect they hold. And the way each person chooses to play his or her hand may be more of an open question than is at first apparent. Ofttimes, everything one needs, one already has, although this may not be immediately evident. As I watched long-passage subjects evading or going out to meet opportunities, I often thought that, for them, passage mainly involved their growing realization of their assets and increasing appreciation of them. One commented,

> What I now see primarily as my "good points" are not my professional success or my bank account, but the inner qualities I am slowly but steadily developing. I assume now that they will continue to be acknowledged and valued by others and that this is an excellent basis for having a satisfactory life.

For instance, maintaining control of the course of passage is seen as critical by the Graduates, whose nightmares center on finding themselves going down the aisle again, before they wake up; but Immediate (Planned) Remarriers have nightmares about their weddings being *halted* on the way down the aisle. Graduates use disclosure of a refusal to pair as a means to scare off potential wooers, however, in all the subgroups, the factor of disclosure is employed to the same end: having the power to influence outcome. Searchers strive for the capacity to be open "transparent" people, trusting that they will then attract "good people" who seek a partner in their kind of a person. Thus, people in both Graduate (solo) and pairing modes (planning repartnering) use disclosure to enhance their aims, even though their ends differ. Graduates want to stabilize into singlehood and Remarriers to normalize into remarriage, while for Searchers, the stable and "normal" condition is, first of all, an inner state. Thus, similar means can be shrewdly utilized to achieve ends that differ enormously and are based on wildly dissimilar definitions of one's situation.

If Graduates are compared to Searchers even more closely, it is not the issue of *pairing* that finally and fundamentally distinguishes them. It is their attitudes toward control. The Graduates make a point of not even considering pairing, because they reject what Searchers accept and define as positive: that being partnered is equivalent to being less in control, from both groups' perspectives. Even "looking" or being at all open to pairing means that one is less able to predict tomorrow, to say nothing of "tonight." It is not that one category of men and women understand this fact, while the other does not see it. Rather, they disagree on the value or *meaning* of unpredictability. Women Graduates often address this issue squarely:

> I look at my friend, Blanche, who lives in New Hampshire. She is such a nice person! Let me read you part of her last letter. Here— the part about her bumping into a man friend when walking over to the common. She says, "He hadn't called me lately. We chatted a moment about nothing much. I found myself flirting with him. He seemed quite pleased with the encounter, so I asked him to dinner and he accepted. I guess our scenario is still running."
>
> Doesn't she have a wonderful sense of humor! She must be fifty-five, but she has a great approach to life! She's always been warm, untidy, and humorous. I've never had that kind of joie de vivre. I budget ahead, pay each bill as it arrives, and have to have everything tied down in advance.
>
> I'd love to, what do they call it, "hang loose," but I'm not cut out for it. Look at my desk, how organized it is. I just couldn't trust men again. I couldn't go through all the courtship stuff. Not in middle age! I'm a devout coward! Don't laugh; I mean it. But I love to listen to the women at the office and to get Blanche's news. What soap operas!

Control is an important property of passage for Comfortable Courters. While the Graduates use disclosure to prevent pairing ideas on the part of others, the Courters use disclosure to recruit prospects and sponsors. However, both disclose to friends in order to get their cooperation in facilitating their goals, to help them get more control over passage, in other words. Both the Courters and the Graduates use a passage as preparation for retirement; but the Graduates believe that for this time of life to be "stable" and "safe," it must be partnerless. Otherwise, it would not be nearly so controllable. With relatives to sustain them in old age, they do not need a partner; they have an entire family with members from several generations, and they view this as much more reliable an arrangement than remarriage. One woman Graduate talked about passing up a man she liked a lot:

> It would be nice to have a companion, but as I said, I'm not used to having to account to anyone for anything. The man I was most tempted to marry, I finally introduced to my cousin. She's a fine person. Most of her energy had gone into caring for her father until her late forties, and she had never married. I'd been married twice (once widowed and once, divorced). They have had an excellent marriage. The three of us are good friends, and they looked after my son when I was away and he got into some difficulties at college. They are planning their retirement in Mexico and it will not involve having as much money as they had thought. I have to put in only four more years at the institute and then I can start traveling almost full time. I wouldn't want to be shut up in some little town or have to consider someone else's wishes.

Brief-passage subjects were very rightly concerned with the question of control, *given their objectives.* "Transition to *what?*" is always a matter to ponder after a divorce, but it was an easy question for people who chose brief passages. They knew what they wanted. Partly, they sought to mute, if not completely subdue the transitional nature of passage. The Courters remarried so quickly, in fact, that it was hard for me to accept the fact that a major variant of passage had been uncovered. Their rapid remarriages seemed to me fortuitous or accidental, rather than carefully constructed. But when I checked their accounts, I found them to be faithful to the facts. They did effect remarriage promptly, often within two days of the final decree, to someone they did not know well when the divorce papers were filed, and they managed to do this by courting seriously (sometimes just during litigation) with a single-minded pursuit of this goal. The Courters control a number of dimensions of passage with the sagacity of entrepreneurs whom they do not otherwise resemble, and their *single-mindedness* is the cement that holds their passages together and leads to an early and satisfactory termination.

The Courters exploit disclosure to the hilt with enormous skill. They are virtually prepared to take out an ad on a billboard describing their virtues. In fact, one Courter male lived in a city where another Courter paid for an ad in which he appeared in a short film in local theaters, pleading his own case as a potential mate, and giving his telephone number. Also, Courters are exceedingly clever both at retaining the interests of a prospect, without offering a commitment themselves, and in arranging their other roles so as to feed directly into the partner hunt. One junior high school teacher used his students as agents. A mother I encountered in fieldwork had two daughters at a local junior high school whose teacher noticed the mother at a school play. He got the daughters to introduce him to her and to say, "You'd make a good pair." The mother agreed with the evaluation eventually, and the man thus remained on the scene to become a stepfather.

All brief- and mid-length-passage subjects tried to control the complexity of passage. Their motto was "Keep it simple!" At first, I checked their statements with great reluctance to accept them at face value. With long-passage subjects so full of enthusiasm for change and so frequently talking about it, in themselves, in their plans, in their ideas about transition, and in partners, I was skeptical about other subjects' ability to stick to their original plans to exit early for ends chosen so quickly. Thus, for a long time, I reinterviewed many people constantly, waiting for a "crack" in the façades of their intentions to manifest itself, until their lack of interest in switching direction or making personal changes in themselves was so well documented as to remain unequivocal. I also did the same with men in my life who appeared interested in exploring partner possibilities with me as a woman, rather than just with me as a researcher. Of these, I gradually learned, that despite all nonverbal clues to the contrary, some men begin passage with a longing for but virtual horror of commitment and never choose to undertake the work (perhaps, in therapy) of trying to understand whether or not it is unconscious fears that propel them away from an outcome to which they instinctively are drawn, while others bite the bullet and forge ahead despite their fears.

The accounts of all earlier exiting subjects displayed a very clear distaste for the unexpected. In addition, these men and women are quite realistic about either preventing the development of interruptions (such as "allowing" oneself to become really interested in someone with characteristics that depart from their plans) or recognizing and "saving" a stalled passage, when opting out suits them better than struggling further. Comfortably courting to a satisfactory outcome demands the systematic exploitation of extensive social networks. Without them, recruiting and hanging onto a prospect is quite likely not to be amenable to control. This Courter's passage was in jeopardy, but he knew why:

It's hard to find a wife when the job market's so unstable. Now I consult, so I often change jobs. With two very late children still in high school, I can't very well take work in New Zealand or Saudi Arabia. Most of my work is for Babcock-Wilcox. It's short-term and right down my alley. I like not having changed their schools, but it's a pretty stodgy suburb. And I'm going crazy taking care of them. Mostly, I switch projects so often, I don't get acquainted. You know, the invitations. And the salary's not what it might be.

The Steadies organize passage on the basis of traditional norms. Taking *family* responsibilities as seriously as they do is a factor that mitigates against an innovative or experimental transition. Steadies want to control the *quality* of the outcome as much as the kind. Making a "good" remarriage means one good for everyone as members of a solidly reconstituted familial unit. They care very much about their children's reactions to a prospect, and they are apprehensive about making misjudgments, to the same degree that Searchers expect to make some. They want a minimum of "unpleasant surprises" now or later on. In addition, they are sensitive to their neighbors' and relatives' expectations and approval. The key indicator to this is the refusal to live together openly, or at all, before a wedding. Flouting neighborhood values or rejecting family traditions does not appeal to them and would not work for them. A woman who went Steady to a stable exit described the feelings of a number of people to whom the remarriage was very important:

Matt and I had gone together for two years, when he popped the question one night when we were out to dinner. I was *so* uncomfortable about it, and *he* was so uncomfortable. It just broke up the evening! He took me home, and then he went home. The following day he came by and we just looked at one another. Then I said, "Who are you? I don't want to hear any more talk like that! Now, we're just going to *forget* it!"

It was another six months before he brought it up again. He said something like, "October 14th would be a pretty good day to get married on"; and I looked at the calendar, and said, "No, the 15th's better." And that was that!

There was no big announcement with the children either. But several days before the wedding, he moved his furniture in, because he didn't have anywhere to stay. So he slept on the couch in the family room. The kids were really prudish about it—they kept checking to see if he was *staying* there! There was never any idea of its being any other way until after the wedding.

Thus, brief- and mid-length-passage subjects used practical solutions that expressed their solid middle-class views. They agreed on the *meanings* of middle age. It was a time to be "sensible." Part of this definition was the belief that the mid-life stage should serve as preparation for launching oneself into a successful old age; in other words, *controlling* far into the future.

The Question of Meaning

Brief and mid-length passages were not chosen by subjects unaware of the social and cultural changes filtering throughout much of society. These people simply did not identify with those developments or with the people who found them interesting and helpful. New Age thinking was foreign to them and rarely appeared even to arouse their curiosity. Curiosity was the "juice" of life for many long-passage subjects. But when brief- and mid-length-passage subjects said "our generation," they meant people who used to dance to the music of Glenn Miller, but who no longer did much dancing.

The goals of the Courters and the Steadies alike was to control for a sensible, uneventful remarriage. To them, it was reassuring to move ahead to the goal on a well-worn, familiar path. One subject discussed this:

> I was surprised to be so comfortable with my second husband, especially when we weren't kidding ourselves that we were terribly in love or anything. It was just *comfortable!* One of my friends said, "Stop worrying about what you've done! What's *wrong* with being *comfortable?*"
>
> It's funny how the little things added up.
>
> Like the family dinner hour, for example. Albert was *always* home from the office on time. Having dinner on schedule was important to him. He made the children aware of his expectations about that. He was so dependable and happy as a stepfather. The children were reassured, too. If Peter didn't pull out my chair, he'd say, "What's the matter with this crowd? Your mother is the beautiful woman I love! Peter, you get the honor of seating her! Jump!" Then he'd kid about the food—"Look at these gorgeous mashed potatoes! What am I supposed to serve them with?" Ginny would rush to the kitchen for a spoon. It was as all-American as a Norman Rockwell cover. It took me, all in all, about three years to get accustomed to being *comfortable.*

At the time of this chapter's writing, all early and mid-length exiters interviewed in depth repeatedly in the case studies (as well as those available in similar categories with whom I had less consistent communication) were once more contacted. Not one of those people had changed place of residence, jobs, partners, or life-styles. They all described themselves as "still settled in." This fact confirmed what came to be my expectations for them, because I learned a lot about them in the intervening years.

In contrast to the early exiters, change is a veritable leitmotif for all long-passage men and women. Their transitions are individualistic, idiosyncratic, and, in many respects, unstable. To my mind, the Runner males are the most conventional among these people, despite their nonconforming sexual lives, but I would like to fill out the picture of Sorters and Searchers to show the connections between their passages and their earlier if somewhat submerged interests. These links were strengthened or consolidated during the 1960s and 1970s so that, at the time of passage, their lives exhibited a congruence that encompassed more than their aspirations and current affluence. This fact became increasingly apparent in the course of my study, and as it did, I paid more attention to it.

In the first marriage (or even before it), Sorter and Searcher men and women were interested in social change and often social justice, although in some cases, this concern for social reform developed slowly and partially, from things that happened to them in the regular course of existence. However, it was an important *tendency* that began fairly early in life and was manifested in varying degrees in their subsequent attraction to the cultural transformation that followed the sixties, including conservationist issues, the human potential movement, and New Ethic ideals. These kinds of interests (or the basis for them) were newly stirred in the 1960s and deepened in the 1970s. This had a significant influence on their largely nonconformist private lives and on the extent to which financial success became secondary to the importance they put on the personal realm.

For instance, they had approved of or supported various artistic and political movements of the 1960s and began to take active roles in the antiwar protest which brought them more in touch with others of like mind, much as the children of some of them became each others' (or their) comrades. Some met peers through their children's circles of acquaintanceship or the nucleus of people active in a particular cause; and these circles often involved people of different ages interacting as peers. A few of my long-passage subjects had already gotten to know one another through such networks, some time ago, and somewhat serendipitously. Two of my research subjects, for example, came to be involved with student activists from Chicago, Berkeley, and Columbia, since, at the time, the latter were their students or friends; and subjects became privy to their policy deliberations and accustomed to their redefinitions of social reality. The mutuality of their interests (particularly in opposing many policies of the Johnson and Nixon administrations) helped to generate friendships that crossed traditional social boundaries. However, by and large, the Runners were apolitical. But among the Sorters and the Searchers were a number of people who had taken at least a minor part in the formulation and articulation of a number of ideological positions promulgated in the sixties. One result of this was that some men and women were more comfortable with the views of people junior to them in other ways, or otherwise not seen as "normal" peers, than with the people in their own age groups. There were a substantial number of these people for whom this type of social realignment simply took place indirectly, rendering age or status less relevant to them as a sorting mechanism in subsequent interaction, such as pairing interests. Therefore, as a social phenomenon, what sociologists call "age-grading" became less decisive for their associations and their self-definitions than would otherwise have been the case; and their later interest in a New Age society or community cannot be seen as a distinct departure from their earlier lives.

For varying lengths of time, and in varying *combinations*, they had been active as pacifists, feminists, radical theorists, writers of social or literary criticism, group-work leaders (one had learned leadership techniques originally through his corporation and the National Association of Manufacturers, an early sponsor of the Bethel, Maine, training group), and seekers.

Looking Ahead

They had been longtime members of the American Civil Liberties Union (ACLU), worked for integration in Southern cities of their residence, campaigned for Eugene McCarthy, or raised money for the farmworkers in California. One had researched legal issues for the integration movement, one had contributed to policy analyses on prison reform, and one had been the first woman to sit on a jury in her particular Southern state. Several had also supported the community mental health movement, both as professionals and in their roles as private citizens. One had lived in the first racially integrated suburban housing development in his part of the country; one had traveled with a well known rock band; and one had followed black music, especially jazz as it evolved in the Chicago area, from his college days.

One prefaced his first marriage (into an aristocratic Dutch family) with a living-together arrangement when he and his eventual bride, who considered themselves Socialists, were graduate students in Europe. Several subjects came from families that had been active in the labor movement at an earlier time, and the grandmother of one was an intimate of Emma Goldman. One had debated leaving a corporate career to enter a Protestant seminary (to study for the ministry); another published poetry and studied music; another taught abroad; and one had classical musicians for parents. One had gone to Africa before this was common; two had made original contributions in the world of arts and crafts; one began a very successful firm; another implemented a Peace Corps program.

In many ways, Sorters and Searchers had been marginal people socially or men and women who had "compartmentalized" their lives relatively early in their first marriage. Two had been involved in the founding of a church; two were the children of a Jew who had "passed as non-Jewish" (a fact they learned of in early adulthood); and one was the child of parents

275

who changed careers in mid-life, leaving the corporate world to become art dealers in a cooperative husband-wife effort. Another had an abolitionist ancestor; and the family of still another had connections to the Zionist movement in Israel. One person had been named for a father of the Russian revolution; another wrote a play produced in a little-theater setting. Several had founded Women's Centers or bureaus for the retraining of women or lobbied for Displaced Homemakers' legislation. One had founded a chapter of Amnesty International; one learned before her mother's death that her birth had been preceeded by a pregnancy that her parents had chosen to terminate by abortion because they did not "feel ready for parenthood"; and several had been raised by freethinkers who did not so term themselves. Most of them were products of interfaith marriages and/or the children of immigrants. A majority of the subjects considered their parents to be unhappily married, most of them regarding the parental marriage as lackluster at best, continuing only because of a lack of alternatives.

At present, a number of these multiple-degree holders earn their livings with their hands. (Of these, one has a deep love for and wide knowledge of American history, and once taught in a federal penitentiary.) Another founded a children's library and recorded books for the blind. One man's company put a Lear jet and pilot at his disposal; he had worked his way through college as a hod carrier. Another, who went on to study abroad and "live very well," went to college carrying a brown paper bag containing a pair of pajamas—and got there by bus.

Two subjects went on religious retreats as earnest young parents. A woman who trained as a labor organizer became a stockbroker, and had been raised in a trailer. A woman who had spent a year in Grenoble and repeatedly returned to the Côte d'Azur had once taken in roomers. Another woman had started out watching other women's children and scrubbing their floors.

Several knew the political process as best friends of a candidate or as staffers. A large number of them had long been interested in human rights. Many had marched for the rights of homosexuals or in peace rallies, or taught in Vietnam Day teach-ins. Two were "purged" from their college faculties. One had been hospitalized during a breakdown; two more had to do their's "on their own." One woman had taught in an inner-city ghetto before she was twenty. Another had been raped. One woman had been ashamed of a mother who kept insisting "It's as easy to fall in love with a rich man as a poor man" and had chosen the latter, who eventually gave her a life of luxury. One woman had always been told to wear "her best underwear on a trip" in case of a "car crash," and sometimes she later went without any at all.

However, one subject had had divorced grandparents, and *only one other was the child of a divorce.* Thus, the majority of long-passage subjects came from intact homes and thought their parents quite unhappily married and staying together from convention and a lack of courage or other opportunities. In most cases, people had neither a firsthand knowledge of a happy marital pairing nor of what they considered to be effective parenting techniques. Their childhood homes had been full of conflict, resignation, or formality, and sometimes, ill health.

Therefore, these men and women had lived in, but at the same time, apart from the mainstream. They continued to consider themselves "professionals" after divorce to a much greater extent than did earlier exiting people. They thought of themselves as trailblazers only to a modest degree, and they had lived ostensibly conventional lives during their first marriage. Just before, or some time after the divorce, they began to take their credentials for granted, and their professional roles became secondary to their personal roles. While they still enjoyed their work, they no longer identified with it so strongly. Professionalism, as a concept and as a way of life, was being questioned by many, but not all of them. Some also questioned the institutions in which one was a "professional"; however, Searcher women who compartmentalized life the most strictly did not. One woman said she thought "people were more important than institutions" in discussing a divorce she had effected which greatly upset her family.

In all long-passage accounts there was a story about a turning point, which marked a person's turning away from occupational commitments in order to make more frequent or more complete investments in personal life. Often this meant taking a leave of absence, sometimes without salary, or abandoning some part of a career role. Men gradually moved away from always viewing their work roles as the core of their identities. Some women switched direction occupationally or began to lay plans for taking some time out, as this one did:

> Now that I have a promotion which will give me a chance to manage a production function for my company, I bought myself some expensive silk underwear. I didn't even know Dior made matching sets; I bought three! I also told my new boss that I plan to take a leave of absence next year.

One woman became more demanding of the men in her life:

> I'm looking around for a new man. I don't see John anymore. The physicist I was spending so much time with told me that a woman who had been his lover had just come back from Europe. He planned to divide his time between us. Apparently it was alright with her, but I explained to him that it wasn't with me. But I'd like to go on having him for a friend. We see each other once or twice a week. I am not interested in just affairs anymore.

Looking Ahead

It's time for me to pay more attention to taking care of myself.

Another subject said,

It's interesting that the alternative Olympics are canceled. I think the Berkeley City Council is right. We live in the most highly politicized community in the United States, and with a protest expected, it'd be more trouble than it's worth to us. Someone pointed out that black athletes wouldn't attend, because, in the ghetto ten miles away, infant mortality rates are three to one for black versus white babies. That's true—and *it's important.*

If I were still teaching, I'd talk about that. But I have a different way of looking at the world. Let's run it down! I like being able to set my own schedule. I am not a case of *teaching* burnout; I really got burned out with the *academy,* as a place. Now I want work which attracts me, as the academy no longer does.

A number of other subjects became more demanding of themselves. One man said,

I am learning not to be as afraid as I was, and hence, I don't opt out for a "safe" course so often or someone easy to get along with and pliable who offers mainly security, as readily as I once did. In fact, I'm back in therapy to complete some unfinished work.

And, a woman observed,

I am less attached to the outcome in a love relationship, although more ready to fight openly for the possibilities I see in one. I am glad to initially explore possibilities with fewer early guarantees and less defensive if this openness to life is not seen by a man for no more and no less than it is. I think this a great improvement, since I can now gently let go of an admirer who is more alarmed than pleased about what is starting to transpire between us. I can accept it more gracefully, in other words, than I once could. I have learned that it is much better to let whatever is inside of the other person just well up unmistakably with a great deal of force than to try to repress signs that our relationship is bringing up emotional conflicts. I also have learned how to "stand by" a man who is testing me to see if I actually mean that I can and will respect my commitment to him despite the fact that he is subjecting me to a lot of tests. Generally, there are important reasons for his doing so, and to keep the door open between us, I feel I must understand rather than fault him for it. At the same time, I can let go, when it seems appropriate or he asks me to, with less self-doubt and with no need to hurt him in parting.

Long passages are complex. In the case of Runners, it is because they are so active socially. They go out a great deal, and they have many friends. Since they tend to have a succession of sexual partners and a great deal of casual sex, I wondered about how they handled the possibility of herpes or other venereal infections, but I was too polite to ask such a question. It is, however, one that tends to worry the Sorters and Searchers. Runners go through a series of people and a series of affairs rapidly. In the case of Runner women, they strictly compartmentalize their professional and private lives. I called these people Runners in Place because they don't go anyplace, so to speak. They neither appear to seek many changes nor to make changes, except substitutions of sexual partners. Runners are busy, attractive people, and I predict you already know and like some if you are a city resident, whether or not you recognize them as such.

Sorters are busy people, but they are less glamorous and a bit more "down home" than Runners. In general, they have lower incomes, but this is not always true. They are not so apt to be found driving Alfas loaded with expensive cameras, the latest in tennis rackets, and a case of the most expensive wines. Nonetheless, Sorters have a good time, too. They are rarely "between relationships" for any length of time. (Sometimes there seems to be a waiting list of prospects.) Sorters tend not to get very unstrung over a breakup, compared to Searchers, who may temporarily appear to be about to "go around the bend." As you know, Runners don't go through breakups since they do not attempt to pair, even briefly. The purpose of not pairing may, of course, be to avoid breakups.

Runners are not very impressed with psychotherapy, but most Sorters use psychotherapy at least once. The Searchers tend to use a therapist or a therapy group in an intermittent, ongoing way. It is common for a Searcher, whose Searcher pal expresses great distress, to suggest "Why don't you give your therapist a call and go in to talk it over?" Searchers regard this sort of thing as "preventative medicine," quite as much as it once was remedial. Most Searcher men and women call upon a therapist to help them get through the divorce or make faster progress after it. Both the Sorters and the Searchers, but especially the latter, put a lot of time, effort, and thought into what they call "my personal trip." One spoke about his efforts:

> Since my life has changed, I am no longer anxious as much of the time. I do miss some of the old "bennies" from the old life-style, like the money I had then. But I've been able to do a fair amount of "self-work."

This is a typical theme running through Sorter and Searcher accounts, "I've done a lot of work to change *me.*"

While long passages are complex, the Running passage is the least complicated, although it is by far the busiest. Not wanting to pair saves Runners as many complications as they intend it to save, and their added time goes right back into more running, more dinners out, more weekend travel and parties, and more sports. The Sorters and Searchers spend an inordinate amount of time on prospective partnerships; and, many of these love affairs fail. Unlike the Courters, who want closure on pairing and push ahead to it with great success, Sorters and Searchers compulsively examine every aspect of a tentative partnership.

Talking together is a major feature of a Searcher pairing. Since a Searcher's partner is apt to be another Searcher, each can undertake a (romantic) life review with the expectation of the tactful interpretative input of the other person—until a storm brews and breaks out in a quarrel. One Searcher woman said,

> I waited four years for him to stop calling me the same kind of woman his former wife was—when he got mad. It finally happened, and I wasn't ready for it, nor for the tag line he added, "You're not *anything* like Martha; you're the *least* powerful woman I've ever been with." Since I think all of his other women except me have been battle-axes, I just said, "Thank you."

Because Searchers tend to be very wary of conventional marriage, they need to be able to settle into a partnership a bit, while still being able to consider it provisional. Sorters tend to let a relationship develop or fail, but Searchers think that "things can be worked out." If the partner doesn't believe this also, a Searcher might as well prepare to write that person off as a "treasured former intimate," on the spot. However, as a concept, permanence is not taken as essential to life by either Sorters or Searchers. A common remark of both is, "We have no expectations for this partnership." Partnerships, like passages, are also viewed by both groups as ends in themselves whatever their durability, and they are valued for the lesson they provided or the delights they once brought. Most Searchers expect to pair permanently but only after they deserve this goal (that is, they have earned the right to it by learning to understand themselves and to interact successfully). One woman Searcher described her tentative love relationship:

Looking Ahead

We have talked and talked throughout our relationship. Sometimes we have thought we talked too much. We don't have any plans. We have been together for several years now. The fact that we are not striving for marriage or for "marriage when we have accomplished this or that"—seems to free us up to be open. I had been married for a total of twenty-five years before this, but I never felt free to be "open."

Although it forecloses on a quick repartnering, Sorters structure their pairings loosely so they will not resemble traditional marriages. For Searchers, too, both partners usually think that the point of pairing is to enjoy its warmth, without finding a partnership coercive, artificial, or constraining—in short, duty bound. If people experience a pairing in this way, they tend to leave it. Thus, the first marriage (if not their parents' marriage) remains a reference point for these men and women for a longer time and to a greater extent than they seem to recognize. An additional factor is that a specific aspect of a new pairing often reflects a significant change related to "the times," such as the woman's now being a full-fledged professional.

Whether or not these pairings result in legal marriages, they display certain modern characteristics, not the least of which is a division of labor based on egalitarian convictions as well as convenience. Tasks are assumed or assigned on the basis of such criteria as, "Who is free to do it?" or "Who likes this kind of task?" or "Who hasn't washed dishes lately?" Another criterion is "Who is in a crisis and needs a hand?" For many couples, lowering standards for keeping house is a means to save on energy output.

Another means toward conserving energy is the casual manner in which these couples live in contrast to the first marriage (for instance, men do not spend all summer mowing the lawn —they rarely have lawns—and women do not entertain at all elaborately). The casual living reflects at once a rejection of suburban customs, a narrowed social circle, and the intention to live well. Searcher pairs generally keep to themselves a great deal of the time and enjoy "the simple life."

The Sorters and the Searchers as Prophetic Models

While long-passage men and women subjects talked about their experiences of life and what they wanted in middle age (usually referred to simply as "now"), they often failed to take much note of the connection between the first marriage and their present ideas about, for instance, what constitutes a desirable pairing. However, they did talk about another factor also connected to their earlier histories. This was their sense of being much more capable of obtaining for themselves the satisfactions they now desire. This sense grew in the intervening years since the first marriage was contracted, and it came from the ways they were forced to deal with the experiences they met, or the ways in which they failed to deal with them satisfactorily, and their resolution to overcome these problems. By divorcing, they felt they gained a chance to make good use of what they were learning about themselves and the world, and this was an ongoing wish, particularly within a partnership.

Some long-passage subjects seemed to become "change agents" themselves. Indeed, the values they honored after divorce have influenced stably married couple life. In particular, the interpretation that Sorters and Searchers put on pairing—that couplehood after childrearing is not a "family matter" but a *couple-focused* business—has broken ground for married couples who do not wish to do late parenting nor center their lives on the existence of children (who neither need nor wish to have their parents' constant attention, since they are busily exploring and building on their own). The assumption that a forty-five-year-old mother with no dependent children at home should promptly go into a depression is seen as ridiculous by long-passage women who enjoy their work and see their work as mothers mainly as something to look back on.

One Searcher woman long accustomed to the sympathetic clucking of several of her traditionally married women friends, upset that she did not receive from her children the standard courtesies so dear to her counterparts and their continuation of the motherhood role, finally said,

> The children are out *there* somewhere. From what I can ascertain, they are fine, if slightly surprised that I do not pursue them or feel bereft. My therapist congratulated me awhile ago for having let go so completely; if that idea bothers *you*, make an appointment yourself!

In this way, they have made it acceptable not to feel guilty when one is not at all sad about children's departure. For some time now, a number of studies have shown that the "empty nest" syndrome is not present in many well-educated women; and, if anyone suffers when children leave, it is more apt to be fathers, interestingly enough.[1] Long-passage men and women tend not to talk about these questions as much as they just act on their attitudes, such as by failing to express the expected regrets. Many of them not only do not suffer any sense of loss at having adult children, they believe that such an image of sadness or expectation of it is perhaps a residual from an earlier time in history. Searchers have led the way in showing both single friends and stably married peers that just as they once threw all their energies into their children and their professional careers, later they invest all their resources in the pleasures of couplehood, with the added advantage of having more money and almost always, a great deal more leisure and serenity.

Among the Searchers, then, *conventional* marriage is seen as a family matter; it is no longer much related to pairing. Thus, it is of little interest to them, just as the running mode is of little interest to them, as it does not match up with their beliefs or standards either. This is not to say that marriage as such does not interest them. It does; but they tend to assume that most people using the term mean to imply marriage *as traditionally known and practiced*. The reservations they feel about *conventional* marriage are so deep that they sometimes omit the necessary explanation to newcomers about their philosophies of life (that is, that they are not rejecting *nonconventional* marriage as an option, in any sense). Thus Searchers becoming acquainted with an appealing prospect may go through a period of receiving what seem to be completely incongruous responses from a new lover, who has not yet realized that each is using the term, "marriage," quite differently. One subject said matter-of-factly,

> I am just about prepared to hand out a card summarizing my thoughts on this matter for anyone who appears interested. For anyone *really* interested, I could provide a list of readings which would reveal the line of argument by which I arrived at my present hopes for a partnership. When you let the ideas go untended and just act them out along the way, partners tend to forget how serious you are on this point, and also everybody starts getting tripped up by (private and unconfirmed) notions of what the other thought about something that took place, what it *means*.

Also, in the first marriage, couples were together primarily in their roles as parents with mobility aspirations. They were the "company people," or they were status seekers trying to ensure the family's financial future, without foreknowledge of the fact that they might later look askance at affluence, wondering "Is this all there is?" The emotional life of the marital partnership was a neglected side because of the importance to children of the partners' role performance as parents and the relevance to aspirations of using the first decade or two of marriage to consolidate status.

In most reports of the first marriage, the bond was expressed in a dependence on social roles, or it was ignored, to survive by itself, like an unwatered plant. The social side came to dominate the psychological side of marriage. To put it another way, the marital bond "got lost" in parenting and in following opportunities for increased status, or never was strong.

These facts partially account for the Searcher delight in, concern about, and obsession with the emotional state of a partnership. The interest in sexuality might appear quaint to younger people coming to maturity in the sexual revolution, but it is directly related to the lack of any vital intimacy in the first marriage and to the Searchers' awareness, in middle age, of having had sexually impoverished first marriages. In addition, because of new contraceptive technology, the connection between sex and the reproductive function has been severed. One of my subjects had had an early vasectomy (at a second marriage) about which he remained well satisfied, having two natural and three stepdaughters.

The effects of the sexual revolution are perhaps most evident in the case of Runner women, but the impact of the sexual revolution on the lives of Sorter and Searcher women cannot be overestimated and is not always unmixed. This is true, because sexuality remains an area with more problems and less mutuality of expectations than one would hope. There is always the probability of both parties to a sexual interlude being unprepared for the erroneous assumptions or expectations the other person may hold for one or both parties to be thrown for a loss. Because Sorter and Searcher women (and men, too) tend to be seen as and view themselves as somewhat liberated people, they can get into situations where this notion is not confirmed. One woman subject spoke of this in recounting two situations. One involved her being with a man who assumed that her friendliness (as a "liberated woman") was an invitation for persistent sexual overtures which embarrassed and alarmed her. The other was a situation in which her agreeing to a sexual interlude not only brought up her old fears about conventional marriage, but resulted in her friend's assumption that she would then ask him for sexual relations on a regular basis, which astonished, embarrassed, and discomforted her even more than had the first incident. But both alerted her to the fact that she could hardly consider herself very "liberated." Thus the term, "liberated," with respect to either gender roles or sexual attitudes sometimes struck subjects as ironically inappropriate.

The impoverishment of one's emotional and sexual life in the first marriage may be a direct source of much of the running behavior among both men and women. But for all long-passage people, whatever the numerous consequences of the sexual revolution have been, two significant ones appear to be (a) a rise in expectations for sexual life, especially among women, and (b) a new type of pairing which is not complicated by concerns about pregnancy or family life, or very much connected to it. All of this has encouraged a new kind of "mating dance" between these sorts of men and women, which are major influences on all styles of mid-life. They are important changes that arose unexpectedly in the lives of these subjects, most of whom went virginally into a first marriage.

Nevertheless, the potential link between sexual expression and the possibility of commitment remains obvious, and how to handle it tends to be a major problem for some long-passage people. Changes in perceptions about sex or about mid-life or about dating or pairing underlie many current shifts in attitudes among people in long passages. Above all, many people are altering some of the meanings they once attached to age. At the present, these people and others like them are contributing to a redefinition of mid-life and age-appropriate behavior that more closely approximates the lives they actually live, rather than the lives they once thought they "ought" to be living.

An ongoing theme of this book that now merits a closer look is the relationship of education and upward social mobility to the changes possible for my subjects. The equation at the heart of their stories is that education equals mobility and money, and the experience of having had the opportunities of education, mobility, and money equals greatly enhanced choices. Among the highly mobile Searchers, the effects of this were that education led to a degree of experience with money and mobility that resulted in adaptability, which gave them a feeling that abundantly rich options lay within their grasp after divorce. In tandem, there appeared to be twin prizes for the taking: *(a)* the truly intimate heterosexual partnership and *(b)* the enlarged interior journey, perhaps a matter of the spirit. However these are defined by any one individual, the enactment of these goals operate as part of a feedback loop to the very married. Both of these groups, the formerly married and the stably married (in first marriages), seemed to be somewhat unconscious participants in the feedback process.

Nevertheless, one remark I often heard from long-passage subjects was "Sometimes I feel I have taken too independent a direction or gave up too much for what I have, but I run into old friends and. . . . " The benefits of education and money are almost inestimable; and to many people, the gains from not being readily satisfied (and being willing to take risks) are incalculable. At times, each group looks at the problems of the other and sighs with relief; but at other times, long-passage people are the "time and space explorers" that they set out hopefully to be as young marrieds who wanted "their share." In many respects they are pacesetters to a large audience.

What other conclusions should be drawn from the study? First, implicit similarities among the various categories can be made more explicit. If the sexual theme is taken out of running, and the Runners' small networks of "buddies" are considered as "family" kinds of networks, which is how they are used, the Runners' alternatives are not so different from those of the Graduates. Both categories of men and women establish a rigid status quo early on. Even their gap in income is superficial compared to the similarity in their approaches to pursuing control over their lives and to holding change to a minimum or keeping it from entering life. One Runner said flatly, "I don't *allow* myself to fall in love."

Courters and Steadies adopt relatively uneventful solutions, full of decorum. Of two former Enforced Remarriers, one is now repartnered in the Sorter mode, but this does not look like a stable pairing to me, because this pairing seems to have been a response to a setback that again generated the subject's increased interest in "security," which may not provide the subject with sufficient motivation to remain in the partnership long. The second passage seems to be a response to the reverse situation, a triumph that enhanced the subject's opportunities for running in a direction of considerable interest, which may prove transitory (only an experimental detour). Nonetheless, these two are back in the passage experience. Their passage-management competence is much increased because of their more adequate stock of resources, among which is their prior experience of passage. One observed, "In looking back, one advantage of having the sky fall on you is that it never knocks you quite so flat again." And the other found, "There's a certain excitement in living out 'on the edge' with nothing handled well, but not very much."

With respect to other observed similarities, sorting and searching are quite comparable phenomena. Sorters lack the intensity of Searchers and also incline to take both passage and a partner less seriously. They also take themselves less seriously. This almost seems to be a matter of temperament. Sorters are much less preoccupied with questions about meaning. Therefore, they spend much less time debating what this or that *means* and just go ahead with their lives. But Searchers are engrossed with the "why?" and want to understand not only themselves but everyone else. Still, in many ways their coping styles are fairly comparable. In a general sense, Searchers function as the "ideologues" if not the consciences of Sorters and other onlookers.

A theme uniting Sorters and Searchers is their positive perspective on middle age. For the women and men in these modes of passage, the glass is not "half-full" at mid-life, it is overflowing. In terms of the way they both view "time," mid-life is the proof that there is not only time left, there is more than enough of it. Thus Sorters and Searchers tend, much of the time, to be people who are extremely pleased with life.

There are differences in personality structure behind the relatively conservative choices of earlier exiting people and the Sorters' and Searchers' expansive venture-taking bets on themselves and their ability to handle life. These latter people do hedge their bets with careful attention to their professional roles and an inclination to "fence off from view" their private lives, a prime example of the way they control disclosure for the purpose of self-protection.

Nonetheless, their coping strategies are grounded in their adventurousness and their great resiliency (they pick themselves up, dust themselves off, and strike out again with the determination of twelve-year-olds on roller skates, after a misadventure). Searchers are astute at innovating successfully because they are also not too caught up in "saving face." One Searcher woman, trying to set out on a new bicycle she bought to save taking her car to work gave this order to onlookers, "Don't watch me! I'm shy," to which they responded with hoots and applause as she pedaled off. An important related characteristic is their enormous stock of optimism.

The Sorters and the Searchers were the study's strongest survivors, because they were too tenacious to view mid-life divorce as merely the occasion to "cut your losses." They were aware of and used this expedient well when it was called for, but they put much more energy and resolve into enlarging their lives. They also tended to have a good sense of humor and to use humor as a mechanism for handling discomfort; it relieved continuous control. And all of them believed in the value of persistence. One said, "My former wife is a demon bridge player who taught me that the person who wins at the bridge table or in life may be the person who hangs in the longest."

Searchers' commitments to their goals were not very conditional, because they planned to reconstruct their lives for however much time it would take. The Sorter-Searcher choice was built on a rather formidable intent to "grow" as a person, which appeared to succeed in many respects. One of the goals that fascinated Searchers was the opportunity to increase at mid-life the number of options available to them, enabling them to express their identities as more fully functioning adults (that is, who were less neurotic) than had been the case before.

The Sorter-Searcher passage casts light on a number of salient questions pertaining to stage of life. To Sorters and Searchers, viewing mid-life as a static period of deficits in which nothing can be expected to happen in terms of growth,

Looking Ahead

is refusing to celebrate life. If they were asked, "Is middle age a time for renunciation and settling down in anticipation of a difficult old age?" they would reply, "Quite to the contrary!" This belief is a conviction they are *living,* as they are now living out some of the alternatives presently available to anyone who formerly viewed mid-life from so dismal a standpoint. Careers, marriages, and divorces are probably as "good" as the uses people put them to, and the Sorters and the Searchers I studied would add mid-life to this list. In many cases, these subjects were really happy and self-accepting for the first time in their lives.

People can and do adapt and change throughout life, to a much greater extent than used to be recognized. The Sorters and Searchers are contributing to our understanding of this by being models for possibilities, because they are *acting* on their new definitions. The power of self-definition as a tool in the self-determination process is now more widely utilized, since a plethora of formerly potentially stigmatized groups have demonstrated its value. Middle-aged singles have been able to convert a sometimes previously disadvantaged social role into all manner of personal opportunities and gains.

In particular, many long-passage people have shown how much women can profit from facing and incorporating social change into their lives with respect to gender issues. This they have done without "taking anything away from" the men who are their intimates. The presence of "new women" in the lives of some of my long-passage male subjects was seen by them as their gain. Many men are shedding some parts of the traditional male role which they see as burdensome and not necessary to their enactment of masculinity.

Another contribution of Searchers is that they are acting as prototypes in learning how to remove the adversary character from divorce, love, marriage, and breaking up, and they are teaching others that there are better positions to adopt after divorce than perpetual hostility toward prior mates. Sometimes they fail; but their attempts to make life into something more than a zero-sum game (such as, "If I win; baby, you *lose!*") is a worthwhile effort that deserves our good wishes. It is an experiment not without its own kind of pain, and it is one in which many onlookers may also have a stake without knowing it.

Adult development and aging should be interesting topics to a population that, like our's, is steadily becoming older, or "graying," and particularly when the ranks of the middle aged will soon include some of the research subjects' oldest children. In terms of adult development, then, what other life-cycle implications remain to be noted?

First, in reviewing the case material on long-passage subjects, it appears that the early first marriages were often contracted *(a)* out of a desire to escape the constraints of small-town life, *(b)* out of conventional wishes to marry, and *(c)* out of an unconscious effort to avoid dealing with the psychological task of individuation, by reentering the world of the family through early marriage. One of the maturation tasks that will repeatedly face you throughout adulthood, if it is a piece of "unfinished business," is establishing yourself adequately enough to be able to function emotionally without unresolved dependency needs constantly tripping you up or forcing you into unconscious choices that you do not recognize as such and later come to regret very much. As the decades roll on, not having taken care of this work of individuation can become more and more expensive.

Some of my research subjects spoke of marital problems in the first marriage and subsequent love relationships that I suspected were the problems of an adult who had postponed arriving at emotional maturity, only to have to pay and pay for this postponement. In other cases, the postponement seemed a permanent state of affairs, effected by going through continual romances and remarriages, almost like a lifetime spent in a revolving door.

My point is simply that, if the work of individuation (like dealing with separation from parents or not continually having to have someone to lean on) is not yet accomplished, you have the choice in middle age to try to see it through. You also then have time left to enjoy the numerous rewards of having done so. The foremost among these would likely be the establishment of a truly intimate, stable partnership of two relatively autonomous people, who have chosen each other freely because the partnership enhances the life of each, rather than from dependencies such as having to have someone to prop one up constantly. It is the dependent person, as a rule, who is in an enormous hurry to partner, because to this individual, being alone is equated with being lonely (or in danger). The other side of the dependency coin is the person who cannot pair no matter how much this is longed for, because he or she is unable to acknowledge a need to have and depend on a reliable loved one. There would have to be a number of intermediate steps between an emotionally immature person's becoming strong enough emotionally to eventually achieve a mature partnership commitment; most of the steps would have little to do directly with partnering. Only when a person can both accept support and stand alone can he or she make an actual choice about taking a partner. People who cannot stand on their own feet accept a partner they are in conflict about but can't leave, or try to become indispensable to that person. Feelings that one is not a worthy object of love intensify fears of abandonment and together these fuel relationship crises.

Another version of problems I sometimes saw among my subjects, was the more dependent person continually claiming that the lover made unreasonable claims upon him or her, and repeatedly breaking up with someone he or she was quite well-suited to and crazy about, out of fears of being "trapped" by the pairing. In these cases, the subject's own dependency needs were so enormous (and unrecognized by him or her) that the person in question handled them by the mechanism of projection. In thus putting the situation of "neediness" out on the valued potential partner, a number of people convinced themselves that the lover would be a devourer once they were paired or married. Then they sadly went on to someone else, with no more likelihood of success, because they had only denied the root of the problem and justified their own flight from dealing with reality. The latter process then becomes, essentially, a flight *from* happiness. Thus I saw some Searcher couples put a lot of time into wasted efforts to pair successfully that involved their being seized upon by attractive but essentially immature lovers suffering the terrors of expecting impending abandonment—whose motives were limited to wanting to forestall having to face life by and for themselves. What these premature hopefuls were usually in touch with, then, was simply their own inability to work at a commitment (they sought for themselves) in a fairly adult fashion. Therefore, in transition, the Aztec two-step is commonly seen in couples. This is how it goes: "You move closer to me, and I'll run away; if you feel rebuffed and withdraw, I'll be back to pursue you." In addition, becoming frightened as a desired pairing or remarriage is nearly effected is also quite common and can be quite dramatic, but it is quite different from successive love affairs in which one or both persons always ask for "more time" and are too busy being distant to take steps to advance the courtship or make concrete plans for their future as a couple.

Some people began to suspect that their succesive partners had this kind of emotional problem, only to have to confront finally the possibility that they themselves sought the protection of incompleted love affairs, in the sense of not being carried to happy (paired) conclusions. In these cases, some of my subjects then saw that they had themselves been *contributing* to the unsuccessful outcomes they had endured; and they then attempted to understand if the payoff they actually sought was to enjoy the preliminaries of a romantic affair without having to invest themselves in the work necessary to harvesting the much greater benefits of a major love commitment. A typical question a subject then posed to her- or himself (during an interview with me) was "What am I unconsciously getting out of these eventually unsatisfactory affairs that I must want, more than I wish for a partner?" And some of them then tried to remedy matters, generally by moving gradually away from people who seemed unable to act on a wish to pair. This step often led to their subsequently choosing more wisely and being much less inclined to attribute partnering difficulties to the other person. In so learning how to start taking responsibility for what was happening to them, a number of subjects moved into a more self-contained mode of singlehood and from there, into solidly contracted and permanently gratifying partnerships.

Some of the long-passage subjects were on the horns of a dilemma; therefore, while they did not want to partner with someone as bound-to-mate as a Courter, they also realized that some formerly marrieds are working on maturation issues that will bear great fruit if the work is accomplished, but if not, they will merely be people with unfinished business that will result in unfinished stories that are never going to coalesce. The question of whether a divorce at mid-life represents a straightforward separation from a prior mate or also (or, instead) represents the basic task of psychological individuation has been well discussed by Dorothy Cantor and is not a point original with me.[2] But it probably relates in important ways to the Searchers' discovery that they had to go on an odyssey in partner searching, and to their enthusiasm about doing self-work. It is worthwhile to speculate hereon that although many Searcher subjects underwent agonized periods during passage where only "calling on their best efforts" and full supply of personal courage would suffice, they managed to do this and were considerably strengthened and encouraged by their success at it. Many long-passage people, furthermore, may have indirectly accomplished the process of individuation in therapy which they entered for what they believed at the time were more concrete, specific, and limited reasons. There is always the possibility of selecting a really astute and competent counselor who is able to enlarge the therapeutic process so that it encompasses more achievement than a person coming in for help may suspect is necessary or even be willing to attempt to accomplish. Such a development may account for the fervor of some subjects' remarks about their self-work and its yields to them.

At any rate, without so naming it (or always understanding it), some of the Sorters and the Searchers seem to me to have signed on for a passage trip into emotional maturation. I think this was true whether or not some subjects were aware of it and quite apart from the extent of progress they made ultimately. And with regard to their partnerships, when they achieved a new kind of human connectedness (partnering well) while simultaneously accomplishing the liberating degree of "individuation" necessary for being able to pair, this double victory was heady stuff indeed, and their glowing reports certainly appropriate. At any rate, their accounts of passage are remarkable for their conviction that they can properly perceive themselves as very fortunate men and women.

At the very least, their stories of their lives direct our attention to how freeing and deeply sustaining it can be to realize this kind of a goal if you have been dragging through life without it; for no matter how long it takes you to plant your flag on top of the mountain named "Mount Maturity," it is enormously gratifying to be able to do so. In addition, questions of self-esteem and self-mastery always underlie our struggles over love and the dependency-autonomy balance we must find. Attempts at some degree or form of pairing brought many challenges to the forthrightness and self-esteem of many of my subjects and none more demanding than their strivings toward being capable of a healthy interdependence. People with a strong self-concept and truly adult ways of going at life and the cherished other can pair without a sense that their boundaries will be violated; in this regard I mean that they are able to build, use, and enjoy interdependence with the loved one.

Thus an important factor for outcome was the psychological maturity of any particular long-passage subject. This is a point that deserves to be made directly, since in our culture so many aspects encourage us to feel that it is our exteriors (our physical appearances or financial worth) that most fundamentally affect our chances. I do not believe this now to the extent I once did before completing the study, since, when exterior characteristics were equally positive between two subjects whose passage success I was comparing, often it clearly was the psychologically stronger person who "won a partner" conclusively and happily.

I sometimes watched with dismay extremely attractive subjects who were promising prospects for someone, (when examined and weighed on external criteria such as appearance or intelligence), go round and round in the same futile circle, repeating the same tragic lack of basic trust in other humans. Basic trust in oneself and in the lover is a fundamental requirement for victory in the game of love. First putting one's trust in life may be the only brief substitute love allows its eventual beneficiaries, unless it could be said that obtaining and actually seeing through working with a good therapist amounts to the same thing. I hope some of my readers just noticed that I have used the word "tragic" for the first time in this book. I do so deliberately. I see nothing inherently tragic in divorce, mid-life or, for that matter, the aging process, although I know this runs counter to some people's definitions. I do, however, think that the penalties that a lack of basic trust brings one can hardly be overstated.

Thus, emotional maturity is one more element, and a crucial one, whenever one considers one's chances (and consequent choices) in pursuing any kind of a postdivorce goal. The issue of one's chances can be seen in the language with which people pose the typical questions they ask themselves during transition about how well it is going. Naturally enough, these questions address not simply one's goal but one's likelihood of attaining it, or one's worth. "What am I worth on the remarriage market?", "What are we worth as a family headed by a single parent?", or "What am I worth as a single parent getting on with my life?" are all ordinary questions during the postdivorce transitional process. Other common questions are "What am I worth as a sexual partner?", "What am I worth as a lover?" or "as a lifetime companion, come what may?" A very important (and also common) question that people seem to be less consciously asking themselves when they are not yet out of passage is "What is this kind of satisfaction (or relationship, or life) worth *now, to me?*" A few subjects who were Searchers told me they asked themselves finally a somewhat different kind of question that one can only expect to answer partially in the conduct, not simply of a passage, but of the rest of life: "Life, what am I worth and what are you *worth* to me?" Put more simply, this is an important question, too, because what we think we cannot afford to have, or do, or risk, or be, (or what we feel we cannot afford to miss having, doing, risking, and being) tells us *who we are*.

For many subjects in long passages, mid-life, then, is not only the time to get a second chance, as is true for many earlier exiters as well; it is also the time one gets another chance to start asking oneself some of the really interesting questions. This fact was apparent at many levels to many subjects. One subject spoke about being advantaged recently by finally getting to have a "good adolescence." Despite its being quite late and "off schedule," it was a valuable experience used as a piece of emotional work, developmentally:

> Most people have dreadful adolescences, in my opinion. I know I did. And I agree that adversity strengthens a person. But a good childhood, or a "good" adolescence is also a life enhancement. The idealized picture which most of my generation missed out on—as do many young people today—has a lot to be said for it. After my divorce, I went back and had mine. I knew perfectly well what I was doing. I now feel a lot better about myself, and having had such a happy growing time makes it easy to settle down to being a more productive person.

To Sorters and Searchers, a happy pairing is the foremost goal that these men and women go back and try to claim, and what they learn in the process contains lessons for others.

Another issue remains. What about the children? They were raised in the midst of all of the familial and societal confusion. Some are now in their thirties, and they have made some fateful choices of their own.

In some histories, the personal growth of their parents seemed to be the element that reunited the generations, or such reconciliations offered both sets of people new moments together to look back on with gratitude. Other children remained closed to their parents throughout and after passage.

The order of the day in some histories was still estrangement; in other cases, each generation set aside the blaming to get along with life, independently. Thus peace has not been declared in all subjects' histories. Many parents now feel that the price for some of their early choices or lack of understanding along the way has been the forfeiting of their children's companionship and regard for them. But the early mobility trip was a *joint* (family) *venture*, and some ties from this period sent out new shoots, as this subject reported:

> One of the things I supposed I would forfeit by becoming a committed professional was the grandchildren. For sixteen years, much of what I could have given to the children went into my work. I didn't make much of an investment in them after they had children of their own. But middle age continues to have nice surprises. A bonus for me is that I am starting to know the grandchildren. My oldest is sixteen now, and I really didn't know much about what kind of a person she is. But I got a note from her which her mother didn't know she had written, telling me she thinks she is interested in my field.

It is now well documented that many people handle the mid-life divorce transition well. Middle age has been used by many subjects as the auspicious chance for new beginnings which appear "healthy" by any number of standards. Women have learned a great deal from their efforts to become newly self-sufficient human beings. Men long ago saw the connections between money and sex (love) and used them. More women are starting to see them. There is another aspect of gender to examine. Career women, such as the one just quoted above, did not expect their work commitments would lead to very much closeness with their children in later life. This was a loss of a previous tradition they valued and a large loss for both generations in their mutual experiences of adulthood, despite being forever in different stages simultaneously. Some saw this as a gain, others saw it as a "price." But many long-passage women in my study found that such feared either/or choices were not always necessary. It appears that career commitments do not inevitably cost a woman lack of access to the warmth of *family* ties, even as a remarried but *unconventional* mother.

At any rate, some women are beginning to think that career commitments perhaps do not force a woman to develop her own competence at some dire cost. Some women in my study were asking themselves, "Maybe this isn't going to have cost me *anything* important?" Thus, as the contraceptive advance has allowed some women to separate sex and reproduction if they wish, and, as women are able to separate work and love so that one does not extinguish the other, "the times" seem to be giving some women a chance to "put them back together again" or, in other words, to "have it all," as they once thought only men could do.

Much of what now goes on in long passages results from the recent collision between traditional values and contemporary problems—in which mid-life looked likely to become a minefield littered with casualties. Many of my subjects found the old traditions no longer sustained them. One said, "We are stranded in the present." Like the school dropouts who were victims of an oppressive educational system with no place for them, some of my subjects felt they did not "fit in" when they found that the old traditions no longer had the *power* to nourish and guide them, in the circumstances in which they found themselves on the mobility trail.[3] This problem is reminiscent of the ways in which the Old World traditions of some subjects' grandparents sometimes failed to help them meet the consequences of migration. Thus subjects often reported they finally began to feel like outcasts, pushed out of the family, because its tenets were hollow in the face of their own experiences. Despite the danger of overstating the case for the utility of the group movement, to people who "needed a group of their own" in order to make a fresh start while carrying the old story within them, New Age ideals have been a godsend. They have given these people a sense of being able to lead an ethical (seriously adult) life in terms of some practical and concrete ideas. The "new culture," expressed in the New Age thought which it encapsulates, has become a new dogma, a new truth. Thus, for some people, the group movement functioned as a church. This phenomenon is entirely in keeping with the histories of Sorters and Searchers, who have by no means been *only* people who "made it." They have also been concerned with the moral and ethical questions of their time. (In some cases, it was because they had "made it" that they were particularly concerned.)

Furthermore, since the group movement discarded the medical model of health and illness, people could move toward healthy growth through an empowering *learning process*, that is, self-help. For people who so often adapted to regional customs and advantages and who frequently had to deal with setbacks in their careers or marriages, the group movement served a vital function. It assisted them in discovering new qualities in themselves that enabled them to participate more wholeheartedly in aspects of life with which they were not acquainted or were not doing well. It helped them learn more about themselves, such as why they were failing in some areas of life and ignoring or running away from other areas. This enabled them to move in new directions, and it helped them gather their courage and upgrade their "smarts" for doing this. It gave them a place to mourn with others dealing with a fresh loss, and it gave them a home. In the embrace of the group movement, people could expect to be listened to with respect, supported in their efforts to change wisely, and applauded for having the capacity to take risks. To the movement's many detractors, a good question to pose is, "Exactly where would *you* have sent them?" These research subjects were "You can't go home again!" people, for whom the Methodist Sunday school, the Episcopal Altar guild, and the Kaddish were, at best, only fragrant echoes, such as one might recall a grandmother's muffins or pitching hay to the stock. These people were carriers of the contemporary.

To goal-directed subjects who had used whatever was at hand, and who needed some means through which to continue to view life as an adventure, (perhaps a spiritual journey), the movement was a perfect mechanism for a new form of mobility. One person said,

> It is absolutely necessary for human health and happiness to be in loving relationships. One can adjust to their lack, but that wounds people. Of course, we don't always get what we want, but life also brings us many ways by which to learn how to gather the strength to cope when this happens.

Long-passage men and women tend to approach the topic of aging by suggesting that each successive decade may hold its gains. The misery of the first marriage, their knowledge of their having somehow agreed to pay a very high price for affluence, and their present heightened sense of having vastly increased abilities for getting from private life the degree of satisfaction they obtain in their work, leads many to try again. In other words, the rewards that you had to wait for, or the ones that you barely dreamed of in your original calculations, are present for you to reach out for in middle age.

Although it has not been addressed directly, the main problem for many long-passage individuals has simply been generated by the shift of large numbers of people into an urban existence from families with fairly recent rural backgrounds. For instance, one subject remembers very well his father chopping off the head of a hen in the backyard in preparation for Sunday dinner and another remembers hating to have to go with her brother to drive the cows into the barn from the pasture nightly.

The bounty of an industrial age spread before these people from early adulthood appearing as life's smorgasbord; but, while they had their heads and their feet in the "future," their hearts were left behind in a rapidly receding past with which they soon became uncomfortable. As the mushrooming technology swept them along in its path, they became the first of this new migrant wave to try to assimilate what had taken place. Along with their answering machines, and their IUDs, their conferences abroad, and their BMWs, many of the women still retained the family Bible or a packet of Civil War letters. One man has memories of an immigrant father who left the Amsterdam waterfront at seventeen, and another of a grandfather who never again saw the cattle country and the mists of the Pyrenees or *his* own father, who had given him a leather pouch of gold coins for the voyage to the New World.

Other products of the technological revolution have been a decrease in family size and a dramatic extension of the human life-span, both of which have radically altered mid-life as a stage. I have said little about these phenomena, but they have had a fateful impact on the family and on society. Prior to these developments, (and still the case in traditional, nonindustrialized societies), middle age was regarded as a time in which you tried to keep going in hopes of seeing your last child safely launched. The specter that hung over life in your grandparent's day was not, "What will there be to talk about when we're just a twosome?" but, rather the threat of not living to see the last youngster grown. It was a practical consideration and a logical hope, because it was often an unmet goal.

Today, people in the upper-middle-class stratum, in particular, as well as much of society, in general, will have a long period of time in which to have a vigorous mid-life that little resembles traditional portrayals of middle age. Among the changes they will witness and assimilate will be that many of their children will divorce and a large number of their stably married children will postpone parenthood until they forgo this option altogether and remain child-free. In the process, the length of a stable first marriage will continue to increase, and among the married middle-aged in this group, people will be occupied trying to figure out just how they will use this time together. In other respects, too, people's ideas and notions about the purposes to which an adult life should be put will undergo more shifts. The "new demographics" will carry along the "new culture"; it will more often be lived than debated because electronic technology and new ecology have simply changed the conditions of existence.

In the Western nations, people are picking their ways through the fall-out from a life-span revolution. The New Age themes irrevocably interwoven into the lives and reports of the Sorters and Searchers are merely illustrative of a broad societal change to which these people have tried to respond appropriately. Some of their attitudes and patterns of behavior can be expected to spread throughout the wider society because these will be adaptive choices and life philosophies for many people. I predict that, just as there is no longer any one "mass market," there will be a proliferation of life-styles at mid-life. In addition to making partner substitutions, some men and women will sample various life-style alternatives, also in succession. In the meanwhile, among my Sorter and Searcher subjects, people simply take for granted being in a

New Age, just as they take for granted their answering machines, their sound systems, their new nutrition, the remote control on their televisions, and their time-share condominium vacation homes.

But the new technology will not be the most important component of life in the years ahead, despite its great power. *The ideas we hold rule our hearts.* The present ideological revolution is nothing less, and it will lead to more new images of middle age and other significant life experiences. The patterns by which more and more people are living will simply become customary parts of life. Fewer people will perceive a divorce decree as a license to hate, but will use it as the occasion for the best cooperative spirit they can muster. Families animated by a spirit of harmony and concern for the welfare of all its members will continue to delight onlookers. While people will probably continue to accept the state's ratification of a marriage, fewer people will feel that they need a license to love. A life of singlehood that exemplifies the best virtues of responsibility and generosity will more often receive the applause that such an accomplishment merits. New social patterns will be widely adopted for the simple reason that they "work," the circumstances of life being what they are, in the stream of time.

The new definitions on which all of the foregoing rest will become familiar, like the keepsakes they begin to replace. Life will be less static, more fluid, and more organic. People who are capable of living without the support of "old rules and old roles" will be fun to know and fun to be. They will be more adaptable and, thereby, more healthy. People will choose for themselves more often, rather than being manipulated by the marketing expert rejecting the ersatz product and the counterfeit experience in favor of the real, not the simulated life adventure. Adversarial lines will be drawn less frequently and less rigidly, because more and more people will walk away from competition and learn how to build cooperative networks. More people will understand that *living has always meant changing;* and that in loss there is at least a basis for renewal. People will appreciate and feel closer to nature, seeing that they are a part of rather than separate from the natural world. When required to do so, people will move in and out of relationships more easily, learning how to bond authentically and whole-heartedly more quickly, and to relinquish more readily and in a spirit of comradeship. The primary human task is, after all, not to find a way to avoid loss; but rather to find the capacity to mourn a loss and then to create an on-going life that is, *in the face of loss,* full of purpose and meaning. Lifton has made this argument well.[4] More people will be struck by the fact that, in themselves, all of the adult years (be they early, middle, or late) constitute quite an adventure. More and more people will find ways and reasons to use this time well.

In the past several decades, the "new frontier" was, for many people wanting to live fully rather than shrink from new experience, the interior life. I predict that the next new frontier will be the aging process. While aging is a completely "natural" phenomenon, there is nevertheless a current explosion in bio-chemical research, some of it directed to work on the aging process.[5] It now appears that some of the negative factors associated with aging which we presumed were "supposed" to accompany this process are not only not inevitable, they are also reversible. Aging is not only a matter of chemistry and biological "clocks," it is a process with significant behavioral and attitudinal components as well. This can be stated in another way: people will continue to do after passage out of divorce what they do in it, to protect what they hold most dear and value the most highly as essential. Their beliefs will determine their ways of being in the world, as men and women.[6]

FRESH STARTS

People who have faith in mid-life, in themselves, and in others may well also go out to meet old age with a comparable intention to make something "good" out of it, to be "open" to whatever it brings, and to "let it be."

The Sorters and the Searchers together make up a group of people whom I regard as a new social type. I call them the "young middle aged." Many of them seem to be able to feel at home almost anywhere, which is perhaps their greatest (if unintended or unconscious) achievement. Their emergence as a group in the United States seems to me entirely congruent with our national history. To these men and women and many others beginning to share some of their views, mid-life as a stage is proving to be newly unfettered, rife with confusion, and exuberantly alive. So far, it is also barely charted country. With any luck at all, some of the formerly married among them will be able to look back over their lives from the vantage point of a deeply satisfying old age to recognize that they were among the first settlers of the latest new world, the earliest inheritors of modernity's most recent boon, the new mid-life stage.

Notes

Chapter 1

1. The fact that our roles are expressed in an *integrated* combination (or a totality which amounts to a Gestalt) was first pointed out to me in a conversation with Leonard Schatzman in 1978, during which he used the term, "configuration." This is an important point, in my judgment.

2. Richard Schickel, *Singled Out, A Civilized Guide to Sex and Sensibility for the Suddenly Single Man or Woman* (New York: The Viking Press, 1980). This book by a divorce veteran is both practical and humane.

Chapter 2

1. John Seeley et al., *Crestwood Heights, A North American Suburb* (London: Constable, 1958). This study of an upper-middle class suburb adjacent to a Canadian city is a classic on the belief systems among these kinds of couples in North America at the end of the fifties. Reading it now also shows how much values are changing in the same types of populations.

2. Landon Y. Jones, *Great Expectations, America and the Baby Boom Generation* (New York: Ballentine, 1980). Jones's insufficiently appreciated study of the demographics of the baby boom is a triumph that should be read by all "baby boomers," at the very least.

3. David Reisman, Nathan Glaser, and Reuel Denny, *The Lonely Crowd, A Study of the Changing American Character* (Garden City, NY: Doubleday, 1955).

4. Lawrence Durrell, *The Poetry of Lawrence Durrell* (New York: E. P. Dutton and Company, Inc., 1962), p. 7. The poem is titled "Poem" and in its entirety reads:

Notes

Find time hanging, cut it down
All the universe you own.

Masterless and still untamed
Poet, lead the race you've shamed.

Lover, cut the rational knot
That made your thinking rule-of-thumb

And barefoot on the plum-dark hills
Go Wander in Elysium.

Chapter 3

1. Judith S. Wallerstein, and Joan Berlin Kelly, *Surviving the Breakup, How Children and Parents Cope with Divorce* (New York: Basic Books, 1980). This somber book casts a great deal more light on the extent to which parental divorce can be confusing and disruptive to the children than it does on the specific mechanisms by which one-third of their sample of divorced families, followed for five years, coped. Further study to delineate in detail exactly what mechanisms work best for formerly marrieds and their children would be of great assistance to parents in this situation. Of considerable significance to my research is Wallenstein and Kelly's discovery that most children want the parental marriage to *continue* no matter how bad it is in the parents' view. In other words, an intact home may be seen by children as to be preferred over happy (single or re-paired) parents. This supplements the prior studies which report that a psychologically "dead" (empty shell) or damaging intact marriage is less healthy for children than a successful divorce.

The rather high and general level of satisfaction about the divorce that I saw in many of my subjects (instead of the guilt one might have expected to find) also relates to their continual criticism of *their* parents, who seemed to them to have sacrificed a great deal of everyone's happiness for the purpose of keeping the parental marriage intact at virtually any cost. One might speculate that regardless of the conscientiousness with which a parent might decide for or against divorce, it can be hard to be a hero or heroine to one's children.

2. C. Wright Mills, "Situated actions and vocabularies of motive," in *Symbolic Interaction,* eds. Jerome Mavis and Bernard Meltzer (Boston: Allyn and Bacon, 1940), pp. 904–913. Jacqueline Wiseman has also used the phrase "vocabularies of identity" with respect to the accounts people give of their actions and motives.

Chapter 6

1. Robert O. Blood, Jr. and Margaret Blood, "Amicable Divorce: A New Lifestyle," *Alternate Lifestyles* 2, no. 4, (1979), pp. 483–499. This remains the best single

discussion I know of on the "cooperative, goodwill divorce" and the cluster of values that are associated with this type of cooperation and mutual support. We might speculate on the great decrease in psychological costs to parents and children alike whose family breakups are mediated by the parents' ongoing concern *for each other* as well as for their children. The Bloods' model is as applicable to the breakup of living-together-arrangements as it is to marriages and the research was based on both kinds of ruptures. An interesting concomitant of the amicable breakup is that it leaves the separating couple with a sense of gratitude for their prior joint life.

2. Ibid.

Chapter 7

1. John F. Cuber and Peggy B. Haroff, *Sex and the Significant Americans* (New York: Appleton-Century, 1965).

2. Robert Broadhead, "Professional Identities and Private Life" (Ph.D. dissertation, University of California, San Francisco Medical Center, 1979).

3. Cuber and Haroff, *Sex and the Significant Americans*.

4. Peter J. Stein, *Single* (Englewood Cliffs, NJ: Prentice-Hall, 1976). See also Robert Staples, *The World of Black Singles, Changing Patterns of Male/Female Relations* (Westport, Conn.,: Greenwood Press, 1981). Both of these books are valuable. Staples shows in great detail how the formerly married (or always single) are both pulled toward a further exploration of singlehood and simultaneously pushed away from marriage by impersonal social forces that impinge similarly on both blacks and whites, in many cases.

5. John Lennon and Yoko Ono, "Beautiful Boy," song from the album *Double Fantasy* (The David Geffen Company, 1980).

6. Bernice L. Neugarten, "Age groups in American and the rise of the Young-old" (Paper presented at the Annual Meeting of the American Association for the Advancement of Science, 1974).

7. Bernice L. Neugarten and Joan W. Moore, "The Changing Age–Status System," in *Middle Age and Aging, A Reader in Social Psychology*, ed. Bernice L. Neugarten (Chicago: University of Chicago Press, 1968), pp. 5–21.

Chapter 8

1. Marjorie Fiske, (Lowenthal) and David Chiriboga, "Transition to the Empty Nest: Crisis, Challenge, or Relief?" *Archives of General Psychiatry* 26 (1972). These life stage researchers at UCSF's Human Development Program pointed out that women were relieved at children's departure, and if anyone was discomforted by it, it was fathers. This correlates with my finding that aging ceases to be a central concern for women just as it becomes alarming to men in middle age. Departure of children is thus apparently a negative marker for some men but usually a positive life event for

Notes

women, in a general sense. Thus the "empty nest" syndrome was posited by male family sociologists originally. They were speaking of pangs true for some of them but were not necessarily describing a symptom of the lives of women. This definition of middle age as a "time of regret" when children grow up and leave home lingers in our culture, however, and for women with no other identity at middle age (except "mother"), it is still persuasive. See also Lillian Rubin, *Women of a Certain Age; the Mid-life Search for Self* (New York: Harper Colophon, 1981). It is important to remember that women's options at mid-life are strongly class-linked, that is, related to educational level attained.

2. Dorothy Cantor, "Divorce: Separation or Individuation?" (unpublished paper presented at the Annual Meeting of the American Psychological Association, Los Angeles, 1981). Cantor contends herein that many individuals who did not complete the psychological work of individuation in young adulthood accomplish this task later on, with divorce as indirect result.

3. For a powerful distillation of the vast emotional and cultural range of the gap between past and present life experiences, I recommend reading a pair of recent novels by the distinguished American author, Herbert Gold. *Family* (New York: Arbor House, 1981) depicts with much love the tradition from which the novel's protagonist had come, and *True Love* (New York: Arbor House, 1982) portrays with equal amounts of honesty the new world he found he had come to inhabit, prepared for it or not.

4. Robert Jay Lifton, *The Life of the Self, Toward a New Psychology* (New York: Simon and Schuster, 1976). See especially chapter 5, "Survivor as Creator," in which Lifton discusses his research on victims of the atomic holocaust in Hiroshima, whom he sees as symbolic of the plight of Everyman and Everywoman today, because "not only holocaust but rapid social change makes survivors of us all." Lifton suggests that to experience personal losses at so deep a level as to have "touched death" but still to be able to "rejoin the living" can be a "source of insight and power," adding that this is true for "those who have permitted themselves to experience fully the end of an era, personal or historical."

5. John Mann, *Secrets of Life Extension* (Berkeley: And/Or Press, 1981). See also Durk Pearson and Sandy Shaw, *Life Extension, A Practical, Scientific Approach, Adding Years to Your Life and Life to Your Years* (New York: Warner Books, 1982). Both of these excellent books draw on recent research on the aging process. The second faithfully reports the original scientific papers which constitute a body of work giving support to hopes that application of recently discovered principles can both arrest and *reverse* some of the consequences of aging heretofore taken as "natural."

6. The question of the interplay between one's perceptions of one's social identity and one's value system is complicated since so many of the ways in which we view our own existences are based on dimly perceived and unconsciously held beliefs. The works of Strauss and his associates at UCSF and that of other Symbolic Interactionists trained in the University of Chicago tradition comprise a school of thought about how we build our social selves. The work of the late Erving Goffman also greatly advances our understanding of the "hows" and "whys" of our self-presentation to our fellow humans.

The notion that one's self-presentation is often inauthentic, spurious, and merely manipulative is borne out, of course, by the numerous examples of "media hype" which now abound. However, it is my judgment that we have, consequently, tended to overlook the importance of the fact that how we act *is* who we are—and hence, a great deal of the time and very high stakes ride on our self-portrayals. These can be, then, of great moment.

Bibliography

Allon, Natalie, and Fishel, Diane. "Urban Courting Patterns: Singles Bars." Paper read at the Annual meeting of the American Sociological Association, New York, 1973.

Andreas, Carol. *Sex and Caste in America.* Englewood Cliffs, N.J.: Prentice-Hall, 1971.

Astin, Helen; Parelman, Allison; and Fisher, Ann. *Sex Roles: A Research Bibliography.* Washington, D.C.: Center for Human Services, 1975.

Bach, George R., and Deutsch, Ronald M., *Pairing.* New York: Peter H. Wyden, 1970.

Barbach, Lonnie Garfield. *For Yourself: The Fulfillment of Female Sexuality, A Guide to Orgasmic Response.* Garden City, N.Y.: Doubleday, 1975.

Barbach, Lonnie Garfield, and Levine, Linda. *Shared Intimacies, Women's Sexual Experiences.* Toronto and New York, Bantam Books, 1982.

Barnett, James H. *Divorce and the American Divorce Novel 1858–1937: A Study in Literary Reflections of Social Influences.* New York: Russell and Russell, 1968.

Bart, Pauline. "Mother Portnoy's complaints." In *Transaction*, no. 8, (1970): 69–74.

Barthelme, Donald. "The bill." In *Women in a Changing World: Collected Writings By Women and Men Caught between Conflicting Values*, edited by Uta West, pp. 123–5. New York: McGraw-Hill, 1975.

Becker, Howard S. "Personal Change in Adult Life." In *Middle Age and Aging*, edited by Bernice L. Neugarten, pp. 40–53. Chicago: University of Chicago Press, 1968.

———. "Problems of inference and proof in participant observation." *American Sociological Review* 23 (1958): 652–60.

Becker, Howard S., and Geer, Blanche. "Participant observation: analysis of qualitative data." In *Human Organization Research*, edited by Adams and Preiss. Homewood, Illinois: Dorsey Press, 1960.

———. "Participant observation and interviewing, a comparison." In *Symbolic Interaction*, edited by Manis and Meltzer. Boston: Allyn and Bacon, 1972.

Becker, Howard S., and Strauss, Anselm. "Careers, personality, and adult socialization." *American Journal of Sociology* 62 (1956):253–263.

Bibliography

Becker, Inger. "Men, beware of women." In *Encounter: Love, Marriage, and Family*, edited by Ruth Albrecht and E. Wilbur Brock. Boston: Holbrook, 1972.

Bem, Sandra L., and Bem, D.J. "Case study of a non-conscious ideology: Training the woman to know her place." In *Beliefs, Attitudes, and Human Affairs*, edited by D.J. Bem. Belmont, Ca.: Brooks Cole, 1970.

Bensman, Joseph, and Vidich, Arthur J. *The New American Society, The Revolution of the Middle Class*. Chicago: Quadrangle, 1971.

Berger, Bennet M. "Suburbia and the American dream." In *Urban America, Conflict and Change*, edited by J. John Palen and Karl Fleming. New York: Holt, Rinehart and Winston, 1972.

Berger, Michael. "Men's new family roles—some implications for therapists." *The Family Coordinator* no. 28, (1979) 4:638–646.

Berger, Peter L. *Invitation to Sociology*. Garden City, N.Y.: Doubleday, 1963.

Berger, Peter, and Luckmann, Thomas. *The Social Construction of Reality*. Garden City, N.Y.: Doubleday, 1967.

———. Bernard, Jessie. "Age, sex, and feminism." *Political Consequences of Aging, the Annals* (1974):120–137.

———. "Marriage: Hers and his." *MS* (1972):46–49.

———. "The status of women in modern patterns of culture." *The Annals* 375 (1968):6–14.

———. *The Future of Marriage*. New York: Bantam, 1972.

Bird, Caroline F. "The case against marriage." In *The Future of the Family*, edited by Louise Kapp Howe. New York: Simon and Schuster, 1972.

Black, C.E. *The Dynamics of Modernization*. New York: Harper and Row, 1966.

Block, Jeanne Humphrey. "Conceptions of sex roles: Some cross-cultural and longitudinal perspectives." *American Psychologist* (1973):512–26.

Blood, Robert F. *Marriage*. New York: Free Press, 1962.

Blood, Robert O., Jr., and Blood, Margaret C. "Amicable divorce: A new lifestyle." *Alternative Lifestyles* 2, no. 4(1979):483–499.

Blumer, Herbert. "Collective behavior." In *New Outline of the Principles of Sociology*, edited by A. Lee. New York: Barnes and Noble, 1956.

———. "Collective definition." In *Symbolic Interactionism: Perspective and Method*, pp. 163–70. Englewood Cliffs, N.J.: Prentice-Hall, 1969.

———. "Science without concepts." In *Symbolic Interactionism*, edited by Manis & Meltzer. Englewood Cliffs, N.J.: Prentice-Hall, 1969.

———. "Society as symbolic interaction." In *Human Behavior and Social Process*, edited by Arnold M. Rose. Boston: Houghton Mifflin, 1962.

———. "Social problems as collective behavior." *Social Problems* 18(1971):298–306.

Bohannon, Paul F., ed. *Divorce and After, An Analysis of the Emotional and Social Problems of Divorce*. Garden City, N.Y.: Doubleday, 1970.

Bowlby, John. *Attachment and Loss*. Vols. 1, 2. New York: Basic Books, 1973.

Bradley, Michael et al. *Unbecoming Men: A Men's CR Group Writes on Oppression and Themselves*. Washington, New Jersey: Times Change Press, 1971.

Branden, Nathaniel. *The Psychology of Romantic Love*. New York: Bantam, 1980.

Brecher, Edward M. *The Sex Researchers*. Boston: Little, Brown, 1969.

Brecher, Ruth, and Brecher, Edward, eds. *An Analysis of Human Sexual Response*. New York: The New American Library, 1966.

Brenton, Myron. *The American Male*. Greenwich, Conn.: Fawcett Publications, 1966.

Brim, Orville. "Theories of the male mid-life crisis." *The Counseling Psychologist* 6, no. 1(1976):2–9.

Bibliography

Brim, Orville G., and Wheeler, Stanton. *Socialization After Childhood*. New York: Wiley, 1966.

Broadhead, Robert. "Professional Identities and Private Life." Ph.D. dissertation, University of California, San Francisco Medical Center, 1978.

Brown, Norman O. *Life Against Death*. New York: Random House, 1959.

Browning, Harley L. "Timing of our life, the social consequences of the biologically complete life." In *A Guide to the Study of Society*, edited by Irving Horowitz and M. Strong, New York: pp. 137–42. Harper and Row, 1971.

Buhler, Charlotte. "The course of human life as a psychological problem." *Human Development* 11, (1968).

Burton, Arthur. *Modern Humanistic Psychotherapy*. San Francisco: Jossey-Bass, 1967.

Callenbach, Ernest. *Ecotopia*. Berkeley: Banyan Tree Books, 1975.

Carter, Hugh, and Glick, Paul. *Marriage and Divorce, A Social and Economic Study*. Cambridge: Harvard University Press, 1970.

Cauhapé, Elizabeth Broadhurst. "Aspects of interest in research on midlife; predictions of a new life-cycle stage." Paper, Human Development Program, University of California, San Francisco Medical Center, 1975.

———. "A study of the use of social networks in mid-life post-divorce adjustment." Proposal to the Committee on Human Experimentation, University of California, San Francisco Medical Center, 1974.

———. "Developments in the American middle-class family." Community College Social Science Quarterly, October 1972.

———. "Insights from Simmelian theory applied to an analysis of a singles' organization." Paper, Department of Social and Behavioral Sciences, University of California, San Francisco Medical Center, 1974.

———. "Treatment Modalities in Sex Therapy: Sex Role Implications for Practitioners." Paper presented to the Northern California Association of Marriage, Family and Child Counselors, Sacramento, Calif., 1976.

———. "Qualitative research methods: Participant observation and interviewing in the case of the urban social world of a singles." Paper, Department of Social and Behavioral Sciences, University of California, San Francisco Medical Center, 1975.

———. "Mid-life Divorce as a Status Passage, A Symbolic Interactional Analysis of the Management of Multiple Roles." Ph.D. dissertation, University of California, San Francisco Medical Center, 1980.

Chesler, Phyllis. *Women and Madness*. Garden City, N.Y.: Doubleday, 1973.

———. About Men. New York: Simon and Schuster, 1978.

Chafetz, Janet Saltzman. *Masculine/Feminine or Human? An Overview of the Sociology of Sex Roles*. Itasca, Ill.: F.E. Peacock Publishers, 1974.

Chiriboga, David A. "Marital separation and stress: A life course perspective." *Alternative Lifestyles* 2, no. 4(1979):461–71.

———. "Perception of well-being." Paper, American Psychological Association, New Orleans, 1974.

———. "Time and the life course." Paper, American Gerontological Society, Miami Beach, 1973.

Cleveland, Martha. "Divorce in the middle years: The sexual dimension." *Journal of Divorce* 2, 3 (1979):255–262.

Cohen, Jessica Field. "Male roles in mid life." *The Family Coordination* 28, no. 4(1979):465–472.

Collins, Randall. "A conflict theory of sexual stratification." *Social Problems* 19(1971):3–21.

Coser, Lewis. *The Functions of Social Conflict*. Toronto: Free Press, 1964.

Bibliography

Coser, Rose Laub, ed. *The Family, Its Structures and Functions*. New York: St. Martin's Press, 1974.

Coser, Rose Laub, and Coser, Lewis A. "The principle of legitimacy and its patterned infringement in social revolutions." In *Cross-National Family Research*, edited by Marvin Sussman and Betty Cogswell, pp. 119–130. Leiden, Netherlands: Brill, 1972.

Crane, Diana. "Fashion in science: Does it exist?" *Social Problems* 16, 4(1969):-433–440.

Cuber, John F., and Haroff, Peggy B. *Sex and the Significant Americans*. New York: Appleton-Century, 1965.

Cutter, Neal E., and Bengtson, Vern L. "Age and political alienation: Maturation, generation and period effects." In *The Annals of the American Academy of Political and Social Science, Special issue: "Political consequences of aging,"* 415(1974):-160–75.

Daedalus Special Issue. 1976 "Adulthood." American Academy of Arts and Sciences. Boston, Mass.

Daniels, Arlene Kaplan. *A Survey of Research Concerns on Women's Issues*. Washington: Project on the Status and Education of Women, Association of American Colleges, 1975.

David, Deborah, and Brannon, Robert, eds. *The 49% Majority: The Male Sex Role*. Menlo Park: Addison Wesley, 1976.

Davis, Fred. "Haight-Ashbury's hippies and the future society." In *Society As It Is*, edited by Glen Gaviglio and David Raye. Boston: The Macmillan Company, 1971.

———. "Why all of us may be hippies someday." In *Sociological Realities, A Guide to the Study of Sociology*, edited by Horowitz and Strong, pp. 80–87. New York: Transaction Textbook, Harper and Row, 1971.

DeLora, Joann S., and DeLora, Jack R. *Intimate Life Styles, Marriage and its Alternatives*. Pacific Palisades, Ca.: Goodyear, 1972.

Denzin, Norman K. *Sociological Methods, A Source Book*. Chicago: Aldine, 1970.

———. *The Research Act*. Chicago: Aldine, 1970.

———. The Logic of Naturalistic Inquiry." *Social Forces* 1, no. 2(1971):166–82.

———. "The methodologies of symbolic interaction: A critical review of research techniques." In *Social Psychology Through Symbolic Interaction*, edited by Stone and Farberman, pp. 447–465. Lexington, Mass.: Xerox College, 1970.

Dobriner, William M. *Class in Suburbia*. Englewood Cliffs, N.J.: Prentice-Hall, 1963.

Douglas, Jack D. ed. *Existential Sociology*. New York: Cambridge University Press, 1977.

Durrell, Lawrence. *The Poetry of Lawrence Durrell*. New York: E.P. Dutton, 1962.

Epstein, Cynthia Fuchs. "Ten years later: Perspectives on the woman's movement." *Dissent*. 1975.

———. *Woman's Place: Options and Limits in Professional Careers*. Berkeley, and Los Angeles University of California Press, 1970.

Epstein, Cynthia Fuchs, and Goode, William. *The Other Half, Roads to Women's Equality*. Englewood Cliffs, N.J.: Prentice-Hall, 1972.

Erikson, Erik H. "Identity and the life cycle." *Psychological Issues*, monograph 1. New York: International Universities Press, 1957.

———. "Inner and outer space: Reflections of womanhood." *Daedalus* 92, no. 2 (1964):582–606.

Fasteau, Marc Feigen. *The Male Machine*. New York: McGraw-Hill, 1974.

Bibliography

Flacks, Richard. "Growing up confused: Cultural crisis and individual character." In *Intimacy, Family and Society*, edited by Skolnick and Skolnick. Boston: Little, Brown, 1974.

———. "The liberated generation: An exploration of the roots of student protest." *Journal of Social Issues* 23 (1967).

———. *Youth and Social Change*. Chicago: Markham Publishing Co., 1971.

Foote, Nelson H. "Identification as the Basis for a Theory of Motivation." *American Sociological Review* 26 (1952).

———. "Love." *Psychiatry* 26: (1953):245–251.

———. "Sex as Play." *Social Problems* 1 (1954):161.

Francoeur, Robert T., and Francoeur, Anna K. *The Future of Sexual Relations*. Englewood Cliffs, N.J.: Prentice-Hall, 1974.

Fullerton, Gail Putney. *Survival in Marriage, Family Interaction, Conflict, and Alternatives*. 2nd ed. New York: Holt, Rinehart and Winston, 1977.

Gagnon, John H. *Human Sexuality in Today's World*. Boston: Little, Brown, 1977.

Gagnon, John H., and Simon, William, eds. *The Sexual Scene*. Rutgers, N.Y.: Transaction Books, 1970.

Geiger, H. Kent. *Comparative Prospectives on Marriage and the Family*. Boston: Little, Brown, 1968.

Glaser, Barney G., and Strauss, Anselm L. "Awareness contexts and social interaction." In *Symbolic Interaction*, edited by Manis and Meltzer Boston: Allyn and Bacon, 1972.

———. *Status Passage: A Formal Theory*. Chicago: Aldine, 1971.

———. *The Discovery of Grounded Theory*. Chicago: Aldine, 1967.

Glick, Paul C., and Norton, Arthur J. "Marrying, divorcing and living together in the U.S. today." *Population Bulletin* 32, no. 5. Washington, D.C.: Population Reference Bureau Inc., 1979.

———. "Perspectives on the recent upturn in divorce and remarriage." *Demography* 10, no. 3 (1973).

Glick, Paul, and Parke, Robert. "The cycle of family life." In *Life in Families*, edited by Helen MacGill Hughes, pp. 31–9. (1971).

Glick, Paul, Weiss, Robert S., and Parkes, Colin Murray. *The First Year of Bereavement*. New York: Wiley-Interscience, 1974.

Goffman, Erving. *Behavior in Public Places*. Glencoe, Ill.: The Free Press, 1963.

———. *Frame Analysis, An Essay on the Organization of Experience*. New York: Harper and Row, 1974.

———. "On face work: An analysis of ritual elements in social interaction." *Psychiatry* 28(1955).

———. *Stigma*. Englewood Cliffs, N.J.: Prentice-Hall, 1963.

———. *The Presentation of Self in Everyday Life*. New York: Doubleday, 1959.

Gold, Herbert. *Family, A Novel in the Form of a Memoir*. New York: Arbor House, 1981.

———. *True Love*. New York: Arbor House, 1982.

Goldstine, Daniel et al. *The Dance-Away Lover and Other Roles We Play in Love, Sex, and Marriage*. New York: Ballantine Books, 1977.

Goleman, Daniel. "One thousand, five hundred and twenty-eight little geniuses and how they grew." *Psychology Today* (1980):28–43.

———. "Still learning from Terman's children." *Psychology Today* (1980):44–53.

Bibliography

Goode, William. *After Divorce.* New York: Arch Press, 1956.
———. *The Contemporary American Family.* Chicago: Quadrangle Books, 1971.
———. *World Revolution and Family Patterns.* Glencoe: Free Press, 1963.
Gordon, Michael, ed. *The American Family in Social-Historical Perspective.* New York: St. Martin's Press, 1973.
Gough, Kathleen. "The origins of the family." *Journal of Marriage and the Family* 33 (1971):760–770.
Gove, Walter R. "The relationship between sex roles, marital status, and mental illness." *Social Forces* 51:34–44.
Hacker, Helen Mayer "Women as a minority group." *Social Forces* 30 (1951):60–69.
Haley, Jay, and Hoffman, Lynn. *Techniques of Family Therapy.* New York: Basic Books, Harper Torchbooks, 1967.
Havighurst, Robert J., and Feigenbaum, Kenneth. "Leisure and lifestyle." *Middle Age and Aging,* edited by Bernice L. Neugarten. Chicago: University of Chicago Press, 1968.
Heiman, Julia; LoPiccolo, Leslie; and LoPiccolo, Joseph. *Becoming Orgasmic: A Sexual Growth Program for Women.* Englewood Cliffs, N.J.: Prentice-Hall, 1976.
Heller, Joseph. *Something Happened.* New York: Alfred Knopf, 1974.
Hill, Reuben et al. *Family Development in Three Generations.* Cambridge, Mass.: Schenkman, 1970.
Hochschild, Arlie Russell. "The sociology of feeling and emotion: Selected possibilities." In *Another Voice,* edited by Millman and Kanter, pp. 280–307. New York: Octagon, 1975.
Hoffman, Susanna M. *The Classified Man, 22 Types of Men and What to Do about Them.* New York: G. P. Putnam's Sons, 1980.
Holmstrom, Lynda Lytle. *The Two-Career Family.* Cambridge, Mass.: Schenkman Publishing Co., 1972.
Horowitz, Irving L. *Ideology and Utopia in the U.S. 1956–1976.* New York: Oxford University Press, 1977.
Huber, Joan, ed. *Changing Women in a Changing Society (Special Issue), American Journal of Sociology* 78, no. 4 (1973).
Hughes, Everett. "Cycles, Turning Points and Careers." In *Men and Their Work,* pp. 11–23. Glencoe, Ill.: The Free Press, 1958.
———. "Dilemmas and contradictions of status." *American Journal of Sociology* 50 (1945):353–59.
———. *Men and Their Work.* Glencoe: Free Press, 1956.
———. "Social change and status protest: An essay on the marginal man." In *Phylon,* pp. 58–65. 1949.
———. *The Sociological Eye,* bks. 1, 2. Chicago: Aldine, 1971.
Hunt, Morton. *The World of the Formerly Married.* New York: McGraw-Hill, 1966.
———. *The Affair.* New American Library, 1973.
Hunt, Morton, and Hunt, Bernice. *Sexual Behavior in the 1970s.* Chicago: Playboy, 1974.
Huxley, Albert. *The Doors of Perception.* New York: Harper and Row, 1964.
Inkeles, Alex, and Smith, David H. *Becoming Modern, Individual Change in Sex Developing Countries.* Cambridge: Harvard University Press, 1973.
Irwin, John. *Scenes, Looking at New Lifestyles: "Fern Bars", Discos, Encounter Groups, Surfing, Drugs, Skiing and Much More.* Beverly Hills: Sage, 1977.
Johnson, Karen Sue. "Single men and ♀ in the U.S. since the turn of the century." Ph.D. dissertation, University of Texas at Austin, 1977.
Jonas, Doris, and David, Jonas. *Sex and Status.* New York: Stein and Day, 1980.

Bibliography

Jones, Maxwell. *The Therapeutic Community.* New York: Basic Books, 1953.

Kaplan, Helen Singer. *The New Sex Therapy.* New York: Brenner/Mazel, 1974.

Keleman, Stanley. *Sexuality, Self and Survival.* Berkeley: Lodestar Press, 1971.

———. *Somatic Reality, Bodily Experience and Emotional Truth.* Berkeley, CA: Center Press, 1979.

Keniston, Kenneth, and Carnegie Council on Children. *All Our Children: The American Family Under Pressure.* New York: Harcourt Brace Jovanovich, 1978.

Kerr, Carmen. *Sex for ♀, Who Want to Have Fun and Loving Relationship With Equals.* New York: Grove Press, 1978.

Knudsen, Dean. "The declining status of women: Popular myths and the failure of functionalist thought." *Social Forces* 48 (1969).

Koller, Marvin R. *Families, A Multigenerational Approach.* New York: McGraw-Hill, 1974.

Komarovsky, Mirra. "Cultural Contradictions and Sex Roles: The Masculine Case." In *Changing Women in a Changing Society,* edited by Joan Huber pp. 111–122. Chicago: University of Chicago Press, 1973.

Krantzler, Mel. *Creative Divorce.* New York: Evans, 1974.

———. *Learning to Love Again.* New York: Thomas Y. Crowell, 1977.

Kuhn, Thomas S. *The Structure of Scientific Revolutions.* 2nd ed. Chicago: University of Chicago Press, 1971.

Kypers, Joseph, and Maas, Henry S. *From Thirty to Seventy.* San Francisco: Jossey-Bass, 1975.

Laing, Ronald D. *Knots.* New York: Random House, 1970.

———. *The Politics of Experience.* New York: Ballantine, 1967.

———. *The Politics of the Family.* New York: Pantheon, 1971.

Lederer, William J., and Jackson, Don D. *The Mirages of Marriage, an original look at the marital relationship with no-nonsense procedures to help solve its problems.* New York: W.W. Norton, 1968.

Lefebvre, Henri. *The Explosion, Marxism and the French Upheaval.* Translated by Afred Ehrenfeld. New York: Monthly Review Press, 1969.

Lessing, Doris. *A Proper Marriage.* New York: New American Library, 1952.

———. *The Summer Before the Dark.* New York: Alfred Knopf, 1973.

Levinson, Daniel et al. *The Seasons of a Man's Life.* New York: Ballantine Books, 1978.

Lewis, Robert A.; Freneau, Phillip J.; and Roberts, Craig L. "Fathers and the post parental transition." *The Family Coordinator* 28, no. 4(1979):514–20.

Lewis, Robert A., and Pleck, Joseph H., eds. *The Family Coordinator, Special Issue: "Men's Roles in the Family"* 28, no. 4 (1979).

Libby, Roger, ed. *Alternative Lifestyles, Changing Patterns of Marriage, Family and Intimacy.* Beverly Hills: Sage, 1978.

Libby, Robert, and Whitehurst, Robert. eds. *Renovating Marriage.* Danville, Ca.: Consensus Publishers, 1973.

Lifton, Robert J. ed. *The Woman in America.* Boston: Houghton Mifflin, 1965.

———. *The Life of the Self.* New York: Simon and Schuster, 1976.

Lindesmith, Alfred A.; Strauss, Anselm L.; and Denzin, Norman K. *Social Psychology.* Hindsdale: Dryden, 1974.

Lipman-Blumen, Jean. "How ideology shapes women's lives." *Scientific American* 226, (1972).

Lipset, Seymour Martin, and Bendix, Richard. *Social Mobility in Industrial Society.* Berkeley: University of California, 1960.

Bibliography

Little, Marilyn. *Family Break-up: Understanding Marital Problems and the Mediating of Child Custody Decisions.* San Francisco: Jossey-Bass, Inc., 1982.

Loether, Herman J. *Problems of Aging, Sociological and Social Psychological Perspectives.* Belmont, Ca.: Dickenson, 1967.

Lofland, Lyn H. *A World of Strangers, Order and Action in Urban Public Space.* New York: Basic Books, 1973.

Loge, Betty. "Role adjustments to single parenthood: study of divorced and widowed men and ♀." Ph.D. dissertation, University of Washington, Seattle, 1978.

Lopata, Helena Z. ed. *Marriages and Families, A Trans-actional Society Reader.* New York: D. Van Nostrand, 1973.

Lowenthal, Marjorie Fiske. "Psycho social variations across the adult life course; frontiers for research and policy." *The Gerontologist* 15, no. 1 (1975).

Lowenthal, Marjorie Fiske, and Beeson, Diane. "Perceived stress across the life course." *In Four Stages of Life.* San Francisco: Jossey-Bass, 1975.

Lowenthal, Marjorie Fiske, and Chiriboga, David. "Transition to the empty next: Crisis challenge or relief?" *Archives of General Psychiatry* 26 (1972).

Lowenthal, M.F.; Thurnher, Magda; and Chiriboga, David. *Four Stages of Life.* San Francisco: Jossey-Bass, 1974.

Luckman, Thomas, and Berger, Peter L. "Social mobility and personal identity." In *Readings in Sociology,* edited by Brigitte Berger, pp. 202–7. New York: Basic Books, 1974.

―――. "Social mobility and personal identity." *The European Journal of Sociology* 5 (1964):331–44.

Lyman, Stanford M., and Scott, Marvin B. *A Sociology of the Absurd.* New York: Appleton-Century-Crofts, 1970.

Margolis, Diane Rothbard. *The Managers: Corporate Life in America.* New York: Morrow, 1979.

McHugh, Peter. *Defining the Situation.* New York: Bobbs-Merrill, 1963.

McNall, Scott, and Young, T. R. *Paradigmatic conflict in American sociology: Towards a critical sociology, an annotated bibliography: 1972–77.* Fort Collins, Col.: The Red Feather Institute, 1977.

Manis, Jerome G., and Bernard N., Meltzer, eds. *Symbolic Interaction: A Reader in Social Psychology.* 2nd ed. Boston: Allyn and Bacon, 1972.

Mannheim, Karl. *Essays on the Sociology of Knowledge,* edited by Paul Kecskemeti. London: Rontledge and Kegan Paul, 1952.

Marcuse, Herbert. *Eros and Civilization.* Boston: Beacon Press, 1955.

―――. *One-Dimensional Man, Studies in the Ideology of Advanced Industrial Society.* Boston: Beacon, 1968.

Markle, Gerald. "Sexism and the Sex ratio." Paper, American Sociological Association, New York, 1973.

Maslow, Abraham. *Religions, Values and Peak-Experiences.* Columbus: Ohio State University Press, 1964.

―――. *Toward a Psychology of Being.* Princeton, N.J.: D. Van Nostrand, 1962.

Masters, William, and Johnson, Virginia. *Human Sexual Inadequacy.* Boston: Little, Brown, 1970.

―――. *Human Sexual Response.* Boston: Little, Brown, 1966.

Masters, William; Johnson, Virginia; and Levin, Robert J. *The Pleasure Bond, A New Look at Sexuality and Commitment.* New York: Bantam, 1975.

Mattson, Phyllis H. "Between separation and integration: Through the transition with PWP." Paper, American Anthropological Association, Mexico City, 1974.

Bibliography

Mayleas, Davidyne. *Rewedded Bliss; Love, Alimony, Incest, Ex-spouses, and Other Domestic Blessings.* New York: Basic Books, 1977.

Mazur, Ronald. "The double standard and people's liberation." In *Renovating Marriage,* edited by Roger Libby and Robert Whitehurst. Danville, Ca.: Consensus Publishers, 1973.

———. *The New Intimacy: Open-Ended Marriages and Alternate Life Styles.* Boston: Beacon Press, 1973.

Mead, George Herbert. *Mind, Self, and Society.* Chicago: University of Chicago Press, 1934.

Miller, Alice. *Prisoners of Childhood, How Narcissistic Parents Form and Deform the Lives of Their Children.* New York: Basic Books, 1981.

Miller, Howard, and Siegel, Paul. *Loving, A Psychological Approach.* New York: John Wiley and Sons, 1972.

Millman, Marcia, and Kanter, Rosebeth. *Another Voice: Feminist Perspectives on Social Life and Social Science.* Garden City, N.Y.: Doubleday, 1975.

Mills, C. Wright. *The Sociological Imagination.* New York: Oxford University Press, 1959.

"Situated actions and vocabularies of motive." In *Symbolic Interaction,* edited by Jerome Mavis and Bernard Meltzer, Boston: Allyn and Bacon, 1940. pp. 904–91

———. "The professional ideology of social pathologies." *American Journal of Sociology* 49 (1943):165–180.

Moulton, Ruth. "Early papers on women: Horney to Thompson." *The American Journal of Psychoanalysis* 35 (1975):207–223.

Moustakas, Clark E. *Loneliness and Love.* Englewood Cliffs, N.J.: Prentice-Hall, 1972.

Neugarten, Bernice L. "Age groups in American society and the rise of the young-old." Paper presented at American Association for the Advancement of Science, 1974.

———. *Middle Age and Aging: A Reader in Social Psychology.* Chicago: University of Chicago Press, 1968.

Neugarten, Bernice L., and Moore, Joan W. "The changing Age-status system." In *Middle Age and Aging,* edited by Bernice Neugarten Chicago: University of Chicago Press, 1968.

Neugarten, Bernice L.; Moore, Joan W.; and Lowe, John C. "Age norms, age constraints, and adult socialization." In *Middle Age and Aging,* edited by Bernice Neugarten Chicago: University of Chicago Press, 1968.

Nicholaus, Martin. "Text of speech delivered at the ASA convention on August 26, 1968." In *The Sociology of Sociology,* edited by Larry Reynold and Janice Reynolds, pp. 274–78. New York: McKay, 1970.

Nichols, Jack. *Men's Liberation: A New Definition of Masculinity.* New York: Penguin Books, 1975.

Nye, F. Ivan, and Hoffman, Lois W. *The Employed Mother in America.* Chicago: Rand McNally, 1963.

Nye, F. Ivan, and Benardo, Felix M. *The Family: Its Structure and Interaction.* New York: MacMillan, 1973.

Oestreicher, Emil. "The theory and practice of social change." Course at The New School for Social Research, New York City, 1973.

O'Neill, William. "The origins of American feminism." In *The Other Half: Roads to Women's Equality,* edited by Cynthia Epstein and William J. Goode, pp. 159–164. Englewood Cliffs, N.J.: Prentice-Hall, 1971.

———. *Divorce in the Progressive Era.* New York: New Viewpoints, 1973.

O'Reilly, Jane. "The view from my bed." *Ms,* 1973.

Bibliography

Paley, Grace. "The used-boy raisers." In *Woman in a Changing World: Collected Writings by Woman and Men Caught Between Conflicting Values,* edited by Uta West pp. 88–94. New York: McGraw-Hill, 1975.

Park, Robert E. "Human migration and the marginal man." *American Journal of Sociology* (1928):881–893.

Park, Robert E.; Burgess, Ernest W.; and McKenzie, Roderick D. *The City.* Chicago: University of Chicago Press, 1967.

Parks, C. Murray. "Psycho-social transitions: A field for study." In *Social Science and Medicine,* vol. 5, pp. 101–115. Great Britain: Pergamon Press, 1971.

Parsons, Talcott. "Age and sex in the social structure of the United States." *American Sociological Review* 7 (1942):604–616.

————. *Essays in Sociological Theory.* Rev. ed. New York: The Free Press, 1949.

————. "The feminine role and the kinship system." In *Essays in Sociological Theory,* pp. 184–94 Glenco, Ill.: The Free Press, 1954.

————. *Family, Socialization, and Process.* Glencoe, Ill.: The Free Press, 1955.

Perinbanayagam, Robert S. "Social conflict." Course at the New School for Social Research, New York City, 1971.

Peterson, Linda, and Enarson, Elaine. "Blaming the victim in the sociology of women: On the mis-use of the concept of socialization." Paper, Pacific Sociological Association, Center for the Sociological Study of Women, University of Oregon, 1974.

Petras, John W. *Sexuality in Society.* Boston: Allyn and Bacon, 1973.

Pinard, Maurice. "Marriage and divorce decisions and the larger social system: A case study of social change." *Social Forces* 44 (1966).

Plateris, Alexander A. *Divorces: Analysis of Changes: U.S. 1969.* Washington, D.C.: U.S. Government Printing Office, 1973.

Pleck, Joseph H., and Sawyer, Jack. *Men and Masculinity.* Englewood Cliffs, N.J.: Prentice-Hall, 1974.

Polanyi, Karl. *The Great Transformation.* Boston: Beacon Press, 1944.

Polatnick, Margaret. "Why men don't rear children: A power analysis." *Berkeley Journal of Sociology* 28 (1973–74):45–86.

Pomeroy, Wardell B. *Dr. Kinsey and the Institute for Sex Research.* New York: Harper and Row, 1972.

Putney, Snell, and Putney, Gail J. *Normal Neurosis: The Adjusted American.* New York: Harper and Row, 1964.

Ramey, James. *Intimate Friendships.* Englewood Cliffs, N.J.: Prentice-Hall, 1966.

Raschke, Helen J., ed. "Special issue on ending intimate relationships." In *Alternative Lifestyles, Changing Patterns in Marriage, Family and Intimacy* 2, no. 4 (1979).

Rasmussen, Paul K., and Ferraro, Kathleen J. "The divorce process." *Alternative Lifestyles* 2, no. 4 (1979):443–61.

Riesman, David; Glaser, Nathan; and Denny, Reuel. *The Lonely Crowd.* Garden City, N.Y.: Doubleday, 1955.

Reiss, Ira L. "How and why America's sex standards are changing." In *The Sexual Scene,* edited by John Gagnon and William Simon pp. 43–57 Chicago: Aldine, 1970.

————. "The sexual renaissance in America." *The Journal of Social Issues* (special issue) 1966.

Reuther, Rosemary. "The personalization of sexuality." In *The Future of Sexual Relations,* edited by Robert T. and Anna K. Francoeur pp. 42–49. Englewood Cliffs, N.J.: Prentice-Hall, 1974.

Revere, V. "The remembered past: Its reconstruction at different life stages." Ph.D. abstract, Committee on Human Development, University of Chicago, 1971.

Bibliography

Robinson, Paul. *The Modernization of Sex*. New York: Harper and Row, 1976.

Rogers, Carl. *Becoming Partners: Marriage and Its Alternatives*. New York: Delacorte, 1972.

Rogers, Natalie. *Emerging Woman, A Decade of Midlife Transitions*. Point Reyes: Personal Press, 1980.

Rosow, Irving. "Forms and functions of adult socialization." *Social Forces* 44 (1965).

Roth, Julius. *Timetables*. Indianapolis: Bobbs-Merrill, 1963.

Roth, Philip. *My Life as a Man*. New York: Bantam, 1970.

Rosenbaum, Marcia. "Funneling Options: The Career of the Woman Addict." Ph.D. dissertation, University of California, San Francisco Medical Center, 1979.

Rosenberg, Bernard; Gervet, Isral; and Honghton, William. *Mass Society in Crises, Social Problems and Pathology*. 2nd ed. New York: Macmillan, 1971.

Rosenberg, Marie Barovic, and Bergstrom, Len V., eds. *Women and Society, A Critical Review of the Literature with a Selected Annotated Bibliography*. Beverly Hills, Ca.: Sage, 1975.

Rossi, Alice. "Equality between the sexes: An immodest proposal." In *The Woman in America*, edited by Robert J. Lifton pp. 98–143. Boston: Beacon, 1964.

Roszak, Theodore. *Where the Wasteland Ends, Politics and Transcendence in Post Industrial Society*. Garden City, N.Y.: Doubleday, 1972.

———. "Review of Lasch." *Berkeley Monthly* June 1980.

Rubin, Lillian. *Women of a Certain Age; the Midlife Search for Self*. New York: Harper Colophon, 1981.

———. *Intimate Strangers, Men and Women Together*. New York: Harper & Row, 1983.

Safilios-Rothschild, Constantina. *Toward a Sociology of Women*. Lexington, Mass.-/Toronto: Xerox College, 1972.

Scanzoni, John. *Sexual Bargaining: Power Politics in the American Marriage*. Englewood Cliffs, N.J.: Prentice-Hall, 1972.

Scanzoni, Letha, and Scanzoni, John. *Men, Women and Change, A Sociology of Marriage and Family*. New York: McGraw-Hill, 1976.

Schatzman, Leonard, and Strauss, Anselm L. "A sociology of psychiatry." *Social Problems* 24, no. 1 (1966):3–16.

———. *Field Research, Strategies for a Natural Sociology*. Englewood Cliffs, N.J.: Prentice-Hall, 1973.

———. "Social class and modes of communication." *American Journal of Sociology* 60 (1955).

Schutz, A. *Collected Papers*. The Hague: Nijhoff, 1962.

———. *On Phenomenology and Social Relations*, edited by Helmut T. Wagner. Chicago: University of Chicago Press, 1970.

———. *The Phenomenology of the Social World*. 2nd ed. Evanston, Ill.: Northwestern University Press, 1967.

Schutz, Alfred, and Luckman, Thomas. *The Structure of the Life World*. Translated by Richard Zaner and Tristram Englehardt. Evanston, Ill.: Northwestern University Press, 1967.

Schickel, Richard. *Singled Out, A Civilized Guide to Sex and Sensibility for the Suddenly Single Man or Woman*. New York: The Viking Press, 1980.

Scott, Marvin B., and Lyman, Stanford M. "Accounts." In *Symbolic Interaction*, edited by Manis and Meltzer. Boston: Allyn and Bacon, 1972.

Seeley, John. *The Americanization of the Unconscious*. New York: International Science Press, 1967.

Bibliography

Seeley, John et al. *Crestwood Heights, A North American Suburb.* London: Constable, 1956.

Seidenberg, Robert. *Corporate Wives—Corporate Casualties?* Garden City, N.Y.: Doubleday, 1975.

Sheresky, Norman, and Mannes, Myra. *Uncoupling: The Art of Coming Apart.* New York: Viking, 1972.

Simmel, Georg. *Conflict and the Web of Group Affiliations.* New York: The Free Press, 1955.

———. "Friendship, love and secrecy." *American Journal of Sociology* 11 (1906):457–466.

———. "The metropolis and mental life." In *Images of Man*, edited by C. Wright Mills, pp. 437–448. Glencoe: The Free Press, 1950.

Skolnick, Arlene, and Skolnick, Jerome. *Intimacy, Family and Society.* Boston: Little, Brown, 1974.

———. *Family in Transition, Rethinking, Marriage, Sexuality, Child-Rearing and Family Organization.* 2nd ed. Boston: Little, Brown, 1977.

Slater, Philip E. *The Pursuit of Loneliness, American Culture at the Breaking Point.* Boston: Beacon Press, 1970.

Snodgrass, W. D. *After Experience, Poems.* New York: Harper and Row, 1958.

Spence, Donald L. "An interactionist approach to the life course." Paper, Gerontological Society, San Juan, 1972.

Spence, Donald L., and Lonner, Thomas D. "Divorce as development: A sociological hypothesis." Paper (expanded version), American Sociology Association, Denver, 1971.

———. "Divorce and the life-course of middle aged women." Paper, American Sociology Association. Denver, 1971.

———. "The empty next: A transition within motherhood." *The Family Coordinator* (1971).

Spreitzer, Elmer, and Riby, Lawrence. "Factors associated with singlehood." *Journal of Marriage and the Family* 36 (1974):533–542.

Staples, Robert, ed. *The Black Family.* Belmont, Ca.: Wadsworth, 1971.

———. *The World of Black Singles.* Westport, Conn: Greenwood Press, 1981.

Stein, Maurice; Vidich, Arthur J.; and White, D. M. *Identity and Anxiety, the Survival of the Person in Mass Society.* Glencoe, Ill.: The Free Press, 1963.

Stein, Peter J. *Single.* Englewood Cliffs, N.J.: Prentice-Hall, 1976.

———. "Singlehood: An alternative to marriage." *Family Coordinator* (1975):489–503.

Stone, Gregory P., and Farberman, Harvey. *Social Psychology Through Symbolic Interaction.* Waltham, Mass.: Ginn-Blaisdell, 1970.

Strauss, Anselm L. "Language and Identity." In *Symbolic Interaction*, edited by Jerome Mavis and Bernard N. Meltzer. Boston: Allyn and Bacon, 1972.

———. *Mirrors and Masks: The Search for Identity.* Glencoe, Ill.: Free Press, 1959.

———. *George Herbert Mead: Essays on His Social Psychology.* Chicago: University of Chicago Press, 1977.

———. *The Context of Social Mobility: Ideology and Change.* Chicago: Aldine, 1971.

———. *Varieties of Negotiated Order.* San Francisco: Jossey-Bass, 1979.

Sussman, Marvin B. *Sourcebook in Marriage and the Family.* Boston: Houghton Mifflin, 1974.

———. "Variant marriage styles and family forms." *The Family Coordinator* 21 (special issue, 1972).

Bibliography

Sullivan, Harry Stack. *The Interpersonal Theory of Psychiatry.* New York: W. W. Norton, 1953.

Taibbi, Robert. "Transitional relationships after divorce." *Journal of Divorce* 2, no. 3 (1979):263–269.

Thamm, Robert. *Beyond Marriage and the Nuclear Family.* San Francisco: Canfield, 1975.

The Journal of Social Issues (Special Issue.) The Sexual Renaissance in America. Worcester, Mass.: The Heffernan Press. 1966.

Toch, Hans. *The Social Psychology of Social Movements.* Indianapolis: Bobbs-Merrill, 1965.

Toffler, Alvin. *Future Shock.* New York: Bantam, 1970.

Thomas, W. I. "The definition of the situation." In *Symbolic Interaction: A Reader in Social Psychology,* Jerome G. Manis and Bernard N. Meltzer. Boston: Allyn and Bacon, 1967.

Troll, Lillian. *Early and Middle Adulthood.* Belmont, Ca.: Wadsworth, 1975.

Turner, Ralph. "Role-taking, role standpoint, and reference group behavior." *American Journal of Sociology* 61 (1956):316–28.

Updike, John. *Couples.* Greenwich, Conn.: Fawcett, 1969.

Van Gennep, Arnold. *Rites de Passage.* Chicago: University of Chicago Press, 1960.

Vaughan, Diane. "Uncoupling: The process of moving from one lifestyle to another." *Alternative Lifestyles,* 2, no. 4 (1979):415–43.

Vital and Health Statistics. *Divorces: Analysis of Changes, United States, 1969.* Series 21, no. 22. Washington, D.C.: U.S. Government Printing Office, 1970.

Vital Statistics of U.S. *Marriage and Divorce.* Vol. 3. Washington, D.C.: U.S. Government Printing Office, 1969.

Wallerstein, Judith S., and Kelly, Joan Berlin. *Surviving the Breakup, How Children and Parents Cope with Divorce.* New York: Basic Books, 1980.

Watzlawick, Paul; Weakland, John; and Fisch, Richard. *Change, Principles of Problem Formation and Problem Resolution.* New York: W.W. Norton, 1974.

Wax, Rosalie H. *Doing Field Work: Warnings and Advice.* Chicago: University of Chicago Press, 1971.

Weis, Michael. "Diary of a mad househusband." In *Women in a Changing World: Collected Writings by Women and Men Caught Between Conflicting Values,* edited by Uta West, pp. 64–67. New York: McGraw-Hill, 1975.

Weiss, Robert S. *Going it Alone, the Family Life and Social Situation of the Single Parent.* New York: Basic Books, 1979.

———. *Loneliness: A Book of Readings.* Cambridge: MIT Press, 1973.

Weisstein, Naomi. " 'Kinder, Kuche, Kirche' as scientific law: Psychology constructs the female." In *Sisterhood Is Powerful,* edited by Robin Morgan. New York: Vintage Books, 1970.

Wellborn, Teresa, ed. *Human Sexuality, A Current Bibliography.* San Francisco: Multi-Media Resource Center.

Whitehurst, Robert N. "Changing ground rules and emergent life-styles," and "The monogamous ideal and sexual realities." In *Renovating Marriage,* edited by Roger Libby and Robert Whitehurst. Danville, Ca.: Consensus, 1973.

Whyte, William H., Jr. *The Organization Man.* New York: Simon and Schuster, 1956.

Williams, Robins M., Jr. "Individual and group values." In *Doing Sociology,* edited by Paul Kaplan and Clovis Shepherd, pp. 109–132. New York: Alfred Knopf, 1973.

Wirth, Louis. *On Cities and Social Life; Selected Papers.* Chicago: University of Chicago Press, 1964.

Bibliography

————. "Urbanism as a way of life." *American Journal of Sociology* 44 (1938):1–24.

Wiseman, Jacqueline P. *People as Partners.* 2nd ed. San Francisco: Canfield Press, 1977.

————. *The Social Psychology of Sex.* New York: Harper and Row, 1976.

Wolf, Charlotte. "Sex roles as portrayed in marriage and the family textbooks: Contributions to the status quo." *Women's Studies* 3 (1975):45–60.

Wolf, Kurt H., ed. *The Sociology of Georg Simmel.* Glencoe, Ill.: The Free Press, 1950.

Wortes, Helen and Robinowitz, Clara. *The Women's Movement: Social and Psychological Perspectives.* New York: Halstead, 1972.

Wrong, Dennis. "The over-socialized conception of men in modern society." *Psychoanalysis and Psychoanalytic Review* 49 (1962):53–69.

Yalom, Irvin D. *The Theory and Practice of Group Psychotherapy.* 2nd ed. New York: Basic Books, 1975.

Yorburg, Betty. *Sexual Identity, Sex Roles and Social Change.* New York, N.Y.: Wiley, 1974.

Young, T.R. "The politics of sociology: Gouldner, Goffman and Garfinkel." *Theories and Paradigms in Contemporary Sociology,* edited by R. Denisoff and Serge, et al., pp. 431–441. Itasca, Ill.: Peacock Press, 1974.

Young, Thomas R., and Massey, Goute. "The dramaturgical society: A macro-analytic approach to dramaturgical analysis." Fort Collins, Col.: The Red Feather Institute.

Zubriskie, Philip T. "The storms of middle life: Odysseus and the great goddess." Speech given at the Unitarian Center, San Francisco, February 8, 1978. Franklin at Geary Sts.

Index

Index

Index

Index

and social justice, 273–75; on love, 257; as marginal people, 275, 277; men, 288; openness in, 140–41; pairing strategies of, 141, 142, 164–65, 184; vs. Passionate Searchers, 186, 188, 191, 192, 281, 291, 292–93; as prophetic model, 284–310; vs. Runners in Place, 142, 186; sexual behavior of, 141, 142, 169, 171–79, 183, 280, 281, 287; social life of, 280–81; vs. Steadies, 165; transition in, 272–73; women, 287, 288

identity, 4, 82, 109, 251
identity problems, 41–42
"ideological revolution," 308
ideology of singlehood, 137, 237–41; see also Singlehood
Immediate (Planned) Remarriers, 9, 63–68; on aging, 92–93; case histories, 9, 64–67, 262; vs. Comfortable Courters, 78, 104, 105; control in, 96, 261, 265; courtship in, 9, 108; as covert pairs, 63, 65–66, 68; disclosure in, 96, 265; divorces of, 90, 261–62; instability of, 67; secrecy of, 63, 68, 95–99, 108–9, 265; strategy of, 95–99; success of remarriage in, 67–68; transition of, 108–9, 114
immigrant family backgrounds, 4–5, 276, 303, 306
independence, 94, 168
independent thinking, 12; see also Experimentation
individualism, 141, 142, 155–56, 160–61, 272, 294, 295, 297–98; see also Nonconformism
innovation, see Experimentation
integration (rational), 275
integrity, 158; see also Value judgments and systems
intelligence, 299; see also College, educational experience
interdependency, 299
intimacy, 247; see also Commitment; Love; Personal growth
Intrinsic Marriage, 189
irresolution, 7

Johnson, Lyndon B., 274
Jungian therapy, 193, 229

Kennedy, John F.: assassination of, as benchmark, 22

labor activism, 275, 276
lawyers, 53, 95, 109; see also Litigation
leisure activities, 211–13, 220–21, 223, 286; see also specific activities
Lennon, John, 241
lesbianism, 34
Lifton, Robert Jay, Life of the Self: Toward a New Psychology, The, 309
litigation, 48, 53, 58, 59–60, 62–63, 68, 98
living together, 13, 121–22, 126, 171, 175, 229, 231–32, 270, 275; see also "Staying over"; Trial unions
"locus of control" theory, 111
loneliness, 66, 118–19
love, 15, 21, 257, 259, 262, 290, 293, 294, 299–300; see also Repartnering

McCarthy, Eugene, 275
marriage (first), 273, 275, 284; deterioration of, 30, 287, 288; as duty-bound experience, 12; earliness of, 294; and "facts of family life," 31–40; identity in, 4; length of, 3; as reference point, 283; sexual difficulties in, 214–15, 216, 287; sex-role alterations in, 5–6; stability of, 5; traditional nature of, 168, 194, 233, 277, 286; traditional view of, 150; unsatisfactory nature of, 238, 245, 246, 260, 287, 288; as value judgment, 15
"marrying down," 200
massage, 220
maturation tasks, 294, 297
maturity, see Emotional maturity
men: age concerns of, 16–17; feeling of loss in, 118–19; in passage, 269; sexual behavior of, 120; as single parents, 228;

Index

Comfortable Courters, 219, 231, 281–82; commitment in, 191, 265; control in, 260, 261, 262–63, 266; contribution of, 293–94; courtship in, 14, 238; disclosure in, 265; egalitarianism in, 283; vs. Enforced Remarriers, 131; entertainment patterns of, 230–32, 284; expectations of, 282, 286, 287–88; feminism of, 209–11; former lovers, 191–92, 262–63, 282; former spouses, 228; gain from divorce, 255; goals of, 14, 141, 184, 188, 284, 301; vs. Graduates, 198, 266; health commitment of, 220, 232; housing arrangements of, 144–45; vs. Hunters-and-Sorters, 186, 188, 191, 281, 282, 291, 292; interest of, in social change and social justice, 273–75; on love, 257; as marginal people, 275–77; marriages of, 245–47; marriage vs. pairing of, 194; men, 234–36, 288; openness in, 140–41; pairing in, 188–89, 190–91, 194–95, 208, 213, 230, 231, 237, 238, 239, 241–49, 256, 296; partner's welfare in, 189; as prophetic model, 284–310; romantic orientation of, 136; vs. Runners in Place, 142, 184, 186, 190, 218, 224, 281; self-actualization in, 189; seriousness of, 188; sexual behavior of, 141, 142, 213–22, 223–24, 239–41, 245, 278–80, 281; on singlehood, 237–41; socializing in, 207–8, 283–84; talking aspect of relationship, 282, 283; transitional nature of, 188; urban orientation of, 250; women as, 226–28, 232–44, 288; women professionals as, 195–96, 197–206

Peace Corps, 275
permissiveness, 33
personal growth, 12–14, 23, 141, 151–59; 160–64, 186, 193–94, 211–13, 249–50, 251–56, 263, 269, 273, 278–80, 281, 284–310; case histories, 154–55, 193–94, 211, 212–13, 278–80, 281, 305
personal history, 6
personality types, 6
philosophy of entitlement, 33
physical fitness, 13
playfulness, 46
political activism, 34, 37, 39, 202, 216,

258, 273, 276, 277, 279; see also specific issues
postdivorce strategies, 4; see also Passage(s); specific subgroups
postdivorce transition, see Passage(s)
power struggles, 221–22
prison reform, 275
privacy, 114–15, 141, 172, 173, 248, 249
problem solving, 15, 150–51, 250
profession, professional life, 14, 17, 24–25, 26–32, 40–46, 49, 56, 73, 76, 90, 92–93, 112, 126, 134, 153, 177, 178, 184, 195, 211–12, 213, 217, 237, 245, 248, 250, 255, 261, 276, 277; ceiling on, 138; as secondary to personal growth, 278; of women, 138–39, 195–96, 197–207, 209, 216, 227–28, 229–30, 232–34, 236, 244, 245, 283, 285, 302–3
professional conferences, 205–6
psychotherapy, 110–11, 116, 152, 153, 202, 211, 219, 229, 246, 248, 279, 281, 285, 298, 300; case histories, 161, 193–94, 210–11, 229, 248, 263, 269, 285; see also specific types of therapy

racism, 37
radical theorists, 274
"rebound romances," 115–16
reconciliation, 53, 54, 59, 96, 153, 262
relatives, see Family
religious affiliation, 275–76
remarriage, 8, 65–66; of Comfortable Courters, 267–68, 271–72; as desirable goal, 10, 136; of dissimilar types, 132; of Immediate (Planned) Remarriers, 96; New Age, 14; of Steadies, 270–72; "temporary," 132; see also Repartnering; Wedding plans
repartnering, 54–55, 58, 72, 203–4; as goal, 7, 8, 18; Graduates on, 69; in Immediate (Planned) Remarriers, 63–68; in Passionate Searchers, 241–49; positive value of, 137; postdivorce, 115–16; response to, 4; search for, 4; in Steadies, 165, 271–72; as successful termination of passage, 136; success of, 67–68; see also Courtship; Passage(s); Remarriage

Index

Index

Index

"vocabulary of motives," 58
vulnerability, 193

wedding plans, 83–84, 88–89, 109, 123, 130, 265, 270–71; *see also* Remarriage
will: changing of, 49
wisdom, 159
women: age concerns of, 16, 138; marriage rates of, 200; money concerns of, 16, 116–17; multiple-role management by, 197–205; new roles of, 33, 39, 40, 132, 138, 224–25; primary role identification of, 234, 285, 303; professional career commitment by, 195–96; 197–207, 208, 227–28, 229–30, 233; role conflicts in, 204, 207, 210, 217; as single mothers, 118; structural problems of, 116–17, 130–31, 230; traditional roles of, 33, 207; and younger men, 245, 246
Women's Centers, 276
workaholics, 236
work ethic, 32–33, 34; *see also* Profession, professional life
writers, 274, 276

youth movement, 36, 258, 274; *see also* Children

Zen communities, 38
Zionism, 276